SUN TECHNICAL REFERENCE LIBRARY

SUN TECHNICAL REFERENCE LIBRARY

James Gosling, David S. H. Rosenthal, and Michelle J. Arden
*The NeWS Book: An Introduction to the Network/extensible
Window System*

Mark Hall and John Barry (eds.)
The Sun Technology Papers

Michael Russo
A New User's Guide to the Sun Workstation

John R. Corbin
*The Art of Distributed Applications: Programming Techniques for
Remote Procedure Calls*

George Becker and Kathy Slattery
A System Administrator's Guide to Sun Workstations

Ben J. Catanzaro (ed.)
The SPARC Technical Papers

George Becker   Kathy Slattery

A System Administrator's Guide to Sun Workstations

Springer Science+Business Media, LLC

George Becker
Kathy Slattery
Sun Microsystems, Inc.
2550 Garcia Avenue
Mountain View, CA 94043

© 1991 by Springer Science+Business Media New York
Originally published by Springer-Verlag Berlin Heidelberg New York in 1991
Softcover reprint of the hardcover 1st edition 1991

Library of Congress Cataloging-in-Publication Data
Becker, George.
    A systems administrator's guide to Sun workstations / George
Becker, Kathy Slattery.
        p.   cm. — (Sun technical reference library)
    Includes bibliographical references and index.
    ISBN 978-1-4612-6455-2   ISBN 978-1-4419-8716-7 (eBook)
    DOI 10.1007/978-1-4419-8716-7
    1. Microcomputer workstations.   2. Sun computers.   I. Slattery,
Kathy.   II. Title.   III. Series.
    QA76.525.B43   1991
    004.165—dc20   91-14256

Sun Microsystems, Inc. has reviewed the contents of this book to final publication. The book
does not necessarily represent the views, opinions, or product strategies of Sun or its
subsidiaries. Neither Sun, nor Springer-Verlag are responsible for its contents or its ac-
curacy, and therefore make no representations or warranties with respect to it. Sun believes,
however, that it presents accurate and valuable information to the interested reader, as of
the time of publication.

The Sun logo, Sun Microsystems, Sun Workstation and NFS are registered trademarks of
Sun Microsystems, Inc. in the United States of America and other countries. Sun, Sun-2,
Sun-3, Sun-4, SunInstall, SunOS, SunView, SunCore and OpenWindows as well as the
word "Sun" followed by a numerical suffix are trademarks of Sun Microsystems, Inc. UNIX
is a registered trademark of UNIX System Laboratories, Inc. PostScript and TranScript are
registered trademarks of Adobe Systems Incorporated. Adobe also owns copyrights related
to the PostScript language and the PostScript interpreter. The trademark PostScript is used
herein only to refer to material supplied by Adobe or to programs written in the PostScript
language as defined by Adobe. SPARC is a registered trademark of SPARC International,
Inc. Products bearing the SPARC trademark are based on an architecture developed by Sun
Microsystems, Inc. SPARCstation is a trademark of SPARC International Inc. licensed
exclusively to Sun Microsystems, Inc. All other products or services mentioned in this
document are identified by the trademarks as designated by the companies that market
those products or services. Inquires concerning such trademarks should be made directly to
those companies. The use of general descriptive names, trademarks, etc., in this publication, even if the former are not especially identified, is not to taken as a sign that such
names, as understood by the Trademarks and Merchandise Act, may accordingly be used
freely by anyone.

Typeset by TCSystems, Inc., Shippensburg, PA.

Printed on acid free paper.

9 8 7 6 5 4 3 2

ISBN 978-1-4612-6455-2

Dedication

This book is dedicated to all of our users (past, present, and future) - for all of those "interesting" situations you created, just so we could learn a little more . . . :)

Preface

This Guide to Sun Administration is a reference manual written by Sun administrators for Sun administrators. The book is not intended to be a complete guide to UNIX Systems Administration; instead it will concentrate on the special issues that are particular to the Sun environment. It will take you through the basic steps necessary to install and maintain a network of Sun computers. Along the way, helpful ideas will be given concerning NFS, YP, backup and restore procedures, as well as many useful installation tips that can make a system administrator's job less painful. Specifically, SunOS 4.0 through 4.0.3 will be studied; however, many of the ideas and concepts presented are generic enough to be used on any version of SunOS.

This book is not intended to be basic introduction to SunOS. It is assumed that the reader will have at least a year of experience supporting UNIX.

Book Overview

The first chapter gives a description of the system types that will be discussed throughout the book. An understanding of all of the system types is needed to comprehend the rest of the book.

Chapter 2 provides the information necessary to install a workstation. The format utility and the steps involved in the **suninstall** process are covered in detail. Ideas and concepts about partitioning are included in this chapter.

YP is the topic of the third chapter. A specific description of each YP map and each YP command is presented, along with some tips about ways to best utilize this package in your environment.

The fourth chapter discusses the issues involved in administering the workstation after it has been installed. We present details about installing clients and their home directories, as well as establishing a good working environment.

Chapter 5 provides an overview of the networking in the SunOS environment. The steps necessary to install multiple networks and subnets are presented, along with an overview of some network commands.

Chapter 6 gives a description of ways to increase security. In particular, the steps necessary to install secure NFS or C2 security are discussed. Several of the files that control security are also discussed.

Backups is the topic of Chapter 7. Several different scenarios and procedures are presented, with a description of most of the backup commands.

Chapter 8 provides a step-by-step guide to troubleshooting. Some common error codes are discussed. Also presented are ways to troubleshoot booting, printing and mail delivery problems.

Chapter 9 is the catch-all chapter, containing a combination of miscellaneous information. A discussion of some important files is included with a section on serial communications and another on disk recovery steps. The last chapter lists suggestions for further reading.

Throughout the book, special fonts are used to denote filenames and command names. In general, italics indicate a filename. Some of these are files that you can look at on your workstation or server. Boldface print indicate that the word is also a command. These commands often have at least one manual page associated with it.

Acknowledgments

Special thanks to Laura and Tim and the rest of our families for putting up with us.

We would also like to thank the following folks for reading the earlier versions of this book and for supplying some answers: Chris Drake, Geoff Gall, Bikram Gill, Ray Jang, Scott Mattoon, Ralph Torres, Eric Voss, and Jing May Wang.

Finally we would like to thank Mike and Lance for getting us involved in this project . . . we think!!?

Contents

Preface.. vii
Acknowledgments ix

1. Systems Types   1
    1.1 Client Machines 2
    1.2 Diskfull Machines 4
    1.3 Sun Architectures.................................... 9

2. Installing Sun Workstations   13
    2.1 Preparation... 13
    2.2 Disk Layouts 21
    2.3 Running the Format Utility........................... 35
    2.4 Suninstall 54
    2.5 After Suninstall 83

3. YP   109
    3.1 What is YP? 109
    3.2 YP Maps and YP Makefile 112
    3.3 YP Commands..................................... 141
    3.4 YP Master Server Initialization 149
    3.5 YP Slave Server Initialization....................... 151
    3.6 YP clients 153
    3.7 Problems 153
    3.8 Advanced Topics 155

4. Administering a Network of Sun Systems   161
    4.1 Server Administration............................... 162
    4.2 Workstation Administration 198
    4.3 Wrap-Up.. 209

5. Basic Networking   **211**
    5.1 Network Hardware 211
    5.2 Network Software 213
    5.3 Choosing a Network Class. 214
    5.4 Subnets. 216
    5.5 Setting Up a Single Network 217
    5.6 Adding Multiple Networks 218
    5.7 Useful Commands 220
    5.8 Establishing a Subnet. 224
    5.9 Routing. 227
    5.10 Special Networking. 228

6. Security   **231**
    6.1 /.rhosts,/etc/hosts.equiv and ⁻/.rhosts. 231
    6.2 /etc/ttytab 232
    6.3 Tightening Security. 233
    6.4 Installing Secure NFS 236
    6.5 Installing C2 Security. 237

7. Backups   **241**
    7.1 Backup Concepts 241
    7.2 Output Devices and File Manipulation. 244
    7.3 Backups using **Dump** 246
    7.4 Backups using **Cpio**. 248
    7.5 Other Archiving Commands 251
    7.6 Selection of a Backup Scheme 251

8. Troubleshooting   **257**
    8.1 Error Messages. 257
    8.2 Problems with Booting. 262
    8.3 Problems with Printing 263
    8.4 Forgotten Passwords. 264
    8.5 Problems with Mail. 265
    8.6 Problems with Lockscreen 266

9. Other Important Files and Issues   **267**
    9.1 /etc/rc Scripts. 267
    9.2 /dev/MAKEDEV. 269
    9.3 /etc/inetd.conf 269

9.4 Crontab.. 270
9.5 Serial Communications 271
9.6 Disk Recovery....................................... 276

10. Reference Library   281

Index 283

Systems Types

1

Sun computer systems come in many shapes and sizes, each of which has been designed for a special purpose. Systems such as the 3/50, 3/60, 4/110, and the SPARCstation™ 1 were designed to be used on a desktop by a single user. Deskside machines, such as the 3/260 and 4/260, allow for more expandability and power than the desktop machines, but can still be used by a single user. Both the desktop and the deskside machines are considered to be workstations. The larger, rack mounted machines such as the 3/280, 4/280, 4/390, and the 4/490 were designed to be fileservers.

In the Sun environment, the network is the key ingredient that enables vast amounts of information to be passed among users. Each machine type has a specific role in this environment. The role of the desktop workstation is to provide an easy-to-use interface between user and machine. This is accomplished through windowing environments and application software. Desktop machines offer a smaller overall size than other system types, but not necessarily less power.

The role of the deskside machine has been to offer the same user interface as a desktop on a more powerful machine. Deskside machines have in the past been used to run graphics application packages since more option slots are available for add-on hardware, and more disk space is available than for most desktops. More slots usually meant more memory, power, and expandability. This tradition is quickly changing as more software products require less additional hardware and as the desktops deliver more power. The newer desktop machines now have many more add-on capabilities as well. The deskside machine is now a lower-cost solution for situations that require a fileserver's speed and disk capacity, but in a much smaller footprint.

Most deskside systems have a larger, rack-mounted counterpart which uses the same central processing unit (CPU), but may have more option slots and room for larger disk storage. The major difference between the deskside and rack-mounted server system is packaging.

The role of the rack-mounted fileserver is to support other machines on the network. This support can be in many forms. Some fileservers supply the necessary network information for all the machines on the network. Others can act as servers of particular resources, thus eliminating the need for large disks on all systems and many copies of the same data. Still other servers support the booting and operation of desktop systems that may not have local disks attached. Before any systems can communicate with each other, they must be running SunOS™, and be properly connected to the network. The SunOS 4.0 and 4.0.3 releases contain some key features also found in the Berkeley Software Distribution version 4.3, which was developed at the University of California, Berkeley.

Each system type is determined by how the machine boots SunOS and what network role it performs once the OS is running. If your system boots from a local disk, it is considered to be a diskfull machine. If the system must use resources over the network in order to boot SunOS, it is a client machine. If a system allows other machines to boot from it or to use some of its disk space over the network, it is considered to be a server.

Every Sun system has the capacity to be a client, standalone, or server machine. How you implement your networking environment depends on your needs and budget. You would not want to configure a rack-mounted 4/280 as a diskless client, but it is possible. Likewise, the 3/50 desktop is not a good choice as a server of diskless clients, but given enough disk space, this is also possible.

1.1 Client Machines

Most client machines do not have a local disk from which to boot. Booting and loading SunOS is done through the network, using a fileserver that has been configured to support clients. After loading the boot program and kernel, the root and /usr filesystems are mounted over the network using Network File System (NFS).

Other client machines may use a local disk to boot part of the way, then borrow files from a server to complete their boot process.

The booted client operates in the same manner as most systems with local disks. The difference is a dependence on the network and the fileserver containing its operating system files. If either one is not operating properly, the client machine is literally dead since the operating system files are accessed over the network.

There are two types of client machines, the diskless and dataless client. Each type is dependent on a server in order to run SunOS. A diskless client is fully dependent on the server, while the dataless client uses only the system executables resident on its server.

1.1.1 Diskless Client

The majority of Sun administration centers around the diskless client. A group of diskless client machines are usually assigned to one common server. You may have a number of servers of diskless clients, or just one, depending on the size of your network. Many of the desktop machines in your workplace may be diskless clients.

The diskless machine is an ideal workstation for persons who are not comfortable with floppy disks or tapes. They will never have to see a disk or tape drive, or be concerned with backing up their files. All disk files are resident on the server machine which is administered by the network or systems administrator. This file-sharing reduces the need for purchasing expensive disks for each machine. User and operating system files are easily accessible on the fileserver and can be edited even when the client is not powered up. This model offers a central location from which the user accounts may be archived. The less desirable part of this arrangement is the client's dependency on the server and the network. If one fileserver is down, all of its clients will be down as well. A less critical but more time consuming aspect of the client-server model deals with backups and restores. Whenever a diskless user happens to inadvertently remove one of their important files, it will be your job to have a recent archive available so that it can be restored.

1.1.2 Dataless Client

Dataless clients are a cross between a diskfull and a diskless machine in that they boot from a local disk, but then use NFS commands to mount their /usr files from a server. If the network or server is not reachable, these machines will not work. The local disk contains some system files, an area used to swap processes in and out of memory, and sometimes a home directory. Most often, the home directory will be mounted using NFS commands as well.

Dataless machines are usually systems dedicated to running one main application. This type of configuration allows a local disk to be used more for local processing instead of the network. Local disks can be accessed much faster than the network in most cases so the overall speed of execution is increased when compared with diskless machines. A distant cousin of the dataless machine is becoming quite popular. The swap-local client is a diskless machine when using operating system files, but has its swap space configured locally.

1.2 Diskfull Machines

Diskfull machines are systems that have SunOS installed on a local disk. They boot completely and operate without relying on other systems in the network. Diskfull machines can mount resources over the network, but generally the mounted directories are not critical to the operating system. The system is able to operate on its own without using remote resources. A diskfull machine may also be a single system in a non-networked environment.

Another diskfull machine might be a system that contains a database of the network information. This machine is called the YP master. A diskfull machine may also be used as a gateway or router, when connecting two different networks together. Another common type of diskfull machine is the print server.

Diskfull systems can be broken down into two groups: standalone machines and servers. Standalone machines often do not require the same resources as server machines. Servers usually require more disk space because they will offer resources for other machines to use.

1.2.1 Standalone Machines

A standalone machine can be defined as a system with a local disk that is not a server. The files installed on the local disk are the necessary programs needed to operate the system correctly. The most basic standalone machine has one disk that has been divided into three partitions. Of the three, two partitions are filesystems, meaning they contain files. One filesystem contains the root files while the other houses the executable files. The other disk partition is a kind of a scratch pad which is used for the swapping of processes. More advanced standalone machines may have a number of filesystems, each set up for a special purpose, but all standalone machines must have at least three partitions. Partitioning and disk layouts will be explained in Chapter 2.

The major difference between a standalone machine and a server is that standalone systems do not offer resources to other machines on the network. They are self-contained. A standalone machine is a good choice for the administrator's system since it is not dependent on any other machine for its operation.

1.2.2 File Servers

Fileservers are diskfull machines as well. They must boot from their local disk before other machines can use the resources they have to offer. The fileserver's function is to supply certain files over a network to other machines that do not have the disk resources available locally. The process of making a resource available on the network is called "exporting". Resources that are exported are usually placed in their own partitions or sub-directories for easier maintenance.

It is best to use the fastest and most powerful machines as fileservers. Less powerful machines may be used as servers but clients of these machines will be less responsive under heavy loads. (Consider the number of remote systems accessing a fileserver at any given moment when deciding which systems to use as fileservers.)

A few different fileserver types will be discussed, including diskless client servers, NFS resource servers, and print servers. These are not the only types of fileservers available. You may wish to define your own server type; the possibilities are endless. These three will serve as good examples.

1.2.2.1 Diskless Client Servers

A diskless client server is configured to support the booting and operation of diskless clients. Each client owns a root directory, a swap file, and usually a chunk of home directory space. In the Sun environment, each diskless machine may have at least one user account or login. To minimize confusion, the home directories used by the login accounts should be installed on the fileserver that also contains the root and swap files.

The number of diskless clients that can be configured on a single server is limited only by the amount of disk space and network throughput. Some of the most recent server systems released by Sun boast fifty and sixty diskless client capabilities. While this is true and can be done, it is not an efficient way of managing the network. If possible, support for client machines should be spread out evenly among a number of servers, not all on one.

On some of the older Sun machines such as the 3/280 and 4/280 a maximum of 20 clients per server should be maintained for optimum performance. While disk storage capacities are becoming larger, the single Ethernet® interface on the server becomes the limiting factor in serving diskless clients. The Fiber Distributed Data Interface (FDDI) should alleviate this restriction, when it becomes available.

All client setup and configuration is done on the server. Clients can be set up at the time of server installation, or after installation. If you choose to wait until after installation to configure diskless clients, then care should be taken when partitioning disks to allow for the future growth of the filesystems used by diskless clients.

When a machine is selected as a diskless client server, that should be its only function. The system can become quite loaded down while acting as a disk server for ten or fifteen clients at the same time. The network traffic in and out of the single Ethernet interface for this alone is very high. Try to balance the load among the available machines. One does not want one machine doing all of the work while others are sitting idle.

1.2.2.2 Homogeneous and Heterogeneous Servers   There are two types of diskless client servers, homogeneous and heterogeneous. Homogeneous servers support systems of like architecture, for instance: a 3/280 server that supports five Sun-3™ systems, three 3/50s and two 3/75 would be considered a homogeneous server. In that same context, a 4/280 server that supports three systems, two 4/110s and a 4/260, is also considered to be a homogeneous server. Homogeneous servers require less disk space for executables than servers that support more than one major architecture type.

Heterogeneous servers are set up to support systems of different architectures. Consider a 4/280 with ten diskless clients, five 3/50s and five 4/110s. A Sun-3 server may also support Sun-4™ architecture clients, but as stated before, it is best to use more powerful machines as servers of less powerful machines for performance reasons. Heterogeneous servers need more disk space in the /export/exec directory than homogeneous servers. This is the place in which the executables for machines of different architecture reside. The most space needed in /export/exec for a full heterogeneous server is 200 megabytes, which is enough disk space to hold a full installation of all the different architecture types.

Since Sun-4c and Sun-4 architectures share the same executables, only one copy is necessary. Likewise, the Sun-3 and Sun-3x architectures also share the same executables. One copy is all that is needed to support both of these architectures. Symbolic links are used to point the sub-architecture clients to the correct path to obtain their /usr files.

Both heterogeneous and homogeneous servers share the same concepts regarding disk partitions. As with the standalone configuration, three separate disk partitions are needed to hold the root, swap, and usr files. But diskless client servers need other partitions for diskless client support. This is done in the directories and sub-directories under /export. In addition, a /home partition should be created to hold the user's files. Each partition is discussed in greater detail in the Disk Layouts section of Chapter 2.

1.2.2.3 Resource Server The resource server is a machine with useful programs and utilities installed on it, and might contain application software, the manual pages, or other utilities that can be used by many systems in the local area network. The resources can be NFS mounted by other machines including diskless, dataless, and diskfull clients, as well as other servers. Resource servers are usually dedicated as such and should not be configured to support the booting of diskless clients.

The disk layout of an NFS server would be similar to the diskless client server with the difference being the absence of /export/root, /export/swap, and /export/exec. There may instead be a partition called /export/unbundled configured during installation. This can be filled with unbundled Sun applications, such as OpenWindows,™ or third party applications like FrameMaker™ or Lotus 1-2-3™. Once installed, other machines on the network may use NFS to mount the /export/unbundled directory tree to obtain the respective application. This saves the administrator concern over which software level of each application the users may be running, as well as having one central location to make changes.

A resource server may also contain large database applications. Other systems wishing to use this database can use NFS commands to mount all or selected parts of the database, thereby reducing the CPU cycles on the database server. The installation of a database server would be much different than that of a diskless client server. A somewhat trimmed version of the operating system is all that would be needed, freeing up local disk space for large database files.

Some database applications require raw disk partitions to be used. Frequently the raw partitions must be quite large, often using the whole disk. If you will be using raw disk partitions on database servers, be sure to make a small partition at the beginning of the disk so that the label is not overwritten with raw data.

1.2.2.4 Print Servers Print servers are a luxury. Their sole purpose is to act as a spooler for one or more printers on your network. All print jobs are routed to this machine and spooled.

Print servers need to have more disk space available in the /var directory. Usually a separate partition is created for this purpose during installation. This is done to make certain that enough free disk space is available for many large print jobs that may be spooled at the same time.

Print servers can be configured as diskless clients while using a local disk for spooling. This is one instance of a diskless machine that is acting as a server as well.

The different system types created by Sun can be from any one of the architectures offered. There are Sun-3 desktops, desksides, and fileservers. There are also Sun-4 desktops, desksides, and fileservers. Knowing how to tell the different architectures apart is very important. The next section explains the differences.

1.3 Sun Architectures

Sun computers are available in three major architecture families. Each family is based on a microprocessor or CPU. The Sun-2 family is based on the MC68010 CPU designed by Motorola. The Sun-3 family is based on the MC68020, also from Motorola. The Sun-4 architecture is based on the SPARC CPU. The SPARC® microprocessor is a reduced instruction set computer or RISC™, designed at Sun.

Within each architecture family there are several different machine types that are considered to be systems of like architecture. Each architecture family shares a common set of release tapes. The Sun-3 family can all use the same set of release tapes for installation. They share the same CPU type even though there are many different Sun-3 machines. Likewise, systems in the Sun-4 family can also use the same set of release tapes during installation whether the machine is a 4/110 or a 4/280.

A basic rule to keep in mind is that systems of like architecture may share binary files while systems of unlike architecture may not. The binary files on any UNIX® machine are executable programs that make up the operating system. Most every command or utility is a binary executable file. The UNIX kernel itself is a binary executable file. When a system attempts to execute a binary file of an unlike architecture, a message similar to this is displayed:

```
"Cannot execute binary file."
: Exec format error
```

This situation holds true between SPARC and 680X0 binaries. An exception to this are binaries compiled on the Motorola MC680X0 family of microprocessors. The 68000 family allows programs that are compiled on the older 68010 processor to remain executable by the newer 68020 processor. Taking this one step further, binaries that are created on the MC68020 CPU are executable on the MC-68030. This is why most applications created for Sun-2 machines will execute on Sun-3s. They will not execute as fast as they would if compiled on the 68020, but they do run. Unfortunately, they are not reverse compatible. Programs compiled with the MC68020 cannot be run on the MC68010. The breakdown of Sun machines and architecture families can be seen in Table 1.1.

1.3.1 Application and Kernel Architectures

There is a minor architecture within the Sun-3 family called Sun-3x, based on the MC68030 microprocessor. Major and minor architectures are also known as application and kernel architectures, respectively. Sun-3x is referred to as a minor architecture because it can share the same binaries (/usr) as Sun-3 systems. This becomes apparent when a Sun-3 machine is serving diskless clients of both Sun-3 and Sun-3x architectures. The path to the client's executables resides in the /export/exec directory. The Sun-3 clients mount /export/exec/sun3 for the /usr files. In actuality, /export/exec/sun3 is a symbolic link to the server's /usr directory. Sun-3x machines will also use the /export/exec/sun3 path when mounting their /usr files which saves much disk space for diskless client servers supporting both Sun-3 and Sun-3x architectures.

Only two hardware products currently exist that use the MC-68030; the 3/80 desktop, and the 3/470 deskside machines. Although binaries can be shared between Sun-3 and Sun-3x machines, the kernel specific files cannot. Among the specific files that cannot be shared are the kernel, the boot program, and certain status programs such as **ps** and **pstat.** Other unshared files are libraries and header files associated with building a new kernel. The kernel architecture dependent files are kept in the /usr/kvm/ <arch> directory, where <arch> is the kernel architecture of the machine. The command "**arch** -k" will echo back the kernel architecture of the local system (see arch(1)).

Sun Architectures			
Machine Name	CPU Type	Kernel Architecture	Application Architecture
2/50	68010	Sun-2™	Sun-2
2/120, 2/170	68010	Sun-2	Sun-2
3/50	68020	Sun-3	Sun-3
3/60	68020	Sun-3	Sun-3
3/110	68020	Sun-3	Sun-3
3/75, 3/140	68020	Sun-3	Sun-3
3/160, 3/180	68020	Sun-3	Sun-3
3/260, 3/280	68020	Sun-3	Sun-3
3/80	68030	Sun-3x	Sun-3
3/470, 3/480	68030	Sun-3x	Sun-3
4/60	SPARC	Sun-4c	Sun-4
4/110, 4/150	SPARC	Sun-4	Sun-4
4/260, 4/280	SPARC	Sun-4	Sun-4
4/330	SPARC	Sun-4	Sun-4
4/370, 4/390	SPARC	Sun-4	Sun-4
4/470, 4/490	SPARC	Sun-4	Sun-4

TABLE 1.1. *Sun Architectures.*

A minor architecture for the Sun-4 family of systems also exists called Sun-4c which includes the latest line of desktop machines, the SPARCstation family. This next generation SPARC processor retains some of the same characteristics of the 680X0 family in that it can share the executables of its predecessor, but cannot share kernel specific files. This is the reason that the 4.0.3c release was made. The relationship between the Sun-3 and Sun-3x architectures is the same as that of the Sun-4 and Sun-4c.

Installing Sun Workstations

2

This chapter explains how to install Sun workstations and servers. Because of the array of system types, most installations will be different. The majority of the differences center around the disk partition arrangement. Other differences concern the software categories that are selected. Still other installation differences involve the operating system support files for diskless clients of like and unlike architecture.

2.1 Preparation

When preparing to install a new system to your network, the first task is to select a unique hostname and establish an internet protocol (IP) number for the machine. The IP number chosen depends on the local network address. If using YP, you must also determine the domainname of the existing network or create a new one if one does not exist.

2.1.1 Saving Files

If you are re-installing or upgrading from a previous SunOS release, you should perform a full system backup. At the very least, backup any files that you wish to save before running **format** or **suninstall.** Specifically, the user account files residing in /home/ <server>/<username> and the sub-directories thereof should be preserved. If you are re-installing a server of diskless clients, be sure to backup the /export/root directories so that individual client mount entries and mail files are saved. Other important files that should be saved are listed below:

/etc/passwd
/etc/group

/etc/printcap
/etc/aliases
/etc/fstab
/etc/licenses
/var/spool/mail/<username>

The easiest way to keep the files listed above with the user files is to create a "save" directory in the user's home directory. Then, copy the files to the "save" directory. When this is done, the user's entire home directory can be archived, including the "save" files. After the system is installed, restore the home directory and copy the "save" files back to where they belong.

One of the most important parts of preparing to install a system is defining the layout of the disk or partitioning. Partitioning the disk is a way to group or separate areas of the disk media into manageable sections. Once the operating system is installed, changing the partition arrangement is nearly impossible without extended down time. What follows is a brief discussion of some concepts regarding the **format** utility since this is where some of the disk partitions are defined.

2.1.2 Format Concepts

The main objectives of the **format** utility are to format disks and to adjust the size of the root and swap partitions since they cannot be changed during **suninstall.** The adjusting is done by creating or modifying the disk label.

There are other uses for the **format** utility as well. Nondestructive diagnostic routines can be used to test a suspected bad area on a disk, while utilities such as mapping bad sectors, converting raw block numbers to cylinder, head, and sector numbers are also available.

The **format** utility reads a data file called */etc/format.dat* when invoked without arguments. In this file are entries for every disk type known to SunOS. Each entry contains specifics about every disk such as the number of cylinders, the number of heads, rotation speed, which type of controller it uses, and the number of sectors per track (see format(8s)).

If you are adding a disk device that is not in this file, you may make an entry in */etc/format.dat* if all the disk parameters are known. It is not recommended to change the format.dat file, but if you are to attempt this, make a copy of the original */etc/format.dat* before you change its contents. Save the original, just in case your entry does not work. This is good practice when editing any system file.

Running the **format** utility is usually necessary under these conditions:

- Installing new systems
- Adding new disk peripherals to an existing system
- Adding a new bad block to the defect map
- Testing suspected bad sectors

You should format the disks in your new systems. Although it is unlikely, a disk surface may become damaged during shipping. Formatting may find a problem on the disk that could cause grief after the OS is installed. A better way to find problems on the disk in a less time consuming manner is by using the analyze utility within **format.** One of the options under analyze is to compare the data read with the data written. If errors are found, the compare option makes minor corrections and updates the defect list if necessary. If a large number of disk errors are encountered, something is wrong. Check disk cabling or call for hardware help.

Every disk is equipped with a list of manufacturer defects. The disk manufacturers have tested the disks for many hours to find potential problem areas. They attach a hardcopy to each disk identifying the problem areas, usually as a label on the disk itself. Each defect is mapped with a cylinder, head, and a sector, or a number of bytes offset from the index mark. The defect list is also stored on the disk, in a special pre-determined area. Sun engineering works with the disk manufacturers so that the defect information can be obtained automatically, without a lengthy, manual input session. When a disk is formatted, a map is created from this list that tells the disk not to use these defective blocks. A number of alternate cylinders are set aside to be used instead of the bad sectors. If a new problem is found while the system is up and running, different measures should be taken, depending on which type of disk and controller you have installed.

Storage module disk devices, also called SMD disks, such as the "xy" or "xd" drives, support slip sectoring and mapping, while many SCSI disks do not. Slip sectoring is used when a bad datablock is encountered. The bad datablock can be "slipped" into an unused sector on an alternate cylinder. A spare sector is used instead of the bad sector from this point on or until the disk is re-formatted. On some disks one sector on each track is reserved for slipping. If this sector is used then any further bad sectors must be "mapped" to an unused sector on an alternate cylinder. Both processes attempt to save the data that is located on the bad sector; however, sometimes it does not work, so current backups should be kept for all systems.

Old SCSI disks cannot be "slipped". Their defects must be found and mapped before they are formatted. Defects that are found after the initial disk format may be mapped, but the only way for the changes to take affect is to format the disk again, thus removing all data that may be present on the disk.

The best way to learn all the facets of the **format** utility is to locate an unused disk drive, boot MUNIX and get acquainted with the different menus. While in each menu, use some or all of the utilities. Some tests are destructive to the data on the disk while others are not. Tests that are destructive to the data on the disk are labeled as such and should be avoided if you wish your data to be left intact.

It is not recommended that you attempt to run the **format** utility on your system disk after the installation has occurred. You could accidentally re-label the disk with the wrong parameters, and quite possibly hang the system. You may wish to use **format** to adjust the size of unmounted disk partitions while running SunOS. This technique is dangerous, but if you know what can be changed without affecting the other filesystems on the disk, it can be done. It is frustrating to find plenty of disk space available in the wrong partition, so plan ahead.

In pre-4.X SunOS releases, a utility called **diag** was used to manipulate the label and repair disks. The new **format** replaces the **diag** routine. There are more features available within **format**. Once your disks have been formatted with **format**, the 3.5 **diag** program cannot be used any longer on those disks. You may still load 3.5 SunOS, but you must use the 4.0 **format** routine to do all the disk partitioning and formatting.

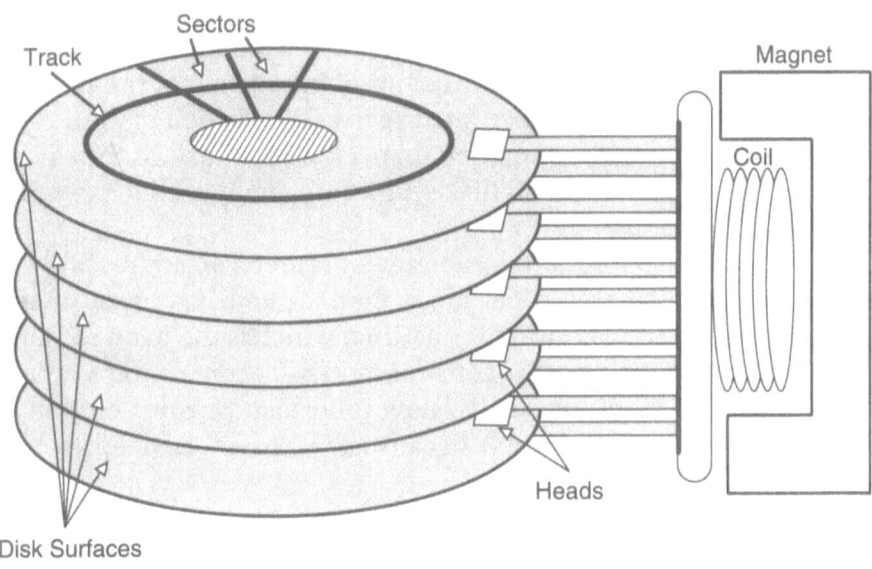

FIGURE 2.1. *Cylinders, heads, and sectors.*

There are many items that can be discussed concerning disk devices. This is not the forum for an in-depth study. However, a working knowledge of disk geometry can be quite helpful in solving those special problems.

Disk technology has come a long way recently. Media densities are growing by the minute and increasingly massive amounts of data storage are available in compact packages. While densities and package sizes can be radically different, all disks have a few things in common: cylinders, heads, and sectors.

2.1.2.1 Cylinders and Heads Most disks have multiple media platters. Each platter surface has at least one read/write head associated with it, and many have two or more. Each head is numbered and can only be positioned over one track at a time. The first data block on most disks is the outermost track, head number zero. Since the head assembly is attached to a fixed armature, all heads are positioned over the same track at the same time. This area is called a cylinder. Tracks are associated with one head while a cylinder is made up of all the tracks, and all the heads.

2.1.2.2 Sectors Each track is divided up into many sectors, where the data is stored. The sectors are lined up next to each other all the way around each track. Sector sizes and layout are implementation specific depending on the density and physical size of the media itself. Disks with more surface area, such as a 5.25 inch platter, can contain more sectors in one track than a 3.5 inch disk, if they use the same density. All SunOS disk sectors are configured to contain 512 bytes of data.

When a disk is formatted, each sector is given an address. This address becomes the physical block number and is written in an area inside each sector during formatting, which is the main reason that formatting a disk is time consuming. Disks containing a large number of blocks are especially slow to format. Smaller capacity disks take less time to format because fewer sectors need to be written.

2.1.2.3 Partitions Partitioning divides the disk up into sections. A partition is a group of sequential cylinders with an absolute start and end point. For example, the first partition on a disk could begin at cylinder zero, sector zero, and end at cylinder ten. All of the blocks or sectors contained between cylinder zero, sector zero, and the last sector, last head on cylinder nine, are part of this partition. The next partition could then begin at cylinder ten, sector zero.

Some partitions may contain filesystems, others may not. When defining a partition that will be used as a filesystem, one must allow for overhead, because not every raw block in that filesystem is used for data. Some overhead blocks, such as the inode table and indirect inode pointers, are needed to keep track of files and directories that will live in the data blocks. This overhead amounts to nearly ten percent of the size of the raw partition. If a partition has 30,000 raw disk blocks, 3000 of these blocks are used for alternate superblocks, the inode table, and indirect inodes.

Still more overhead is used after the filesystem has been made. By default, the writable size of a filesystem appears to be ten percent less than the size of the partition after the filesystem has been made. This is why a partition that you configure to have 100 megabytes of free blocks actually contains about 90 megabytes of free space when empty. If the filesystem becomes full, only root can continue write to the filesystem, which prevents a normal user from causing a system crash by overflowing the filesystem, while maintaining a reasonably efficient block allocation scheme. As the filesystem becomes more populated, the amount of free contiguous blocks decrease. When a filesystem is under 90 percent full, data blocks can be more contiguous, thereby speeding up the time it takes to perform write and read operations.

When determining the actual size of a partition in raw data blocks, or sectors, figure the total overhead to be 20 percent. If you want to make a partition that has 100 megabytes of writeable space, you need to configure the partition to have 120 megabytes of 512 byte blocks, or 234,375 blocks.

2.1.2.4 Filesystems After a partition has been defined with a start and end point, a filesystem can be created. Every UNIX operating system uses filesystems. Filesystems are accessed by the **mount** maintenance command. The first task performed by the **suninstall** program is to look at the partition sizes specified in the disk form so that it can create new filesystems. After the filesystems have been created, some are mounted and filled with the software that was selected in the software form. Other partitions are left empty, save for their lost+found directory. The lost+found directory is used by the **fsck** program when it cannot resolve where files or directories belong.

Filesystems are built with the **mkfs** maintenance command (see mkfs(8)). A friendlier command, is also available called **newfs** (see newfs(8)). **Newfs** reads the label of the specified disk, then passes the parameters found in the label on to **mkfs** which does the actual filesystem construction.

Each filesystem contains a table of contents or a superblock that maintains critical information about that filesystem. The filesystem consistency check program, **fsck**, first looks at the superblock before it continues checking the filesystem. When **newfs** is invoked, backup copies of the superblock are placed throughout the filesystem so that if the original superblock becomes corrupt, the filesystem may be salvaged. Each backup superblock is placed in a different cylinder group, and on a different media platter. Cylinder groups are defined when the filesystem is created by the **mkfs** command. When **newfs** or **mkfs** is executed, the default number of cylinders per group is sixteen, unless an argument is included to change this.

Backup superblock locations are displayed to the screen when **newfs** is invoked. The backup superblock locations for each filesystem created during the installation of the operating system can be found in the */usr/etc/install/files/suninstall.log* file. The *suninstall.log* file contains screen output from each **newfs** that was performed, and keeps a running log of the installation.

When adding new disks to any of your systems first check that they are defined in the kernel, connect the new disk(s), add entries to /dev if necessary, and run the **format** utility to define your partition requirements. Once this is accomplished, use **newfs** to create the filesystems. You may wish to add the new filesystem entries to the */etc/fstab* file so that they are checked and mounted when the system boots. Also be sure to create directories as mount points for the new filesystems.

2.1.2.5 Disk Labels The disk label is where the partitioning information is kept. This information is critical because most partitions contain filesystems. If a disk were to lose the label, all information on the disk may be lost unless a backup label can be found. Simply restoring the original or backup label may recover data that was thought to be lost. The data was never really removed from the media. Since the label indicates where the filesystems begin, the data in those filesystems was simply not available.

A copy of the disk label should be stored offline just in case the primary label becomes corrupt. You can use the **dkinfo** command (see dkinfo(8)), to read the label once the system is running SunOS. The output from **dkinfo** can either be stored in a file or redirected to a printer. The disk label is the first block on the disk. One of the backup labels is placed near the last block on the disk while others are distributed throughout the disk. Another way to save the label information is to create a log book while installing the system and update the log when changes are made.

Now that you know what a partition is, and where the partition information is kept, examples of different disk layouts will be discussed. Because the partition arrangement is usually decided by the person that is installing the system, each specific partition can be placed anywhere, but traditionally, partition "a" is the root partition, "b" is swap space, and "g" is the /usr partition.

2.2 Disk Layouts

The physical layout of disk partitions differs between machine types. The partitions defined for a standalone machine may be very different than those partitions defined on a server of diskless clients. However, all diskfull systems need a root filesystem, a partition for swapping, and a /usr filesystem. Servers that support diskless clients have additional partitions configured for the clients' files.

The Sun partitioning scheme allows a maximum of eight partitions per disk. Only seven of the eight are user-definable. Partition "a" on disk zero is frequently designated as the root filesystem. The "b" partition is then assigned to be the swap space. Partition "c" is the whole disk and should not be changed. The next five partitions can be defined in any manner necessary, as long as one of the five is the /usr partition. The /usr, root, and swap partitions do not have to be on the same disk if others are available. From a performance standpoint, it is better to configure root and /usr on different disks. Balancing the load among all disks provides the best overall system performance, but increases the risk of down time due to disk failure.

2.2.1 Standalone Layout

The partition layout on most standalone machines is quite basic. When the default partition table is used, the layout may be similar to Figure 2.2.

2.2.1.1 The Root Partition Partition "a" is frequently the root filesystem and is sometimes called slash (/). This filesystem serves as the anchor for all other mounts. The UNIX kernel lives in "slash" as well as other important files like /etc/init, /etc/hosts, and the /etc/rc scripts. Every Sun system must have some kind of root filesystem. A listing of the normal root directory is similar to Figure 2.3.

In most system configurations, the default size for the root filesystem is eight megabytes. The size of / is usually not a problem since only four megabytes are used by the system files after a fresh installation. Problems with smaller root filesystems arise after the system has been up for a while, and a user begins getting large

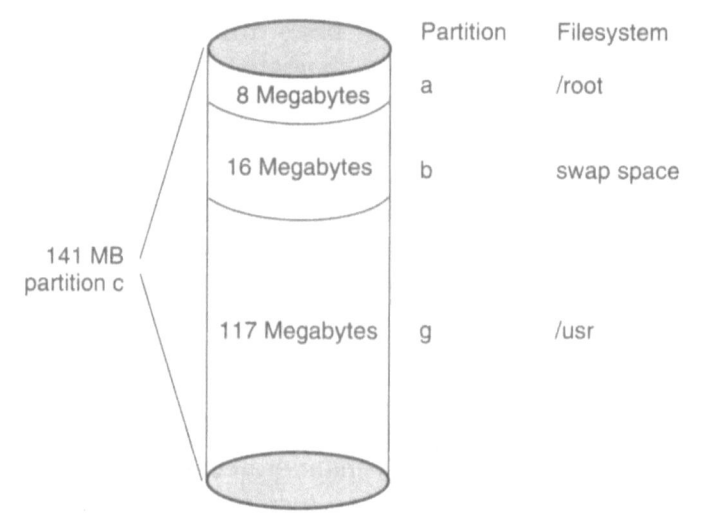

Partition	Filesystem
a	/root
b	swap space
g	/usr

FIGURE 2.2.   *Standalone Layout.*

amounts of email. A tool often used to read email is the window-based **mailtool** program, provided in SunView™. When running, **mailtool** makes a complete copy of the incoming mail file, */var/spool/mail/<username>*, in the /tmp directory. In a normal, standalone configuration, both of these files are created in the root filesystem. Attempting to read a large mail file could cause the root filesystem to become full. If the root filesystem becomes full, system accounting is suspended, as are many other important processes. The system will essentially become frozen until space is freed. This is one of the most common system administration calls. A solution to this problem is to create a separate /var partition during installation. If you choose not to create a separate /var partition, you should increase the size of the root partition to avoid the problem altogether. If the system is already installed, move the large mail file to the user's home directory and tell the user to read it as a mail folder. Other more permanent solutions to this problem can be found in Chapter 8.

Also resident under /var is a directory called /var/adm. The files in this directory can grow endlessly, depending on how often people login to the machine, and how long the machine has been running.

```
blue# ls -la /
total 120:
-rw-r--r--       1    root       101    Apr 24    1989  .cshrc
-rw-r--r--       1    root        53    Apr 24    1989  .login
-rw-r--r--       1    root        70    Apr 24    1989  .profile
-rw-r--r--       1    root         0    Apr 24    1989  .rhosts
lrwxrwxrwx       1    root         7    Mar 30    13:14  bin -> usr/bin
-r--r--r--       1    root    126912    Mar 30    15:38  boot
drwxr-sr-x       2    bin       4096    Apr 10    22:42  dev
drwxr-sr-x       5    root      1536    Apr 10    22:42  etc
drwxr-sr-x       7    root       512    Mar 30    15:39  export
drwxr-xr-x       6    root       512    Apr 24    08:51  home
-rwxr-xr-x       1    root    136185    Mar 30    15:38  kadb
lrwxrwxrwx       1    root         7    Mar 30    13:14  lib -> usr/lib
drwxr-xr-x       2    root      8192    Mar 30    13:09  lost+found
drwxr-sr-x       2    bin        512    Apr 24    1989  mnt
drwxr-sr-x       2    bin        512    Mar 30    15:38  sbin
lrwxrwxrwx       1    root        15    Mar 30    13:14  sys -> ./usr/share/sys
drwxr-sr-x       2    root       512    May 17    13:37  tftpboot
drwxrwsrwx       3    bin       1024    May 22    04:15  tmp
drwxr-sr-x      22    root       512    Mar 30    15:25  usr
drwxr-sr-x       9    bin        512    Apr 24    1989  var
-rwxr-xr-x       1    root    901319    Mar 30    15:38  vmunix
```

FIGURE 2.3. *Listing of a root directory.*

The /tmp directory is used by some system functions such as the **vi** editor and the C compiler. Temporary files are created in /tmp during a **vi** session to provide a backup mechanism should the system go down. You should have enough free space in "/" to allow large files to be edited. The **commandtool** window in SunView also creates a file in /tmp to keep a running log of all the screen text displayed. Each time the system boots, the files in /tmp are removed while directories under /tmp are preserved. The examples above are some good reasons to increase the size of the root partition, or create separate /tmp and /var partitions.

2.2.1.2 The Swap Partition

Swap space is a raw disk partition used as temporary storage of processes waiting to get their turn with the CPU. Swapping usually occurs in the "b" partition of the primary system disk. All systems need some form of swap space. From an administrator's standpoint, don't cheat on swap, because some applications require a large amount. The default partition size for swap space on most Sun systems is often too small. More space should be configured as the size of a system's memory increases.

A good rule for calculating swap size is to create a partition twice the size of the amount of memory installed. If your system has 16MB RAM, then your swap partition should be 32MB, preferably more. Thus you will have an area that is large enough to contain a full memory dump in case of a system panic. In a system panic, all of the system memory that is being used at the time is dumped to an offset in swap. If the swap partition is not big enough to hold all of the memory, the dump will be truncated. This may not concern you directly, but a complete memory dump can help whoever may need to find out why the system crashed.

Other reasons for a large swap space are dependent on the type of load your system will normally incur. Generally, more swap space is needed as the load is increased or as application size increases.

Swap can be increased more easily than a root partition since it is raw disk space. There are other commands that can be used once the system is running to add more swap space given disk resources are available (see swapon(8)).

2.2.1.3 Partition "c"   The "c" partition is always the whole disk starting at block 0 and ending on the last cylinder, last head. The **suninstall** program uses partition "c" as a reference point while the disk partitioning is done in the "Assign disk information" form. Partition "c" in most cases should never be changed. Partition "c" is also used in disk block error reporting. If partition "c" is to be the only partition on the disk, it can be made into a filesystem.

2.2.1.4 The /usr Partition   The /usr partition is where the local system executables live. Most of these executables make up the UNIX operating system. Other files residing in the /usr partition are libraries and header files, the windowing system executables, and the manual pages.

Every system needs to mount /usr either locally or remotely to complete the boot process. If every software category is installed from the SunOS release tape, /usr needs to be no less than 90 megabytes. This does not include disk space for any unbundled applications which may also need to be installed. Your installation may need more disk space for the /usr partition than 90 megabytes. You should know how much disk space your applications need before you do the installation. Applications are easier to maintain if loaded into a separate partition, or on to a resource server.

A normal /usr directory contains the sub-directories and links as shown in Figure 2.4. Notice that a number of entries in Figure 2.4 are symbolic links to other parts of the /usr filesystem. This has been done to keep many of the same pathnames from previous releases consistent. The /usr/spool directory is linked to /var/ spool, and /usr/man is linked to /usr/share/man. If you were to change your working directory to /usr/spool, it would appear that you got there, but your actual working directory would be /var/

```
blue# ls -l /usr
lrwxrwxrwx   1   root      10   Jan 15 20:01   adm -> ../var/adm
drwxr-sr-x   3   bin     5120   Mar 10 13:31   bin
lrwxrwxrwx   1   root      10   Jan 15 19:58   boot -> ./kvm/boot
drwxr-sr-x  13   bin      512   Jan 15 20:01   demo
drwxr-sr-x   2   bin      512   Oct 15 1989    diag
drwxr-sr-x   3   bin      512   Jan 15 19:59   dict
drwxr-sr-x   6   bin     3072   Jan 15 19:17   etc
drwxrwsr-x   3   root    1024   Jan 15 20:02   games
drwxr-sr-x  41   bin     2048   Jan 15 19:23   include
drwxr-sr-x   6   root    1024   Jan 15 20:10   kvm
drwxr-sr-x  22   bin     3584   Jan 15 19:28   lib
drwxr-sr-x   2   bin      512   Oct 15 1989    local
drwxr-xr-x   2   root    8192   Oct 16 1989    lost+found
lrwxrwxrwx   1   root       9   Jan 15 20:01   man -> share/man
lrwxrwxrwx   1   root      10   Jan 15 20:01   mdec -> ./kvm/mdec
lrwxrwxrwx   1   root      13   Jan 15 20:01   pub -> share/lib/pub
drwxr-sr-x   5   bin      512   Jan 15 19:58   share
lrwxrwxrwx   1   root      12   Jan 15 19:59   spool -> ../var/spool
lrwxrwxrwx   1   root       9   Jan 15 19:59   src -> share/src
lrwxrwxrwx   1   root      11   Jan 15 20:01   stand -> ./kvm/stand
lrwxrwxrwx   1   root       7   Jan 15 20:01   sys -> kvm/sys
lrwxrwxrwx   1   root      10   Jan 15 19:59   tmp -> ../var/tmp
drwxr-sr-x   2   bin     1536   Jan 15 19:15   ucb
```

FIGURE 2.4. *The listing of a /usr directory.*

spool. The reason for the links is to remove writable directories from /usr and allow the partition to be mounted read-only.

The three partitions discussed above are the building blocks for all other diskfull system types. Before a system can be a server, it must be able to boot SunOS by itself. Keeping this in mind, the special partition requirements for servers of diskless clients are discussed below, omitting the aforementioned root, swap, and /usr partitions since they function the same way on all diskfull machine types.

2.2.2 Diskless Client Server Layout

Most diskless client server systems contain more than one disk device. In the first example however, a single disk is used to arrange what normally takes eight partitions into only seven partitions. A discussion on multiple disk server systems follows the single disk example.

2.2.2.1 Single Disk Client Server
A diskless client server with only one disk may be partitioned similar to Figure 2.5. The major differences in disk layout between standalone machines and server systems are the additional files and directories that are used by its clients. On diskless client servers, these files and directories are normally placed under the /export directory.

Often the /export directory is itself a disk partition with its sub-directories, /export/root, /export/swap, and /export/exec, also being disk partitions. This arrangement cannot be done on single disk server systems because there are not enough configurable partitions.

2.2.2.1.1 The /export Partition
The /export directory hierarchy contains the root filesystem files, the swap files and system executables for each diskless client that is being served. The default path for the client's root files is /export/root/<client-name>, while the default path for the client's swap space is /export/swap/<client-name>. Every client supported on this server needs a separate root directory and swap file. Both /export/root/<client> and /export/swap/<client> files and directories are created when the **setup_client** script is run, or when a client is configured during the installation process.

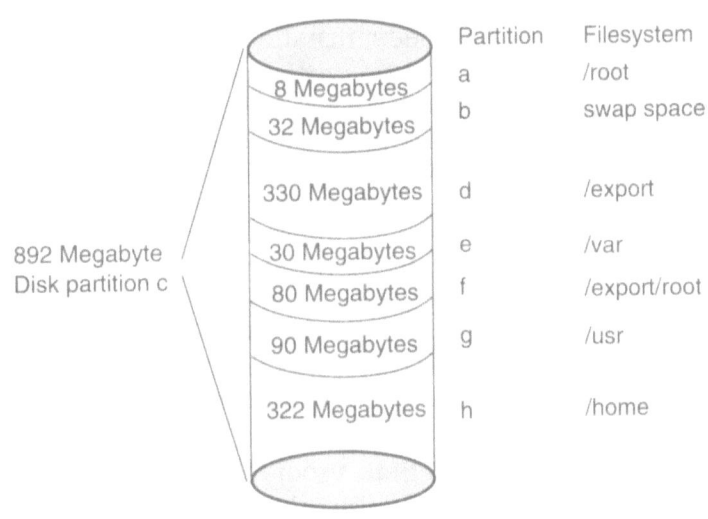

Partition	Filesystem
a	/root
b	swap space
d	/export
e	/var
f	/export/root
g	/usr
h	/home

FIGURE 2.5. *Client server with one large disk.*

Diskless clients also need a directory to mount their system executables or /usr files. These files are kept in the /export/exec/ <arch> directory where <arch> is one of sun2, sun3, or sun4. The/export/exec/<arch> files are a shared resource, so more than one client can NFS mount this resource at a time. Clients of different architectures mount the directory pertaining to their specific architecture type. The root and swap resources for each client are not shared.

The application or major architecture name is used as a path to /export/exec/<arch> because they are binary compatible. Sun-4 and Sun-4c clients share the /export/exec/sun4 directory while Sun-3 and Sun-3x clients share /export/exec/sun3.

Also resident under the /export/exec directory is the sub-directory called kvm. The /export/exec/kvm directory contains kernel specific files pertaining to each architecture served. This is where kernel and application architectures differ. Sun-4 clients mount /export/exec/kvm/sun4 while Sun-4c clients use /export/ exec/kvm/sun4c. Most of the kvm files are used when building new kernels and when new clients are created. A number of the files in /export/exec/kvm/<arch> are copied to the client's root directory when the client setup occurs.

Once the server has been installed, the directories under /export/exec seldom grow. Little writing is done to this directory tree, since all diskless clients use NFS commands to mount their /usr files with the read-only option. The only reason that /export/ exec might need more disk space is if you were to extract more software categories than were originally installed. Still, the greatest amount of disk space needed in /export/exec for a large-scale heterogeneous server is 200 megabytes. A partition of this size covers most of the possible client architectures, except for the Sun-386i™ executables, which are not discussed here.

The /export/root and /export/swap directories use more disk space as clients are added and free up disk space as clients are removed. The files in each client's root directory consume a little more than two megabytes. Some special files and directories used by the system at runtime must also live in each /export/root/ <client-name> directory, so a minimum of five megabytes should be reserved for each client. If each client uses its own /var directory for email, reserve an additional three megabytes just to be safe.

Because the swap space on each machine is usually quite large, the size of the partition containing /export/swap should be considered when installing diskless client servers. A good calculation for swap files is to allow sixteen megabytes of disk space per diskless client, since most diskless clients are configured with eight megabytes of RAM. If you know that your diskless clients have more than eight megabytes of memory, then you can plan for a larger /export or /export/swap. This partition can be adjusted accordingly while in **suninstall**'s "assign disk information" form.

In an ideal environment, /export/exec, /export/root, and /export/swap should each have their own partition assignment as shown in Figure 2.8., later in this chapter. This is not always possible. The partition layout for a single disk server system requires more planning than normal.

In the single disk example, /export was chosen as one disk partition while /export/root was selected as the other. A brief discussion will explain the reasoning behind this choice.

The /export/exec directory is a collection of executables derived from SunOS release tapes. These can be easily restored if the disk were to crash. Also, the /export/swap directory contains nothing more than large files, also painless to re-create. Since /export/ exec and /export/swap can be restored easily, they can be placed in the same partition, /export. The contents of /export in this situation do not change very often because diskless clients mount the /usr files with a read-only option. Frequent tape backups of this partition are not necessary.

The /export/root directory contains the root files for each diskless client served. There are many files under root, such as */var/ spool/mail/<username>* that may be lost forever if not archived before a disk crash. The filesystem containing the client's root files needs to be backed-up daily. Configuring all the root files in one partition makes them easier to backup, while leaving the more constant directories alone.

The normal contents of the /export directory are shown in Figure 2.6. The /export/exec, /export/root and /export/swap directories have been discussed. The last directory normally under /export is /export/share. This directory is used to hold files and libraries that can be shared among all architecture types. These files may include the on-line manual pages, the document formatting macros, some SunView source files and the /sys directory which contains header files and object modules necessary for building kernels.

The /export/share directory is a symbolic link to /usr/share. When support for a new architecture is extracted from tape, some files for that architecture are put into the /usr/share directory on

```
# ls -l /export
total 4
drwxr-sr-x   3   root   512   Oct 16  1989    exec
drwxr-sr-x   2   root   512   Mar 10 18:06    root
drwxr-sr-x   2   root   512   Oct 16  1989    share
drwxr-sr-x   2   root   512   Mar 10 18:06    swap
```

FIGURE 2.6. *Listing of the /export directory.*

your server. This placement demonstrates another reason to leave extra disk space when determining the /usr filesystem size.

2.2.2.1.2 The /var Partition Var is a relatively new directory tree, first used in SunOS 4.0. Var contains the spooling directories for printers, **cron,** and uucp. Var is also the branch in which YP maps reside on the YP master and slave servers. (YP is discussed in Chapter 3.) Other administrative files such as login records and captured console messages are stored under /var/adm.

Incoming electronic mail is put into */var/spool/mail/ <username>.* If you use email extensively, the /var/spool/mail directory can become filled very quickly. Since the default partition table does not reserve a partition for /var, /var is left in the root filesystem. If a separate partition is not designated for /var at installation time, all of the log files, email, and printer spooling that usually take place in /var is actually placed in the root filesystem.

Each diskless client has its own /var that is actually located in the server's /export/root directory. Extra buffer space should be reserved on the server for each client's email and accounting files. Some administrators choose to use the diskless client server or another system as a mailhost. Clients then mount the server's /var/spool/mail directory to receive email. This model illustrates another reason to create a larger, separate /var partition on the server. While the mailhost may sound like a grand idea, the setup and administration can be complicated and time consuming. Still, it is a common configuration, not only limited to supporting email for diskless machines, but to all system types. The listing of a normal /var directory is shown in Figure 2.7.

The adm directory holds administration information. Crash is used as storage for crash dumps, but only if **savecore** is enabled in the */etc/rc.local* script. The preserve directory is used for recovery of files still open by **vi** or **ex** when the system stops abnormally. The spool directory is used for the spooling of print jobs, mail, and uucp jobs. The /var/tmp directory is another place for temporary files. Unbundled Sun applications often leave a directory out here after being installed. The /var/yp directory only exists if the system is using YP, and contains different files depending on the YP type (either server or client).

2.2.2.1.3 The /usr Partition As discussed before, the /usr filesystem is needed on every diskfull machine. On diskless client

```
# ls -l /var
drwxr-sr-x      3    bin     512    Jan 13  04:05    adm
drwxr-sr-x      4    bin     512    Dec 15  15:55    crash
drwxr-sr-x      2    bin     512    Oct 15  1989     log
drwxr-sr-x      2    bin     512    May 20  10:41    preserve
drwxr-sr-x     15    bin     512    May 20  10:39    spool
drwxrwsrwx      2    bin     512    May 20  10:41    tmp
drwxr-sr-x      4    bin    1024    Jan 16  04:50    yp
```

FIGURE 2.7. *The /var directory.*

servers, /usr is mounted by the clients sharing the same application architecture as their server because a symbolic link from
/export/exec/<arch> points to /usr. There is no difference between the /usr partition of a standalone machine and the /usr
partition of a server of diskless clients. When all software categories are selected, both the standalone and the server get the same
files.

2.2.2.1.4 The /home Partition The /home partition is where
user account files are kept. Each login account defines a home
directory in which the user is placed upon a successful login. The
Sun convention for home directories has been to use the /home/
<server>/<username> directory for remote mounts, or /home/
<hostname>/<username> if using a local home.

Home directories are where most users save their work, mail,
and whatever else they need. A partition such as this could grow
quite fast. Standalone /home partitions do not grow nearly as fast as
the home directory space on a diskless client server. Multiply the
normal accumulation of user files by the number of diskless clients
using the same partition to understand why.

The average size of an individual user's home directory does
not need to be larger than 40 megabytes. It is difficult to store and
keep track of much more than this unless the user is working with
large files. Other arrangements should be made for cases when
users have large mass storage requirements.

Diskless systems use NFS commands to mount their home
directory for access to their user account files. Usually one account
is set up for each diskless client. Permissions should be set on user
accounts to keep out unwanted users that mount the same home
directory path, since permissions to restrict this action are not set

automatically. The most secure measure of mounting home directories is to edit each client's */etc/fstab* file to mount only their home directory, /home/<server>/<username>, instead of the whole /home/<server> path. This is more difficult to administer, but may be worth the effort if security is an issue. Another viable option is using netgroups (see Chapter 4).

2.2.2.2 Diskless Client Server with Two Disks In Figure 2.8, the /usr partition has been moved to the second disk as well as some of the other partitions that are used by diskless clients. Notice that there are two home directory partitions, /home and /home1. This is done to spread the load of home directories out among the two disks. Some clients mount /home for their home directory account and others mount /home1. Other ways of specifying alternate home directory paths might be /home/servername1 and /home/servername2, for example.

Regardless of the name, if the path to home directory accounts is not /home/<server> the NFS mount must be set up manually.

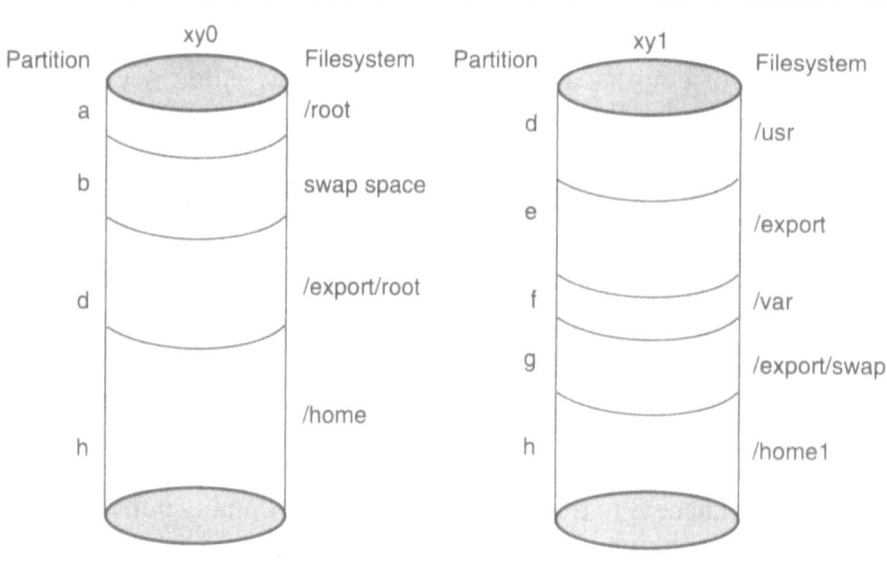

FIGURE 2.8. *Client server with two disks.*

The **setup_client** utility only allows /home/<server> as an option for home directories. This is easily corrected by editing the client's/*export*/*root*/<*client-name*>/*etc*/*fstab* file after the client has been created. Substitute the /home/<server> entry with /home/servername1 or /home/<other-home>.

You can also configure a heavily used partition such as /home between the /usr and root partitions, thereby reducing the amount of distance the heads need to move in between requests. This configuration can increase response times but may not be noticeable because disk access times have decreased dramatically.

2.2.3 Resource Server Layout

The partitioning scheme for a resource server may be similar to Figure 2.9. The /export/unbundled filesystem is created for unbundled applications. Unbundled applications apply to products that are not resident on the SunOS 4.0 or 4.0.3 Release tape set.

Once installed, they are exported for mounting by editing

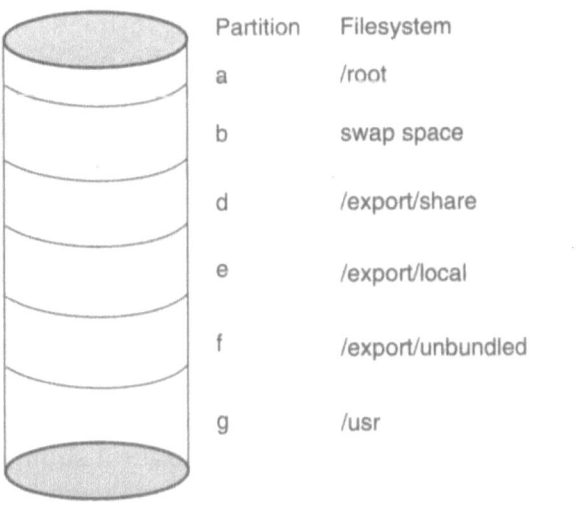

FIGURE 2.9. *Resource serves layout.*

the */etc/exports* file and executing the **exportfs** utility (see exportfs(8)). After the resource is exported, clients wishing to use the unbundled products can NFS mount the application of their choice.

The /export/share partition can be loaded with files that are not architecture dependent. This directory may contain ASCII files such as a names database or a list of current customers. Executable files should not reside in a shared directory unless they are shell scripts that resolve architecture dependencies.

The /export/local partition is filled with useful programs and utilities and will be NFS mounted by networked clients to the /usr/local directory. Sub-directories containing architecture specific executables can be created under /export/local. Then, systems of different architecture type can mount the corresponding architecture directory while retaining the same /usr/local mount point.

For example, Sun-4 and Sun-4c machines NFS mount the /export/local/sun4 directory to their /usr/local. Sun-3 and Sun-3x machines mount the /export/local/sun3 directory and Sun2 machines mount /export/local/sun2. This model saves much confusion when deciding where to put a new executable.

2.2.4 Print Server Layout

A print server is not really a server in the same way as is a diskless client server. Client machines do not mount resources residing on this machine. Print jobs are initiated on clients, and offloaded to the print server for spooling. The print server then queues each job in the order it was received until it is sent to the printer.

In a large network environment, print servers can become quite taxed with print requests from many users. The only real requirement as far as the disk layout for the print server is a /var partition large enough to contain the spooled jobs from many users. You may create separate filesystems for each /var/spool/ <printer-name> if desired.

The layouts discussed in the above figures should be used as a reference. Your machines may have special needs. All possible combinations cannot be discussed here, but these examples should form a basis from which to work. The next section uses

some of the ideas that have been discussed to perform disk partitioning and maintenance.

2.3 Running the **Format** Utility

This section explains how to boot MUNIX and execute the **format**
utility. The normal way to boot MUNIX is by using a local tape
device. If a local tape device is not available, other procedures are
used, and are explained later in this section. Before the boot
process is explained, the SunOS release tapes will be discussed.
Understanding the tape layout can be of great assistance when
booting MUNIX and MINIROOT.

2.3.1 SunOS Release Tapes

The SunOS release tapes are are laid out in sections known as
tape files. Each tape file has a particular purpose for the installation
process. The first file on all release tapes is the boot program. This
tape file is loaded into memory and executed which puts the system into a primary boot state, allowing the remainder of the boot
process to occur.

On most architectures, the full SunOS uses more than one
release tape. The first tape in the set contains a number of special
tape files: the standalone copy program, MINIROOT, MUNIX,
and the munixfs filesystems. The standalone copy program is used
to copy the MINIROOT filesystem on to the system disk. The
MUNIX and munixfs files are used to boot the memory resident
UNIX so that disk maintenance can be performed.

There are a number of **tar** files on the release tapes as well.
Each **tar** file contains a different section or category of the operating system. The categories are selectable in **suninstall**'s software
form, or when using **setup_exec,** which adds executables to a
system.

Table 2.1 shows a typical table of contents for SunOS release
media, which happens to be from a 1/4 inch tape of the SunOS 4.0
release. Tape file number 0, on SunOS 4.0 and 4.0.3 installation
tapes, is the boot program. Tape file 0 as shown in Table 2.1 is
40960 bytes long and is labeled an image-type tape file. When you
type the command **bst**() from the monitor prompt, you are instruct-

SunOS 4.0 Release Tape Table of Contents				
Vol	File	Name	Size	Type
1	0	boot	40960	image
1	1	XDRTOC	4096	toc
1	2	copy	49664	image
1	3	mini-robot	6246400	image
1	4	munix	942592	image
1	5	munixfs	1638400	image
1	6	root	204800	tar
1	7	usr	19046400	tar
1	8	Sys	3276800	tar
1	9	Networking	1024000	tar
1	10	Debugging	4300800	tar
1	11	Sun View_Users	1536000	tar
1	12	Sun View_Programmers	2355200	tar
1	13	Sun View_Demo	614400	tar
1	14	Text	819200	tar
1	15	Copyright	512	image
2	0	boot	40960	image
2	1	XDRTOC	4096	toc
2	2	Install	1126400	tar
2	3	User_Diag	1638400	tar
2	4	SunCore®	1843200	tar
2	5	uucp	307200	tar
2	6	System_V	5324800	tar
2	7	Manual	6246400	tar
2	8	Demo	2764800	tar
2	9	Games	2662400	tar
2	10	Versatec	6144000	tar
2	11	Security	204800	tar
2	12	Copyright	512	image

TABLE 2.1. *SunOS release tape contents.*

ing the system to read the first tape file from the device SCSI tape 0, and load it into memory. When the file has been read and executed, the boot prompt is displayed.

Boot:

Tape file number 1 on release tapes is the table of contents, similar to Table 2.1. The table of contents, or TOC, contains descriptions of each of the tape files including its size and type. Some tape files are loadable sections of the operating system while others are not. The TOC file is consulted when software is being selected for installation. The size of each selected category is compared to the available bytes left in the partition so that the filesystem space is not exceeded. The partition may be expanded if necessary by stealing space from the "free-hog" partition. More on the free-hog partition is explained later in this chapter.

Tape file 2 is the standalone copy program, used to copy the MINIROOT tape file to disk. The copy program is also an image file that can be executed from the boot prompt.

Tape file 3 is the MINIROOT filesystem. This is a complete filesystem containing all the necessary commands and utilities needed to install the operating system onto a machine. The MINIROOT filesystem fits into most swap partitions. Once it has been copied into the swap area, it is booted with special options.

Tape file 4 is also a bootable file, but in a different manner. After loading tape file 0, the boot program, tape file 4 is selected and loaded into memory. This is MUNIX, a completely memory resident filesystem that contains a stripped version of SunOS. MUNIX was designed so that disks could be labeled and formatted in a familiar UNIX environment without the need for any pre-existing disk space. MUNIX allows access to every part of all the disks that are attached to a system. The MUNIX environment is not writable, meaning you cannot save files there. You cannot mount other filesystems while running MUNIX either. Most of the normal UNIX utilities are not available. The only files present are the ones that are necessary to perform disk maintenance.

Once tape file 4 is read, the remaining part of the MUNIX filesystem must be loaded from tape file 5.

Tape file 5 is the filesystem portion of MUNIX. It is a very limited filesystem that is less than four megabytes in size. This is required to allow MUNIX to run on systems with only four megabytes of RAM. The MUNIX filesystem was designed for ultimately one purpose, running the **format** program. MUNIX can also be used to recover data from disks that have problems in the root or /usr filesystems, although MINIROOT is much more versatile for this purpose.

The remaining tape files are the **tar** files used during the installation. Each category selected during **suninstall** or **setup_exec** is read off of the tape, or "un-tarred", and the files placed in their appropriate place.

2.3.2 Booting MUNIX from Tape

To boot MUNIX, insert or load tape 1 from the SunOS release tape set for the architecture machine that is being installed. (If you are loading SunOS 4.0, boot options are different than 4.0.3. In 4.0, the options "-asw" are necessary to properly boot MUNIX. In SunOS 4.0.3, these options are no longer necessary except under certain conditions. Consult the installation guide for specific boot options for MUNIX and MINIROOT.)

From the monitor prompt, enter:

```
>bst()<CR> for SCSI tape devices
>bxt()<CR> for Xylogics tape devices
>bmt()<CR> for Tapemaster devices
```

When the first file on the tape is read and executed, the system responds with:

```
Boot: st(0,0,0)
Boot:
```

To boot MUNIX from tape file 4, enter:

```
st(,,4)<CR>
```

The tape fast-forwards to tape file 4 and begins reading there. Tape file 4 is a special bootable kernel that also loads the MUNIX filesystem into RAM. When the kernel is loaded, you are asked to input the device from which the RAM disk is initialized. Use the same device that you have just booted from. The next question concerns which tape file is to be read to complete the MUNIX boot sequence. Enter the number 5 so that tape file 5 will be read. The output from booting MUNIX is similar to Figure 2.10.

2.3.3 Entering **Format**

When the boot process completes, the pound sign "**#**" appears as your prompt. From this prompt, start the **format** utility by

```
Size: 551824+95496+121944 bytes
SunOS Release 4.0.3 (MUNIX) #1: Mon Apr 24 16:11:49 PDT 1989
Copyright.....
mem = 8192K (0x800000)
avail mem = 7446528
Ethernet address = 8:0:20:6:8f:b0
xyc0 at vme16d16 0xee40 vec 0x48
xy0 at xyc0 slave 0
xy0: <Hitachi DK815-10 cyl 1735 alt 2 hd 15 sec 67>
tm0 at vme16d16 0xa0 vec 0x60
mt0 at tm0 slave 0
zs0 at obio 0x20000 pri 3
zs1 at obio 0x0 pri 3
ie0 at obio 0xc0000 pri 3
Initialize ram disk from device ( st%d[a-h] sd%d[a-h] ft%d[a-g] ):st0
Tape file number? 5
 rd: reading 176, 8192 byte blocks ...............................................................
................................................................................................................
...........................done
root on rd0a fstype 4.2
swap on ns0b fstype spec size 1208K
dump on ns0b fstype spec
#
```

FIGURE 2.10. *Booting MUNIX.*

typing **format**<CR>. If you are installing a SPARCstation 1, a menu selection is displayed instead of the pound sign. See the section below when booting MUNIX on a SPARCstation 1.

The **format** program begins by searching for all the disks that are attached to the system. The output is similar to Figure 2.11. All disks known to the system should be reported in this menu. If not, check cabling and disk addressing to insure that no conflicts exist. You should also check to see if the special device files are present in the /dev directory. In MUNIX, all device nodes are part of the filesystem. If you are running format as a standalone or diskless machine, all device nodes may not be present. For instance: SCSI disk 2 did not show up as a selectable disk, but is attached. Check the /dev directory for "sd2" devices by first exiting the **format** utility and using this command:

    # ls -l /dev/*sd2*<CR>

```
# format
Searching for disks...done

AVAILABLE DISK SELECTIONS:
      0. sd0 at sm0 slave 0
        sd0: <CDC Wren IV 94171-344 cyl 1545 alt 2 hd 9 sec 46>
      1. sd4 at sm0 slave 16
        sd4: <Quantum ProDrive 105S cyl 974 alt 2 hd 6 sec 35>
      2. sd6 at sm0 slave 24
        sd6: <Quantum ProDrive 105S cyl 974 alt 2 hd 6 sec 35>
Specify disk (enter its number):
```

FIGURE 2.11. *Entering format.*

If the result is "No match", then the device files need to be made by running the **MAKEDEV** script as in Figure 2.12. Once **MAKE-DEV** has been run with the correct options, you can re-enter **format** and the disk should be found.

The most logical place to start is with the primary system disk, usually drive 0. Disk 0 contains your root and swap partitions. These are most likely on partitions "a" and "b" respectively. Other disks may be used as the primary disk, but special arrangements must be made, such as changing your EEPROM setting and possibly some kernel modifications.

2.3.4 Selecting Disks

While in MUNIX, the **format** utility will only work with one disk at a time. Select a disk by entering the corresponding menu item associated with the disk when **format** was first invoked. The **format** main menu is displayed as in Figure 2.13.

Many of the main menu selections are paths to sub-menus which perform specific disk maintenance. The command to actually format the disk can only be entered from this menu. The label command can be executed from this menu or while in the partition menu. Selections are made by entering the full name of the utility, or the first non-ambiguous characters at the prompt, followed by a carriage return, <CR>. If you would like to select a different disk to format, entering **di<CR>** at the prompt would display the disk

```
# cd /dev
# MAKEDEV sd2
# ls -l /dev/*sd2*
crw-r-----    1    root    17, 16    Jun 5 10:40    /dev/rsd2a
crw-r-----    1    root    17, 17    Jun 5 10:40    /dev/rsd2b
crw-r-----    1    root    17, 18    Jun 5 10:40    /dev/rsd2c
crw-r-----    1    root    17, 19    Jun 5 10:40    /dev/rsd2d
crw-r-----    1    root    17, 20    Jun 5 10:40    /dev/rsd2e
crw-r-----    1    root    17, 21    Jun 5 10:40    /dev/rsd2f
crw-r-----    1    root    17, 22    Jun 5 10:40    /dev/rsd2g
crw-r-----    1    root    17, 23    Jun 5 10:40    /dev/rsd2h
brw-r-----    1    root     7, 16    Jun 5 10:40    /dev/sd2a
brw-r-----    1    root     7, 17    Jun 5 10:40    /dev/sd2b
brw-r-----    1    root     7, 18    Jun 5 10:40    /dev/sd2c
brw-r-----    1    root     7, 19    Jun 5 10:40    /dev/sd2d
brw-r-----    1    root     7, 20    Jun 5 10:40    /dev/sd2e
brw-r-----    1    root     7, 21    Jun 5 10:40    /dev/sd2f
brw-r-----    1    root     7, 22    Jun 5 10:40    /dev/sd2g
brw-r-----    1    root     7, 23    Jun 5 10:40    /dev/sd2h
```

FIGURE 2.12. *Making the sd2 devices.*

selection menu once again. To view the defect list for this drive, enter the defect menu by typing **de**<**CR**> at the **format** main menu as shown in Figure 2.14.

2.3.5 Viewing the Manufacturer's Defects

Enter the defect list management menu from the format prompt to obtain the "defect" prompt. View the manufacturer's defect list by entering **pr**<CR>. A list of all the defects known on this disk is displayed. Scroll down if necessary by hitting the space bar or <CR> as prompted. When the complete list has been displayed, a total number of defects are reported.

If no defect list was found, you may need to recreate the manufacturer defect list because it is very difficult for vendors to create error-free media. Attempt to extract the original list from the disk by typing **or**<CR>. If this fails, you can enter all the manufacturer's defects manually using the hardcopy list supplied with the disk. Or, you can attempt to create a new defect list using the **create**

```
selecting sd0: <CDC Wren IV 94171-344>
[disk formatted, defect list found]

FORMAT MENU:
    disk            - select a disk
    type            - select (define) a disk type
    partition       - select (define) a partition table
    current         - describe the current disk
    format          - format and analyze the disk
    repair          - repair a defective sector
    show            - translate a disk address
    label           - write label to the disk
    analyze         - surface analysis
    defect          - defect list management
    backup          - search for backup labels
    quit
format>
```

FIGURE 2.13. *Format* main menu.

command, which takes a long time because it writes and reads each sector on the disk to verify its integrity. The only reason you may need to recreate the manufacturer's list is if the disk was previously formatted with an empty defect list.

You may never need to add any defects to the list, but knowing how to do it is always helpful. If you should have to change this list in any way, the changes must be committed before formatting. Attempts to leave the defect menu without committing changes displays a message indicating this. You may also commit the changes while still in the defect menu by using the "commit" utility. If there were not any changes made to the defect list, committing the list is unnecessary. Return to the **format** main menu by typing **q**<CR> at the defect prompt.

2.3.6 Formatting the Disk

Start formatting the disk by entering **for**<CR> at the **format** main menu. You are asked to verify that you do want to format the disk since formatting wipes out everything. A time estimate is made as to when the format should be completed. The estimate format> **de**

DEFECT MENU:
   restore   - set working list = current list
   original   - extract manufacturer's list from disk
   extract   - extract working list from disk
   add   - add defects to working list
   delete   - delete a defect from working list
   print   - display working list
   dump   - dump working list to file
   load   - load working list from file
   commit   - set current list = working list
   create   - recreates manufacturers defect list on disk
   quit
defect>
defect> **or**
Extracting manufacturer's defect list...Extraction complete.
Working list updated, total of 78 defects.
defect> **pr**

num	cyl	hd	bfi	len	sec
1	47	7	7250		
2	48	7	7250		
3	49	7	7250		
4	50	7	7250		
5	51	7	7250		
6	52	7	7250		
7	53	7	7250		
8	54	7	7250		
9	58	4	1450		
10	133	4	28710		
11	134	4	28710		
12	134	4	29290		
13	135	4	28710		
14	135	4	29290		
15	136	4	28710		
16	136	4	29290		
..		...			
.		.....			
73	1426	5	2610		
74	1427	5	2030		
75	1428	5	2030		
76	1429	5	2030		
77	1473	6	290		
78	1537	4	18850		

total of 78 defects.

FIGURE 2.14. *The defect menu*

varies between disks according to capacity. Enter "y"<CR> to begin.

After the actual formatting is complete, a disk test is run to verify that all disk sectors can be written to and read from by the system. The test makes two complete passes on the disk and if errors are found, the block or blocks are added to the defect map. When the two passes are complete, the **format** prompt appears. The default of two passes can be changed if you wish to test the disk for a longer period of time. You may wish to test a disk overnight or over the weekend before you install the operating system. This is accomplished by entering the "analyze" menu, and supplying the appropriate data for the "setup" option.

You cannot interrupt a disk while it is formatting. You may interrupt the verification test by using <Control-C>, although it is not recommended because any errors found during this test cycle are not saved to the defect list.

When both the formatting and the disk verification test is complete, a label is written to the disk that defines a default partition arrangement from data found in the */etc/format.dat* file. Many times the default label needs adjustments to the root and swap partitions tailored to the installation that will occur next.

2.3.7 Partitioning the Disk

In order to adjust the disk partitions to a more suitable arrangement, the disk must be relabeled. The label can be adjusted while in the partition menu. Enter this menu by typing **pa**<CR> at the format prompt. The output is similar to Figure 2.15.

The two partitions to be most concerned with at this point are partitions "a" and "b" on the primary disk. The size of partition "a" is dependent on where partition "b" begins. The next phase of the installation procedure copies the MINIROOT into partition "b". Once this has been done, the size of partition "a" cannot be increased without corrupting the MINIROOT filesystem. If you would like a larger root partition, change it now, before MINIROOT is installed. All other partitions can be modified in the disk form when preparing to run **suninstall.**

SunOS provides predefined partition tables for every disk supported. Some disks have more than one predefined table. For

```
format> par

PARTITION MENU:
   a          - change 'a' partition
   b          - change 'b' partition
   c          - change 'c' partition
   d          - change 'd' partition
   e          - change 'e' partition
   f          - change 'f' partition
   g          - change 'g' partition
   h          - change 'h' partition
   select     - select a predefined table
   name       - name the current table
   print      - display the current table
   label      - write partition map and label to the disk
   quit
partition>
```

FIGURE 2.15. *Partition menu.*

example, the 900 megabyte SMD disk has two partition choices. One choice defines a 128 megabyte partition "b". This would be perfect for a system with 64 megabytes of memory, but most systems have smaller swap space requirements.

The number of blocks per cylinder varies between different disk manufacturers. In this example, a Quantum 105s disk is used. One hundred cylinders on this particular disk is roughly ten megabytes, while 100 cylinders on a CDC WrenIV disk is approximately 20 megabytes. Keep this in mind while partitioning a particular disk.

To view the predefined partition tables, enter **sel**<CR> while at the "partition>" prompt as shown in Figure 2.16. Selection zero is the predefined table, and selection one is the original label that was on the disk when **format** was first invoked. This is good to know if you have made partitioning errors. You can always retrieve the original label as long as you do not exit **format**. Once you do, the next invocation of **format** reads the label again, which then becomes the new "original" label. View the current partition table by entering **pr**<CR> at the partition prompt.

Figure 2.16 shows that partition "a" starts at cylinder 0 and is

```
partition> sel
   0. Quantum ProDrive 105S
   1. original sd4
   2. original sd6
Specify table (enter its number) [1]: 0
partition> pr
Current partition table (Quantum ProDrive 105S):
       partition a - starting cyl        0, # blocks      16170  (77/0/0)
       partition b - starting cyl       77, # blocks      28140  (134/0/0)
       partition c - starting cyl        0, # blocks     204540  (974/0/0)
       partition d - starting cyl        0, # blocks          0  (0/0/0)
       partition e - starting cyl        0, # blocks          0  (0/0/0)
       partition f - starting cyl        0, # blocks          0  (0/0/0)
       partition g - starting cyl      211, # blocks     160230  (763/0/0)
       partition h - starting cyl        0, # blocks          0  (0/0/0)
partition>
```

FIGURE 2.16. *The partition table.*

16170 blocks in size. The data blocks on all disks used by Sun are 512 bytes in size. If you would like to know the actual size of the partition in megabytes, you can multiply the number of disk blocks by 512, but for a quick estimate, divide the number of blocks by 2000. Using the latter approach, partition "a" is roughly eight megabytes. The numbers inside the parentheses are the number of cylinders, heads, and sectors used in the partition. Partition "a" is 77 cylinders long. The head and sector numbers are zeros indicating that this partition ends on a cylinder boundary, as it should.

Partition "b" starts where "a" ends, at cylinder 77, and is 28140 blocks in size, roughly 14 megabytes, which is 134 disk cylinders. A swap partition should not encompass the first cylinder on a disk because swap space is used in raw mode. The disk label may be over-written when swapping occurs. There is no filesystem structure in raw partitions to save critical areas from being used.

Partition "c" is the length of the entire disk, starting at cylinder 0, and ending at cylinder 974. This "c" partition contains 204540 blocks, which is nearly 105 megabytes. The **suninstall** program needs the "c" partition defined as the entire disk.

The only other partition defined on this disk is "g". Partition "g" starts at cylinder 211, which is the sum of the first two partitions, "a" and "b". Partition "a" begins at cylinder 0 and is 77 cylinders in length, partition "b" starts at 77 and is 134 cylinders in length, and partition "g" starts at cylinder 211 (since 77+134=211). Partition "g" is 160230 blocks in size, roughly 80 megabytes, using 763 cylinders on this particular disk. Remember that cylinder 0 counts as a valid cylinder.

The **suninstall** program will not function correctly on disks with labels that contain gaps of unaccounted disk cylinders. If partition "g" started at cylinder 250 instead of 211 in this example, an error message is not reported until **suninstall** starts making new filesystems, which is much too late. All cylinders must be accounted for in the label. **Suninstall** does not check for filesystems with overlapping cylinders, so you must make sure that filesystems do not overlap or your installation may fail. The only exception to this is the partition "c", overlapping the whole disk, although partition "c" is rarely made into a filesystem. It is always a good idea to verify that all disk blocks and cylinders are accounted for in the label. Since partition "c" is always the whole disk, it can be used as a reference point while in this menu. If the number of cylinders used by partitions "a", "b", and "g" are added together (77+134+763=974), the result should be the same number of cylinders that are used by partition "c" (974). This is most helpful when creating a custom partitioning table.

2.3.8 Modifying the Disk Label

Customizing the partition table is done by selecting the partition you wish to change, giving it a starting point and a size. The size can be given in number of blocks or number of cylinders. It is much easier to work in cylinders rather than with the number of blocks since partitions should start and end on exact cylinder boundaries. When one partition is changed, it affects the start or end point of the other partitions in the table. If you want to make the root partition larger than eight megabytes, add a couple more cylinders to its size. That in turn affects the starting point of partition "b", since they cannot overlap. Partition "b" then needs to be adjusted accordingly.

None of the changes made to the partition table are actually written on the disk until the **label** command is executed from this menu or the **format** main menu. Some experimenting can be done without actually writing the current label out to the disk.

In Figure 2.17, partition "a" has been altered. First, the partition name is entered, and the starting point defined. Partition "a" begins at cylinder 0 as before, so a "0"<CR> is entered. The next input sets the size of the partition. The partition size can be entered as the number of blocks or number of cylinders. If you want partition "a" to be 10 megabytes, and 77 cylinders is roughly eight megabytes, then 100 cylinders should be enough. Enter 100 followed by a "/" to indicate 100 cylinders. If 100 is entered without the "/", you would be setting the size of partition "a" to be 100 blocks, which is quite a bit smaller than 100 cylinders. Finally, the partition table is displayed to verify that the changes were made correctly.

Partition "a" still starts at zero, but is now 21000 blocks in size ending at cylinder 100. Partition "b" still starts at cylinder 77. This is the overlapping situation discussed before, and is not allowed. You must change the starting cylinder of partition "b" to be where "a" ends. For example, assume this system has eight megabytes of memory. It is optimum to have at least twice as much swap space as

---

partition> **a**

partition a - starting cyl 0, # blocks   0 (0/0/0)

Enter new starting cyl [0]: **0**
Enter new # blocks [16170, 77/0/0]: **100/**
partition>
partition> **pr**
Current partition table (unnamed):
    partition a - starting cyl   0, # blocks   21000 (100/0/0)
    partition b - starting cyl   77, # blocks   28140 (134/0/0)
    partition c - starting cyl   0, # blocks 204540 (974/0/0)
    partition d - starting cyl   0, # blocks   0 (0/0/0)
    partition e - starting cyl   0, # blocks   0 (0/0/0)
    partition f - starting cyl   0, # blocks   0 (0/0/0)
    partition g - starting cyl 211, # blocks 160230 (763/0/0)
    partition h - starting cyl   0, # blocks   0 (0/0/0)

FIGURE 2.17. *Changing partition "a".*

memory, so the "b" partition should be increased as well. You can make an estimated guess as to the number of cylinders needed for 16 megabytes by comparing the number of blocks in partition "a". If 100 cylinders is roughly 10 megabytes, then 160 cylinders should have enough space to hold 16 megabytes.

Figure 2.18 shows that partition "b" now begins at cylinder 100 and is 33600 blocks in size, which is roughly 16 megabytes. The swap partition is now set.

The remaining partition, "g", must be changed so that there is no overlap. To do this, add the number of cylinders used by partition "a" to the number of cylinders used by partition "b". The result is the starting cylinder for partition "g" (100 + 160 = 260). Since more cylinders have been added to the first two partitions, the size of partition "g" must be reduced. Subtract the original start point of partition "g", 211, from the new start point 260 (260 − 211 = 49). Thus partition "g" must be reduced by 49 cylinders. Subtract 49 from the original size of partition "g" 763 (763 − 49 = 714). This is the new size of partition "g" in cylinders. Adjust partition "g" accordingly, as shown Figure 2.19.

Partition "g" now has roughly 76 megabytes. If you are satis-

```
partition> b

partition b - starting cyl   77, # blocks   28140 (134/0/0)

Enter new starting cyl [77]: 100
Enter new # blocks [28140, 134/0/0]: 160/
partition> pr
Current partition table (unnamed):
    partition a - starting cyl       0, # blocks    21000 (100/0/0)
    partition b - starting cyl     100, # blocks    33600 (160/0/0)
    partition c - starting cyl       0, # blocks   204540 (974/0/0)
    partition d - starting cyl       0, # blocks        0 (0/0/0)
    partition e - starting cyl       0, # blocks        0 (0/0/0)
    partition f - starting cyl       0, # blocks        0 (0/0/0)
    partition g - starting cyl     211, # blocks   160230 (763/0/0)
    partition h - starting cyl       0, # blocks        0 (0/0/0)
partition>
```

FIGURE 2.18. *Changing partition "b"*.

```
partition>g

partition g - starting cyl   211, # blocks   160230 (763/0/0)
Enter new starting cyl [211]: 260
Enter new # blocks [160230, 763/0/0] 714/
partition> pr
Current partition table (unnamed):
     partition a - starting cyl        0, # blocks     21000  (100/0/0)
     partition b - starting cyl      100, # blocks     33600  (160/0/0)
     partition c - starting cyl        0, # blocks    204540  (974/0/0)
     partition d - starting cyl        0, # blocks         0  (0/0/0)
     partition e - starting cyl        0, # blocks         0  (0/0/0)
     partition f - starting cyl        0, # blocks         0  (0/0/0)
     partition g - starting cyl      260, # blocks    149940  (714/0/0)
     partition h - starting cyl        0, # blocks         0  (0/0/0)
```

FIGURE 2.19. *Changing partition "g"*.

fied with this label configuration you can write the new label to the disk. If not, continue to adjust the label to suit your needs. Remember that you can change partitions "d" through "h", as well as any of the partitions on other disks when running **suninstall**. Be sure to check your math by adding the number of cylinders used in the partitions you defined. Their sum should equal the number of cylinders used in partition "c".

2.3.9 Labeling the Disk

After you have defined your custom partition arrangement, the disk label must be written, otherwise the original label is used. The whole process of partitioning is useless without labeling the disk, which can be done from either the partition menu or the **format** main menu by using the **label** command.

```
partition> la
Ready to label disk, continue?y
partition>
```

The new label has been saved to disk, and the system is ready for installation. To proceed with the system installation, the MINI-ROOT filesystem must be loaded on to the disk. Loading MINI-

ROOT can be done while the system is running MUNIX, or by using the standalone copy program from the monitor prompt.

The section below describes how to run **format** on the SPARCstation 1. Following that discussion, instructions on how to load the MINIROOT filesystem can be found. Loading the MINIROOT is the next step towards installing your system. If you are not installing a SPARCstation 1, skip to Loading the MINIROOT.

2.3.10 Booting MUNIX on a SPARCstation 1

The procedure for booting MUNIX on a SPARCstation 1 is the same as for most other systems. When the system has finished booting, a script is invoked containing a menu driven utility which guides you into the **format** program rather than you typing it in. This can be a bit confusing at first because all of the other machines do not use menu options to enter **format.**

The initial prompt asks if you would like to install the MINIROOT, or exit into the shell. You may exit into the shell and invoke **format** from there, or you may continue by selecting "1" to install the MINIROOT. If menu item one was selected, the system polls all of the disk devices and asks which disk you want to be the primary disk, which is usually drive 0. When the primary disk has been selected you are asked if you want to run **format** on this disk. Answering yes puts you into the **format** utility. Answering no begins installing the MINIROOT filesystem into partition "b" of the disk just selected, if a "b" partition was defined. If there is not a "b" partition defined, an error is reported and you are asked to check the partition arrangement. If you have more than one disk attached to your SPARCstation, and you would like to run **format** on that disk as well, you must select that disk before leaving the **format** utility. You may select any of the other disks while at the main menu in **format** by using the "disk" command. Once you leave the **format** utility on a SPARCstation 1, the system begins copying the MINIROOT automatically. It copies and boots the MINIROOT without operator intervention.

2.3.11 Running Format as a Diskless Client

There are some instances when you must install a system without a local tape device. Since you cannot boot MUNIX from a remote tape device, the tapeless system must be temporarily installed as a diskless client. It can then boot over the network so that you can run the **format** program. See Chapter 4 for detailed instructions on how to set up and boot diskless clients.

There are other special requirements when a diskless system is being used to run **format.** The UNIX kernel used by some diskless machines does not contain the drivers necessary for disk devices. Be sure to use the GENERIC kernel for that architecture when booting to cover all possibilities. Copy a GENERIC kernel into the client's /export/root/<client-name> directory before booting.

Another necessity for the diskless client is to verify that the disk device nodes are present in the /dev directory. This can be done, once the system has booted, by changing your working directory to /dev, and listing all devices. If the disk device files are there, **format** should be able to see the disk. If the devices for your disk are not there, you can create them by running the **MAKEDEV** script. You must use the appropriate disk type as the argument to **MAKEDEV.** Only the superuser can make these special files.

```
# cd /dev
# MAKEDEV sd0
#
```

In this example, the SCSI disk zero devices were created. Other arguments to MAKEDEV are xy0 and xd0 for SMD disks, and id0 for IPI disks. If you find that not all the disks attached to your system are being reported when starting the **format** utility, check the /dev directory first. If you continue to have problems, then check the cables, controller, or power to the device in question.

2.3.12 Loading MINIROOT from MUNIX.

When you have completed running the **format** utility on a standalone system, the Sun documentation suggests that you halt the system and install the MINIROOT filesystem using the copy program supplied on the release tape. However, MINIROOT can be copied without halting the system.

After exiting the **format** utility, the system is returned to the root prompt. Insert the SunOS release tape 1 if not already loaded, and position the tape to file 3, then dump the image of tape file 3 into the swap partition as illustrated in Figure 2.20.

The **mt** command is first used to rewind the tape. Once the tape is rewound, it is positioned at the beginning of tape file three. When positioning and reading the tape, a special non-rewinding device must be used, "nrst0". The "fsf 3" option tells the tape to "forward skip file", or fast forward three tape files. If you use rst0 instead of nrst0, the tape would fast forward to tape file three, but then rewind to the beginning of the tape and wait there. It is very important to use the non-rewind device or the wrong tape file may be copied. Figure 2.20 used the SCSI device st0. The **mt** command is not restricted to SCSI devices. You may use **mt** to position 1/2" tapes as well, given the appropriate device name, nrmt8.

The **dd** command in Figure 2.20 uses three arguments, an input file, output file, and block size. The input file is the non-rewinding tape device, which is positioned at tape file 3. The output file is the "raw" disk device /dev/rsd0b, which is SCSI disk 0, partition "b". It is also important to specify the correct disk partition. Dumping this tape file to partition /dev/rsd0a would overwrite the disk label. The final argument sets the block size to 48k, meaning 48k chunks are transferred at a time.

Since the **shutdown, halt,** or **reboot** commands are not resident in the MUNIX filesystem, you must abort the system with the keyboard sequence L1-A, or by using the break key if not on a Sun keyboard. For instructions on how to boot MINIROOT, skip to booting the MINIROOT since you have already copied MINI-ROOT to your swap area. The next section is a discussion of the **suninstall** program.

```
# mt -f /dev/rst0 rew
# mt -f /dev/nrst0 fsf 3
# dd if=/dev/nrst0 of=/dev/rsd0b bs=48k
61+0 records in
61+0 records out
#
```

FIGURE 2.20. *Loading MINIROOT into the swap area.*

2.4 Suninstall

Suninstall is the program used to install the operating system onto your diskfull system. Installations can be carried out on dataless, standalone, and server system types only. Diskless machines can be configured during this process but are not able to boot until their server has been installed and booted. In preparation for the installation you need to gather some information such as a hostname and IP address for the machine being installed, being sure that each is unique. Also identify the YP domain currently in use if you wish to use YP.

You must have a set of release tapes for the architecture of your machine before you can begin. SunOS release tapes are available in two formats, 1/2 inch reels and 1/4 inch cartridges. SunOS 4.0.3c is also available in several dozen 3 1/2 inch floppies if so desired.

Suninstall has changed a bit between SunOS release 4.0 and 4.0.3. The majority of the changes concern the added support of the Sun-3x and Sun-4c architectures. A number of bugs were also fixed in 4.0.3, while the basic installation procedure remained the same. Other changes deal with boot options given when booting MINIROOT and MUNIX. See the 4.0.3 release notes if you are interested in specifics. The boot procedure described below is tailored to the 4.0.3 release.

Suninstall is destructive to filesystems. If any partition information is changed, it is likely that all filesystems must be re-created.

2.4.1 The MINIROOT Filesystem

The **suninstall** program is executed from a small filesystem that is loaded into the swap partition called "MINIROOT" and is approximately six megabytes in size. MINIROOT is copied to the swap area so that other partitions on the disk can be made into filesystems while leaving the contents of MINIROOT intact. The swap area is usually the only partition on the disk that is a raw partition which makes it an ideal area to use during installation. MINIROOT can also be quite useful when corrupt filesystems are in need of repair because you can run the **fsck** program while critical filesystems are un-mounted. MINIROOT is often used in emergency situations to repair systems that cannot boot. After installation, the MINIROOT filesystem is destroyed during normal swap activity.

The files present in MINIROOT are the minimum utilities necessary to support the installation of the system from a local or remote tape device. Any attempt to create or copy files in MINI-ROOT may cause the filesystem to become full. If this happens, it is best to halt the system and re-copy MINIROOT before continuing with the installation. You do not want to be running on a corrupt MINIROOT when installing your system.

These are the basic steps needed to run **suninstall** from a local or remote tape device.

1. Booting from tape or diskless client server.

2. Copying the MINIROOT to swap space on the disk.

3. Booting up the MINIROOT.

4. Entering **suninstall.**

5. Editing the **suninstall** forms.

6. Starting the installation.

2.4.2 Booting from a Local Tape

Every system must boot into a primary boot state before it can continue with the loading of the kernel. Upon successful completion of the primary boot phase, a boot prompt is displayed. A number of options are available once the boot state is reached.

The primary boot state is accomplished by using a local tape device or the network. Figure 2.21 shows how to boot from the tape drive that is attached to the Xylogics tape controller and read file number 0, the boot program. When the boot program is loaded, the boot prompt is displayed.

2.4.3 Installing and Booting MINIROOT

If you have already loaded MINIROOT into your swap partition when the system was running MUNIX, you may skip to

```
Selftest Completed
Sun Workstation, Model Sun-3/200 Series
EEPROM defined Type-4 Keyboard
ROM Rev 3.0, 16MB memory installed
Ethernet address 8:0:20:1:30:20

>b xt(0,0,0)
Boot:
```

FIGURE 2.21. *Booting from tape.*

"Booting the MINIROOT" section below. If not, continue with this section.

There are a number of ways to copy MINIROOT into swap. The first is the most conventional, installing from a local tape device whether it be a cartridge or reel tape. The second involves machines without a local tape device. Since these machines cannot boot from tape, they need to be booted as if they were a diskless client from a server which supports their architecture. A remote machine with a tape drive, called a tapehost, will be used to extract the MINIROOT filesystem over the network and onto the disk. This is explained in the Remote Installation section later in this chapter. First, a local standalone copy is shown.

Figure 2.22 shows how the MINIROOT is copied using the standalone copy program, provided on the release tape. It first instructs the copy program to take the contents of tape file 3, and copy it onto the SMD disk 0 (xy0), partition one (xy0b), normally the swap partition.

```
Boot: xt(,,2)<CR>
Copy:
Copy from: xt(,,3)<CR>
Copy to: xy(,,1)<CR>
Copy Complete:
200+1 records in
200+1 record out
Boot:
```

FIGURE 2.22. *Copying the MINIROOT.*

A common error occurs while entering the "Copy to:" response. If the first disk partition, xy(0,0,0) was entered as the partition to copy the miniroot to, you may destroy the disk label. Since the copy routine uses a program a similar to the **dd** utility, it starts exactly where the partition begins. Partition "a" begins at block 0, where the label lives. If the label gets overwritten, you must reboot MUNIX and relabel the disk by running **format**. Searching for backup labels while in **format** usually succeeds in this situation since there is a menu item specifically for this purpose.

The boot prompt is returned upon successful completion of the copy. After the copy is finished, boot the MINIROOT filesystem as shown in Figure 2.23. When MINIROOT is done booting, the pound sign, "#", also known as the root prompt, appears. It is from this prompt that you invoke the **suninstall** program.

2.4.4 Entering Suninstall

Type **suninstall** from the keyboard, followed by a carriage return, <CR>. The system responds with a message and prompts for verification that you do indeed wish to install SunOS onto this system. Invoking **suninstall** displays the output shown in Figure 2.24.

A response of y continues into **suninstall.** After confirmation, the system responds with a prompt for you to enter the local time zone. Time zones use the format of "US/Pacific" or "US/Central" when appropriate, and "MET" when the time zone spans more than one country, as in Europe. Enter your local time zone name to continue.

Next is setting the current time. The realtime clock on the CPU should be set to a reasonably current time when it comes from the factory. If you have a system whose date is not within a week of the current date, there may be a minor hardware problem. Each CPU is equipped with a battery to keep the time-of-day chip synchronized with the current date. If the system has been powered down for extended periods of time, the battery may fail. Setting the date when the system is powered on may correct the problem. Setting a system's date far into the future may cause many

Boot: **xy(,,1) -sw**   (Booting SunOS 4.0 needs the -asw option)

SunOS Release 4.0.3 (GENERIC) #1: Mon Apr 24 14:51:08 PDT 1989
Copyright (c) 1989 by Sun Microsystems, Inc.
mem = 8192K (0x800000)
avail mem = 7012352
Ethernet address = 8:0:20:6:8f:b0
xyc0 at vme16d16 0xee40 vec 0x48
xy0 at xyc0 slave 0
xy0: <Hitachi DK815-10 cyl 1735 alt 2 hd 15 sec 67>
si0 at vme24d16 0x200000 vec 0x40
st0 at si0 slave 32
st1 at si0 slave 40
sd0 at si0 slave 0
sd1 at si0 slave 1
sd2 at si0 slave 8
sd3 at si0 slave 9
sd4 at si0 slave 16
sd6 at si0 slave 24
tm0 at vme16d16 0xa0 vec 0x60
mt0 at tm0 slave 0
zs0 at obio 0x20000 pri 3
zs1 at obio 0x0 pri 3
ie0 at obio 0xc0000 pri 3
bwtwo0 at obmem 0xff000000
root on xy0b fstype 4.2
swap on xy0b fstype spec size 33667K
dump on xy0b fstype spec
#

FIGURE 2.23. *Booting the MINIROOT*

problems, especially for programs run by **cron.** Most backup programs are affected by this as well since they are date dependent. If
all of the system files are newer that the current date, they will be
backed up until that date is reached. It is not so important that the
absolute perfect time be set at this point, but a close approximation
should be made. There are other commands available to set the
date and time once the system is up-and-running on the network.

To set the date and time at this point, enter a "?". The help
screen informs you how the system time can be set.

When the system time has been set, you are prompted to enter
the primary terminal type. On most standalone installations, this is

Welcome to Suninstall

You are about to install a new version of the SunOS on your system. If this is not a first-time installation and you are upgrading from a previous version of the operating system, then it is strongly recommended that you perform a full backup of each of your filesystems which contain user data. Be advised that as this program runs, it may re-label some of the disk drives and in some cases may initialize new filesystems. After this installation process is complete, you may restore your user data from the backup copies.

Do you wish to continue with the installation [y/n]?

FIGURE 2.24. *Entering Suninstall.*

menu selection 3, the Sun bit-mapped display. Servers are rarely used as workstations, so a terminal such as the TVI925™ or the Wyse 50 is used as the console device.

You may be using a terminal that is not listed here, but may be in the */usr/lib/termcap* file. If you have a VT-100 terminal as the console, you would type "4" (other) and enter **vt** at the next prompt. There are more terminals than you would like to know about in the *termcap* file. If you are using an ASCII terminal, there is more than likely an entry for it.

If you want to see if your terminal type is in the termcap file, you must exit **suninstall.** The only editor available in MINIROOT is **ed.** Use **ed** to open the */usr/etc/termcap* file and search for your terminal type with this command:

/<search string>/<CR>

Exit **ed** by entering a single "q"<CR> at the beginning of a line.

The correct terminal type is needed because the **suninstall** program uses a display library called curses. Your display will be scrambled and unreadable if you select the wrong terminal type.

Select one of these options to continue.

Which type of terminal do you have?
1. Televideo 925®
2. Wyse 50™
3. Sun bitmapped display
4. Other

2.4.4.1 Suninstall Main Menu After setting the timezone, time, and terminal type, the **suninstall** main menu is displayed as in Figure 2.25.

There are five **suninstall** forms that need to be updated with information before the installation can occur, although standalone and dataless installations only use four. Selecting a form from the main menu is done by typing the letter x while the cursor is positioned next to the form or activity you wish to do. Upon completion of each form, a confirmation is needed. After giving confirmation, you are returned to the main menu so that other forms can be selected.

When a form is complete, a plus sign (+) is placed in front of the menu item indicating that a data file has been created for that form. The data files are located in /usr/etc/install.

You may move the cursor around the main menu by hitting the space bar. Cursor movement can also be obtained with control characters shown at the bottom of the screen. An on-line help screen is available, but only shows the different ways to move the cursor around in **suninstall,** so it is really not much help.

```
              Sun Microsystems System Installation Tool

                             Main Menu
        ( on-line help information prints summary of cursor usage )
                 ( + means the data files(s) exists(s) )


                      [ assign host information     ]
                      [ assign disk information     ]
                      [ assign software information ]
                      [ assign client information   ]
                      [ start the installation      ]
                      [ on-line help information     ]
                      [ exit from suninstall        ]
```

```
 [x/X=select choice] [space=next choice] [^B/^P=backward] [^F/^N=forward]
```

FIGURE 2.25. *The suninstall main menu.*

The main menu is set up in a logical order for most installations. The first step of any installation is setting the system type, hostname, and IP address. The next step is configuring the disks or partitioning. The third step involves choosing the software that you wish to have installed onto your system. The next step may be adding any diskless clients that are to be served by this system, if it is a diskless client server. The last step is starting the installation.

2.4.4.2 Assign Host Information
Enter the host form by placing the cursor next to the "assign host information" selection of the main menu and typing **x**. The host form (see Figure 2.26) is where you enter the system type, hostname, the Internet Protocol number, YP type, and whether or not you wish to reboot the system after the installation. If you are attaching this system to a network, your hostname and IP address must not conflict with any other system that is currently in use on that network. IP addresses use

```
HOST FORM     [DEL=erase one char of input data]  [RET=end of input data]

Workstation Information :
      Name  :  noname
      Type  :  x[standalone]  [server]  [dataless]


      Network Information   :
      Ethernet Interface    :  [none] x[le0]  [ie2]
      Internet Address 0    :  192.9.200.1
      Internet Address 1    :
      YP Type               :  x[none]  [master]  [slave]  [client]




Are you finished with this form [y/n] ?
 [x/X=select choice]  [space=next choice]  [^B/^P=backward]  [^F/^N=forward]
```

FIGURE 2.26. *The host form.*

the format of X.X.X.X (meaning 192.9.200.1), where each field is a decimal number between 0 and 255. One often confusing part of networking is being able to tell the difference between the network address and the system address. This difference depends upon the network class, which is discussed in greater detail in Chapter 5. In a nutshell, the network number of a machine using the class C address of 192.9.200.1 is 192.9.200. The host number is 1. When another machine is connected to the same network, it must use the same network number and a different host number (such as 192.9.200.2). Systems should not be assigned the host numbers 0 or 255 because these addresses are used for broadcasting and routing. Host numbers can be any number in between. Network numbers are assigned and registered with the Data Defense Network and Stanford Research Institute (SRI) in Menlo Park, CA., so that systems connected to the Internet can communicate with each other. See Chapter 5 for instructions on how to obtain a registered network number.

The workstation information section is where the hostname and system type are set. The hostname is a unique name for your system. It can be up to ten characters in length. Interesting problems may occur if hostnames exceed ten characters, especially when using YP. Machine names must begin with lower case letters and may contain numeric characters. Before you can enter a hostname, you must clear the field currently filled with "noname" by using either <Control>-U or the backspace key. Then type in the new hostname and a <CR> moves the cursor to the type field.

The type selection defines the system type. A standalone system is a machine that has a local disk, but is not a server. Selecting a server as a system type sets up files on your system that allow it to become an NFS server of some kind, be it a server of diskless clients or an NFS fileserver. A dataless machine is a mixture of a standalone and diskless client in that it has a local disk, but NFS mounts its /usr files from another machine. If selecting dataless, you also need to enter the server's hostname and IP address.

The next section of this form is the network information. Any Ethernet interfaces attached to the system should appear here. This example has two Ethernet connections, ie0 and ie1. This is known as a gateway or router machine. Most machines have only one Ethernet interface. When typing an "x" next to ie0, the cursor is moved to the Internet Address 0 field. A valid Internet Protocol address should be entered in the format mentioned above. The number entered here is the host number of this machine.

2.4.4.3 Setting the YP Type

The options for YP type include none, master, slave, or client. If you are joining an existing domain, your selection should be "client". Master and slave servers are machines that contain YP maps. YP clients use YP servers to obtain network data such as other hostnames and login account information. If unsure as to which selection to make, chose "client". It is easier to turn off YP after the installation is complete. It becomes difficult to join a YP domain after a system has been installed since a number of programs used by YP clients are not available.

When joining an existing domain, enter the domain name carefully. A typing error could cause the system to look for a domain that does not exist. There is no validation checking done to see if the domain name that has been entered already exists. The results of entering a non-existent or incorrectly spelled domain name is not seen until the installation is complete, and the system is booting. The boot procedure freezes while displaying this message over and over:

```
ypserver not responding for domain <domain name>
ypserver not responding for domain <domain name>
```

The solution to this problem is to halt, reboot the system into single user mode, and correct the domainname entry in the */etc/ rc.local* file. Incidentally, this is also how to change the domain name of an installed system.

The "misc information" section of this form asks if you want the system to reboot after the installation is complete. In most cases, rebooting the machine to multi-user mode can be done without problems. If you are installing a YP master server, then the system must be manually booted into single user mode and have YP maps built before the rest of the boot process can occur. If a YP master has this field set to "y", it will display the "ypserver not responding" message when booting. (See Chapter 3 for a more in depth discussion on YP.)

Once the host form has been completed, a message at the

bottom of the form asks if you are finished with this form. If you are done, enter a "y" without a carriage return. This puts you back at the **suninstall** main menu. A response of "n" places the cursor at the top of the form once again.

2.4.4.4 Assign Disk Information The disk form is one of the most important forms in **suninstall**. The failure to create partitions with enough room for files may result in administration problems. There are a few rules to consider when assigning disk information.

1. You cannot make the root partition larger while in the **suninstall** disk form. If you do, your miniroot filesystem will be overwritten, resulting in a failed installation.

2. You cannot overlap partitions. Disk partitions have a specified start and end point which should be on cylinder boundaries. If partitions were to overlap, the filesystems on both partitions would be corrupt. **Suninstall** defaults to the closest cylinder boundary.

3. Have your partition requirements already defined. Know where you will be installing application software and be sure to create enough disk space to hold the programs that run your applications.

4. Every disk installed on your system must be "touched" before a data file can be created. If there are three disks on your system and you only want to alter two of them during the installation, the third disk must be selected and committed by answering "y" to the prompt: "OK to use this partition table [y/n] ?" at the bottom of the form, even if there are not any partitions defined for that disk in the form. The unused disk is ignored during the installation.

Enter the disk information form by placing the cursor next to "assign disk information" selection of the **suninstall** main menu and typing "x". The disk form is displayed as in Figure 2.27.

Any disk that is currently attached to your system should be displayed in the upper left corner of the screen. If you have disks attached that are not shown, check the cables, controller, or power to that device if you would like to configure it now. As discussed

```
DISK FORM    [DEL=erase one char of input data] [RET=end of input data]

Attached Disk Devices  :
      [ xy0] [xy1]  [xy2]

Disk Label                   : x[edit default] [edit existing]
Free Hog Disk Partition      : [d] ]e] [f] [g] x[h]
Display Unit                 : x[Mbytes] [Kbytes] [blocks] [cylinders]




Ok to use this parition table [y/n]   ?
Are you finished with this form [y/n] ?

[x/X=select choice] [space=next choice] [^B/^P=backward] [^F/^N=forward]
```

FIGURE 2.27. *The disk form.*

earlier, the default primary disk on most Sun systems is disk 0. This is the usual place for the root and swap partitions to be configured although any disk can be used as the primary. Systems that do not adhere to this rule are the Sun-3/80, and the SPARCstation 330. When these systems have an internal disk, it is configured as sd6. Systems may be re-configured to boot from different disks if external disk devices are attached, but other procedures may need to be taken to allow automatic booting. External SCSI devices may be in the form of the Sun produced P-box and shoe-box, or any one of the many third-party peripheral SCSI devices available. You may have a system with more than one disk 0, (such as sd0, xd0, or xy0). Select the disk you wish to boot from while remembering that the UNIX kernel used after a machine is installed looks for the swap space to be in the "b" partition of the disk that has the root partition. If you define the root partition to be on disk sd0a, then partition sd0b must be defined as swap. If disk xd0a contains root, then xd0b must be designated as swap. To change this, a modified kernel must be used, specifically designating the swap space to be at a different location.

Select the disk you wish to configure in the same manner as

choosing **suninstall** forms. Position the cursor next to the disk and type an **x** which expands the form into Figure 2.28.

After the menu has expanded, the cursor is positioned over one of the disk label selections. The options are edit default, or edit existing. If you created a custom label when running the format program, you should only select the "edit existing" option. Choosing "edit default" reads the partition arrangement from the /etc/format.dat file, and will most likely cause your installation to fail. If you did not change the partition arrangement while running **format,** you may select either "edit default" or "edit existing".

Default labels are different depending on which system type was selected in the host form. A default label for a system selected

```
DISK FORM      [DEL=erase one char of input data] [RET=end of input data]
-- -- -- -- -- -- -- -- -- -- -- -- -- -- -- -- -- -- -- -- -- -- --
Attached Disk Devices :
      x[ xy0]  [xy1]  [xy2]

Disk Label          : [edit default] x[edit existing] [use data file]
Free Hog Disk Parition : [d] [d] [f] [g] x[h]
Display Unit        : x[Mbytes] [Kbytes] [blocks] [cylinders]

PARTITION  START_CYL  BLOCKS    SIZE  MOUNT PT      PRESERVE(Y/N)
=========================================================
   a         0        64320      32   /              n
   b        64        131
   c         0        174365    892
   d       319        155775     79   /export/root   n
   e       474        97485      49   /var           n
   f       571        194970     99   /usr           n
   g       765        605010    309   /export        n
   h      1367        369840    189   /home          n




Ok to use this parition table [y/n]   ?
Are you finished with this form [y/n] ?
 [x/X=select choice] [space=next choice] [^B/^P=backward] [^F/^N=forward]
```

FIGURE 2.28. *The expanded disk form.*

as a "server" is configured with more disk partitions than the "edit default" selection for a standalone machine. If you are not sure which partitions you need, select "edit default". The necessary partitions for the system type you have selected are shown. Doing this does not, however, inform or offer ideas on how to spread the partitions out among systems with two or more disks. Selecting "edit default" on your second disk shows the same partitions as if it were disk 0.

Choosing the "edit existing" option on a server installation does not give you any clues as to what the default partition names are for server systems. You must remember to enter the /export, /export/root, and /export/swap partitions manually.

2.4.4.5 The Free-Hog Disk Partition

The free-hog partition is used by **suninstall** to give or take disk space from other partitions. It gives away disk space as other partitions are increased. It takes back disk space when a partition is decreased. The free-hog is also used when selecting software in the software form. If the /usr partition needs more space than was reserved in this form, that space is taken from the free-hog while the /usr partition is increased. Another use for the free-hog partition is during the creation of diskless clients.

As each diskless machine is added in the client form, the /export/root and /export/swap partitions are checked to see if they have enough room to fit the client that is being added. If it is determined that more disk space is needed to configure the client, the space is taken from the free-hog partition, granted there is enough extra space in it. The free-hog concept is intended to make installations less confusing for users with limited experience, and to make sure all cylinders are used on the disk. The free-hog was used in pre-4.0 installations to configure space for the "network disk", or "nd" client. The "nd" client used a different protocol when mounting the root and swap space over the network. The root and swap areas for the "nd" client were not part of the same filesystem structure as they are in SunOS 4.0 and above. Raw disk space had to be set aside for each client before the installation happened. It was very hard to find and configure the raw disk space for the "nd" client after the installation. It is much easier to configure disk space for diskless clients in the 4.0 model. If you know how many clients are going to be attached to the server, you can reserve the space without actually setting up the client. You may also wish to buffer the partition sizes with a few extra blocks, just to be safe. When using the free-hog, only the bare minimum is reserved.

If you choose to use the services of the free-hog partition, it should be the largest free partition available on your disk. The choice for free-hog in Figure 2.28 should be partition "h". If a zero-length partition "g" is specified as the free-hog, any attempt to create other partitions on the disk would fail because the free-hog is zero. There is nothing in the free-hog to take from. This is remedied by changing the size of partition "h" to zero, and in so doing, the free-hog grabs the disk space that was used by partition "h", and puts it into partition "g".

The /usr partition should never be designated as the free-hog partition unless you are very careful. As more disk space is pulled from the free-hog, it may reduce /usr to a smaller size than necessary for holding the executables, and would result in a failed installation. Since diskless clients are configured after the software is selected, this is a common problem.

There are two possibilities for defining the free-hog. One is used if there is a limited amount of disk space available. You may want to let the free-hog size your /usr so that valued disk space is put into other partitions. You can do this by setting /usr to be 40MB and selecting a different partition as the free-hog. In the software form, select the categories you wish to install. As more space for /usr is needed, it is pulled from the free-hog. After the software form is complete, /usr is just the right size. The problem with this setup is that there is not any disk space left in /usr for categories to be added later.

The other idea is to know exactly how much space you need for each partition and define it in this form, thereby ignoring the free-hog service. If you have a few extra megabytes to play with, defining the partition sizes manually is preferred.

2.4.4.6 Display Unit   The display unit field in the disk form has no affect on the installation. It is a way to monitor the size of the partitions while using this form. The display unit size is reported in megabytes, kilobytes, blocks, or disk cylinders. Since megabytes seems to be of the most interest, use the first selection (Mbytes). You may wish to view the partition sizes in a different manner.

After all of these selections have been made, it's time to configure the partition sizes. You already know that partition "a" is not going to change. Position the cursor under the MOUNT PT field, and enter a "/" to configure partition "a" to be the root filesystem. After pressing return, the cursor moves under the PRESERVE (Y/N) column.

The preserve option can only be used if a filesystem already exists in the partition. In this example, no filesystems exist. If preserve is selected, a file system consistency check is executed on the partition instead of the **newfs** program (see fsck(8)). The preserve option is intended to be used during operating system upgrades. Certain partitions can be preserved so that the data contained remains intact. The installation aborts if the preserve option is attempted on a partition whose size has changed. The best response to the preserve option is "n" or do not preserve, making sure the system has been backed up before you install it.

Partition "b" on the primary disk is usually swap space. Swap space has no mount point. It is not a mountable filesystem, just raw disk space. You can increase the size of partition "b" on the primary disk while in this form, but should not decrease it. Doing so may cause the MINIROOT filesystem to become corrupt. You should have set the swap partition size during **format**. Do not change it in the disk form unless you are absolutely sure you will not cause harm to the MINIROOT. Partition "b" can be altered on disks other than the primary without ill effects.

Partition "c" begins at cylinder 0 and ends on the last cylinder of each disk. **Suninstall** requires this partition to be defined in this way; do not change partition "c".

The next five partitions are available for custom configuration. The only required filesystem that has not been defined yet is /usr. If all the software categories are going to be extracted from the release tape, /usr should be at least 90 megabytes. Ninety megabytes does not leave much free space after the installation, but if unbundled packages are to be mounted using NFS, it will suffice. The size of your /usr partition also depends on which system type you are installing. There are a number of very helpful forms and examples for calculating partition sizes in the Installation Guide of the Sun documentation.

You cannot exit the disk form without defining all required partitions, which are the root, swap, and /usr. If you try to exit the disk form without specifying a root, swap, or /usr partition, a message is displayed, disallowing you to return to the main menu until the necessary partitions are defined. You are also informed when you have defined two partitions with the same name or mount point. This too requires correction before you may exit the form.

If you are installing a standalone machine, the only partition left to define is /home. Some Sun installations configure standalone machines to use a remote home directory. Others may wish to keep their home directory files stored locally. You cannot specify a remote home directory during **suninstall**. This procedure must be done after the system is installed and booted. When this type of configuration is chosen, the creation of a local home partition is not necessary. If you are installing a server system, or a system utilizing local home space, assign the home partition in the same manner as the others by choosing the size and entering a mount point. You cannot enter a size if it is the free-hog partition.

You may wish to create a separate /var partition, also done by selecting a size and defining a mount point. The /var partition does not need to be large unless you are installing a print server, or a YP master. Create a larger /var for print servers or any system that will be doing a fair amount of spooling. The /var partition should be at least as large as your biggest print job, multiplied by the number of users that may be using the printer at the same time.

Some administrators choose to create a separate /tmp filesystem so their root filesystems are not overflowed with temporary files. This is acceptable and is also done by selecting a size and entering /tmp as the mount point. When this arrangement is used, you must change the permissions on /tmp once the installation is complete so that it can be written to and read from by all. The /tmp directory must have the permissions set to 4777. When a mount point is created, it inherits the properties of its parent directory. If you create a mount point in /, only the superuser (root) has write permissions to that directory. Most windowing systems create files in /tmp when running.

When installing diskless client servers, you must set up the

/export partition by defining a size and creating a mount point. Also, define the /export/root, /export/swap, and /export/exec partitions remembering that if only /export/root and /export/swap are defined, the /export directory ends up in your root partition. This may work for a homogeneous server of diskless clients, but certainly will not suffice for a server of multiple architecture platforms, unless you have created an extra-large root filesystem.

Committing the current partition arrangement is done by answering "y" to the "Ok to use this partition table [y/n]^?" prompt at the bottom of the screen. The next prompt asks "Are you finished with this form [y/n]^?" Responding with a "n" returns the cursor to the "Attached Disk Devices" area at the top of the screen. Select different disks by positioning the cursor next to the device and typing "x". Remember to spread the load of filesystems out among all the disks that are attached. Such a move increases response time for all.

After you have set up your disk partitions, you are ready to select the software categories to install. Commit all disks and answer "y" in response to the "Are you finished with this form [y/n] ?" prompt at the bottom of the screen. After doing so, you are returned to the **suninstall** main menu.

2.4.4.7 Assign Software Information The software form, shown in Figure 2.29 allows you to select software categories to load from the release tape. The architecture information section expects you to select the software for the local or server machine first. Once the base operating system categories have been selected, you may select the heterogeneous software to install.

The path to where the executables reside is always /usr for homogeneous servers and standalone machines. The path where kernel architecture dependent executables reside is always /usr/kvm on homogeneous servers and standalone machines.

For heterogeneous servers, these two paths are changed to the default /export/exec/<arch> and /export/exec/kvm/<arch>, where <arch> is the kernel architecture of the software being selected. These paths are not mandatory. You may choose any partition name granted there is enough disk space to hold all of the executable files. Be aware that other modifications may need to be

```
SOFTWARE FORM [DEL=erase one char of input data] [RET=end of input data]
Architecture Information :
 Type   : [sun2] x[sun3] [sun3x] [sun4] [sun4c]
 Path where executables reside : /export/exec/sun3
 Path where sub-arch dependent executables reside : /export/exec/kvm/sun3
Media Information :
 Device Type : [st0] [st1] [st2] [ar0] [mt0] [x]st0]
 Drive Type  : x[local] [remote]


Choice : x[all] [default] [own choice] [required] [quit]
```

CATEGORY	NAME	BYTES	AVAIL BYTES	Y/N
required	usr	20971520	83447808	y
required	Kvm	2640896	60169421	y
required	Install	970752	57238027	y
desirable	Sys	2917376	683850240	y
desirable	Networking	961536	83447808	y
desirable	Debugging	3401728	55093189	y
common	SunView_Users	1462272	51317271	y
optional	SuView_Programmers	2066432	49694150	y
optional	SunView_Demo	565248	47400411	y
optional	Text	690176	46772986	y
optional	User_Diag	3969024	46006891	y
optional	SunCore	2991104	41601275	y
optional	uucp	270336	38281150	y

```
Are you finished with this form [y/n] ?
 [x/X=select choice] [space=next choice] [^B/^P=backward] [^F/^N=forward]
```

FIGURE 2.29. *The software form.*

done when setting up clients and exporting filesystems if you change the default paths.

The media information section selects the device from which the installation will occur. The possible choices are:

1. st0

2. st1

3. st2

4. ar0

5. mt0

6. xt0

The drive type choices are for a local or remote tape device. If this install is using a remote tape drive, there are two more fields to fill out. The tapehosts' hostname and number must be entered so that the system being installed "knows" which machine has the tape device it is going to use. If an input error is made in either of these fields, you will not be able to read the tape. When the attempt to read the tape fails, re-enter the field with the correct information to continue. Be sure that the Ethernet cable is attached to a functional network.

If your local installation is using 1/2″ tape, your choices for drive type are going to be either an mt0 or xt0. The mt0 selection is for the CDC 1600 BPI tape drive with a Tapemaster controller. The xt0 selection is the Fujitsu 6250 tape drive with the Xylogics tape controller. There is one other 1/2″ tape alternative, the Front Load tape, but this is a SCSI device so the selection is one of st0, st1, or st2.

After setting up the appropriate tape device to install from, the next step is making a list of software to extract. The four choices in this section are: all, default, own choice, and required. Each selection uses a different extract list. It should be pointed out again that if you plan on selecting all software, the /usr partition needs at least 90 megabytes. If you have not left enough room in the /usr partition, the needed space is taken from the free-hog partition. If there is not enough room in the free-hog partition, you are informed and required to define the partition requirements over again in the disk form. Another point to consider when selecting the software list is that if you are letting the free-hog determine the size of the /usr filesystem and you choose the minimum amount of software, your /usr partition may not have enough room to extract other categories after the installation has completed.

Not every machine needs "all" the software installed. Most systems need only the default selection because the categories not installed locally can be mounted over the network. Selecting "all" software for architectures other than the server architecture is a waste of disk space. Categories such as the man pages are not architecture dependent so they can be shared among all architecture types.

Selecting the "default" option chooses the system software that is normally taken for most installations. Even after selecting "default", you are asked if you would like to install any of the remaining sections. You will have to answer "y" or "n" to each category when prompted. What you don't install now can be easily extracted after the installation with **setup_exec** if you have enough disk space left.

Selecting "own choice" is similar to the "default" selection in that you are prompted for a y/n response for every category except the required software. This takes longer since the partition sizes are checked after each y/n response regardless of whether the category was added to the extract list. The "own choice" option is better used when running **setup_exec.** It is mainly for selecting one or two categories.

Once you have decided on the categories to extract, they are displayed at the bottom of the form and the cursor is positioned at the "Ok to use this extractlist [y/n]?" prompt. If this list is acceptable, enter "y". The next prompt, " Are you finished with this form [y/n]?" appears.

If this is a standalone machine, you can start the installation now since you will not be configuring diskless clients. If you are installing a server system that only supports diskless clients of the same architecture, you do not need to install any more software. To start the installation, enter a "y" to quit this form and you are returned to the main menu.

If you would like to add more software of a different architecture type, you may respond to this prompt with a "n". This returns the cursor to the "Architecture Information" section at the top of the form. You may select the architecture of the machines you are going to support, provided you have release tapes for that architecture available. Multiple architecture support is only necessary on servers which support different architecture clients. Select the software in the same manner as described above. The path to where the executables reside changes with every different architecture selected. The base architecture of the machine installs the executables in /usr. The executables for unlike architectures defaults to the /export/exec/<arch> directory. As each different architecture is added, the <arch> directory changes.

The SunOS 4.0.3, 4.0.3c, 4.0.3SPARCserver 390, and 4.0.3SPARCserver 490 releases are each specific to a certain set of systems. 4.0.3 covers the major architectures: Sun-2, Sun-3, Sun-3x, and Sun-4. Sun-4c machines, such as the SPARCstation1 and the SPARCstation1+, may only use the 4.0.3c release, or later. When installing a Sun-4 server that supports diskless 4.0.3c clients, you must be sure to install the 4.0.3c release last. This is due to the library changes in 4.0.3c that affect the Sun-4c architecture. SunOS 4.0.3c is based on 4.0.3, with enhancements for the kernel architecture Sun-4c. The 4.0.3SPARCserver 390 and 4.0.3SPARCserver 490 releases are also platform specific which include extra device drivers to support the Intelligent Peripheral Interface, IPI devices. Both of these releases are based on 4.0.3, not 4.0.3c. If either of these machines are to be servers of diskless Sun-4c clients, the 4.0.3c release must be installed last. A special category in the 4.0.3c release, Sun-4c user, is specifically for this purpose. This category takes only the executables necessary for the proper function of Sun-4c clients.

After the desired software categories and architectures have been selected, exit the form by answering "y" to "Are you finished with this form [y/n]?" prompt. You are once again returned to the **suninstall** main menu. The next menu item sets up diskless clients. Server systems that support the booting and operation of diskless clients can either set the clients up now, or wait until after the installation is complete. It is up to you provided you have left enough disk space to allow the creation of client root and swap files.

2.4.4.8 Assign Client Information Suninstall has the capacity to configure diskless clients on a server during the installation process. When the installation is complete, client systems that have been set up in this form will be able to boot from this server machine. Before you begin entering data in this form, you should have a list of hostnames, IP addresses, and Ethernet addresses for the clients that will be configured. The IP address and hostnames are assigned by you or your network administrator. The Ethernet address is hard coded into an ID PROM on each CPU. It can be obtained by viewing the banner information when a machine is first powered up.

The "Assign client information" menu selection from the **suninstall** main menu is only available if the system type selection made in the "Assign hosts information" form was a server. If you selected the standalone system type, this form is not offered.

In pre-4.0 SunOS releases, configuration of dummy clients during the installation process was necessary to reserve portions of the disk. This was done because it was quite a chore to create new "nd" clients after the installation had already finished. Nd clients used a block of raw disk space for their root and swap. Finding a free chunk of raw disk space on an already configured machine was nearly impossible without adding a new disk. Creating clients after the system is installed is no longer a problem as long as there is enough disk space reserved.

If you are using the services of the free-hog disk partition to expand the size of client partitions as they are added, then you must add a client in this form for every client expected to be using this system. Rather than creating the "dummy" clients, simply reserve the space manually in the disk form, using these rules:

1. For every diskless client, reserve at least eight megabytes in /export/root. If /export/root is not a separate partition, reserve five megabytes for each client in the /export directory. If the server machine is to support ten diskless clients, then the /export/root partition should be at least 80 megabytes in size.

2. For each diskless client, reserve at least 16 megabytes in the /export/swap partition. Some machines may need more and some less. 160 megabytes would be needed in /export/swap for a server supporting ten diskless clients.

If you choose to configure clients during **suninstall**, start with homogeneous clients. Configure all clients of the same architecture type as the server and then move on to heterogeneous clients. Add a client by first selecting the architecture type. This defaults to the architecture type of the server being installed. Attempting to add a client for an architecture that has not been selected in the software form yields an error message and returns to the top level menu of the form (see Figure 2.30). After deciding which clients to add, enter an **x** while the cursor is positioned by the "[create]"

```
CLIENT FORM [DEL=erase one char of input data] [RET=end of input data]

Architecture Type      : [sun2] x[sun3] [sun3x] [sun4] [sun4c]
Choice                 : x[create] [delete] [display] [next arch]

Clients(s) :


Client Information :
  Name                                        :
  Internet Address                            : 192.9.200.200
  Ethernet Address                            : 8:0:20:1:00:00
  YP Type : x[none] [master] [slave] [client]
  Domain name                                 : noname
  Path of Client's Root                       : /export/root
  Path od Client's Swap                       : /export/swap
  Path of Client's sub-arch dependent Execs   : /export/exec/kvm/sun3
  Path of Client's Home                       : /home
  Swap size (e.g. 8M, 8m, 8K, 8k or 8b)       : 16M


Are you finished with this form [y/n] ?
[x/X=select choice] [space=next choice] [^B/^P=backward] [^F/^N=forward]
```

FIGURE 2.30. *The client form.*

choice field. This brings up a list of items that are specific to this client.

First is the client name, also known as the hostname. Enter the name of the client to be configured. Next, enter the IP address of the client then the Ethernet address.

The next item to select is the YP type. It is not recommended that diskless clients act as YP servers. Your choice here is one of "none" or "client". If you select the YP "client" field, enter the YP domain name for which this client will be a member.

The next five "Path" definition fields are supplied by the system. If you have set up non-standard paths to diskless clients root and swap, these fields should be adjusted to reflect those changes. If you are using the default pathnames, just use the <CR> to move the cursor down to the "Swap size" field.

Adjust the swap size depending on the client's memory and/

or application requirements. Sixteen megabytes is a standard since most diskless machines have eight megabytes of memory. There are utilities to increase or add swap space to a system after it has been installed.

When all the client information has been entered, answer a "y"or "n" to the "Are you finished with this form? [y/n]" message at the bottom of the screen. A response of "y" returns to the **suninstall** main menu. If there are more clients that you wish to add, whether they are clients of the same architecture or clients of a different architecture, answer "n". The cursor moves to the top of the form. Select the architecture of the client or clients to be installed and create clients in the same manner just discussed. When all clients are added you can exit this form by answering "y" to "Are you finished with this form? [y/n]" prompt at the bottom of the screen. This returns you to the **suninstall** main menu.

After each form has been completed, it is usually a good idea to see if the partition arrangement has changed in a way that may be detrimental, especially if the free-hog service was used. You may re-enter any of the forms. In particular, re-enter the disk form to make sure that everything is as you have defined it. After selecting the disk, a new field is offered in the disk label section of the disk form, "[use data file]". Select this field to see if the current partition information is correct. Check partition sizes to be sure that the software selected, or the clients configured will fit. One inconvenience about re-entering the disk form is that you will once again have to check the data on all disks, even if you do not change anything. Try not to change any partition sizes because any changes may affect the ability to fit the software selected or diskless clients that will be created. The only acceptable change may be to add another ten percent to your /usr partition, just for padding (thus if /usr is 80 megabytes, add eight more megabytes to it). If you decide to do this, make certain that the partition giving up the disk space is not going to miss it. When in doubt, take it from the /home partition. Regardless of system type, this is an empty partition when the installation is complete.

2.4.4.9 Start the Installation Once satisfied that all forms have been given their necessary information, the installation can begin. Position the cursor next to the "start the installation" field and use the "x" key to begin. The screen clears and the installation begins by labeling the disks and checking or creating the filesystems defined in the disk form.

The output from **suninstall** is redirected to a log file, called *suninstall.log*, which is copied to the /usr/etc/install/files directory once the installation is complete. All other data files used during the installation setup are saved here as well. Some of the other files, such as *sys_info*, *disk_info*, and *media_list* are needed to run the **setup_exec** utility. Do not delete the /usr/etc/install/ files directory. Figure 2.31 is the output from a normal installation.

Midway through the installation, you are prompted to remove the first tape and insert the second. Installations generally take about 1.5 hours after the forms have been completed and take more or less time depending on the system architecture and software selected. Heterogeneous servers take even longer because multiple releases are being installed. Generally, systems with 1/2 inch tape devices install much faster than systems with 1/4 inch tape drives due in part to densities and data transfer rates.

After the install is complete, your system either reboots, or is left at the MINIROOT prompt, depending on what your selection was in the "Assign Hosts Information" form. If you choose not to reboot, halt the system using the L1-A sequence and issue a "b" from the monitor prompt to begin booting. Starting a remote installation is discussed in the next few pages.

2.4.5 Remote Installation

The concepts for remote installations remain the same as for local installs. The only difference is the lack of a local tape device. This is easily remedied by using a server of diskless clients capable of supporting the tapeless machine's architecture type. The **setup_client** utility can be executed on the server to setup services for the new client. The client can then boot over the network, run the **format** utility and copy the MINIROOT to its local disk while running as a diskless client.

The diskless client server of this machine does not have to be the tapehost. Any machine with a tape device located on the local net can be used.

System Installation begin :

Label disk(s) :
xy0

Create/Check File Systems :
sun4 Installation Begin :
0 + 11 records in
0 + 11 records out
Creating root file system.
Extracting "usr" files from "/dev/nrst0" release tape.
Extracting "Kvm" files from "/dev/nrst0" release tape.
Extracting "Install" files from "/dev/nrst0" release tape.
Extracting "Sys" files from "/dev/nrst0" release tape.
Extracting "Networking" files from "/dev/nrst0" release tape.
Extracting "Debugging" files from "/dev/nrst0" release tape.
Extracting "SunView_Users" files from "/dev/nrst0" release tape.
Extracting "SunView_Programmers" files from "/dev/nrst0" release tape.
Extracting "SunView_Demo" files from "/dev/nrst0" release tape.
Extracting "Text" files from "/dev/nrst0" release tape.
Extracting "User_Diag" files from "/dev/nrst0" release tape.
Extracting "SunCore" files from "/dev/nrst0" release tape.
Extracting "uucp" files from "/dev/nrst0" release tape.
Extracting "System_V" files from "/dev/nrst0" release tape.
Extracting "Manual" files from "/dev/nrst0" release tape.
Extracting "Demo" files from "/dev/nrst0" release tape.
Extracting "Games" files from "/dev/nrst0" release tape.
Extracting "Versatec" files from "/dev/nrst0" release tape.
Extracting "Security" files from "/dev/nrst0" release tape.
sun4 installation completed.

FIGURE 2.31. *Screen output during installation.*

2.4.5.1 Booting Diskless while Disks are Attached Even when booting over the network, the standard SunOS kernel expects the root filesystem and swap device to be on the local disk. If the system is not instructed otherwise, disk devices found during the boot sequence are automatically mounted and used. Since most diskless clients do not have disks, this is not a problem. But if you are booting a diskless client that has disks installed, you must use the "-a" (or ask) option.

Using the "-a" option allows you to specify the type and location of the root filesystem, which is either a 4.2 filesystem or an NFS mount. The "-a" option also asks you to specify the type and location of swap space, the root name, and a filename from which to boot:

```
> bie() -a
> Boot: ie(0,0,0) -a
Using IP Address C009C801
Booting from server address C009C806
Root Filesystem type: (4.2, nfs)
Root name:
```

When using the "-a" option, the first prompt is for the root filesystem type. Since you are booting an NFS client, answer "nfs". The "root name?" prompt appears next. The correct response for root name is a carriage return. Any other response causes the system to hang. The file to boot is "vmunix", the SunOS kernel. You may enter a <CR> instead of typing in "vmunix" since it is the default filename to load.

After the kernel is loaded and devices are polled, you are prompted once again to enter the root and swap filesystem type. The client's root partition type is "nfs" and the client's swap partition type is also "nfs". Use a carriage return when responding to the root name and swap name prompts. These fields are best left empty.

After the system completes booting, login as root. Some device special files may need to be made for the disk devices attached to this system. Do this by changing the working directory to /dev and running the **MAKEDEV** script, giving the device that is installed as an argument. When the disk devices have been created, you may enter the **format** utility.

```
machine# cd /dev
machine# MAKEDEV sd0
machine# format
```

After running **format** to partition your disk, exit the **format** utility and return to the root prompt. You must now use the remote tapehost to copy MINIROOT into the "b" partition of the local disk.

2.4.5.2 Remote Copy of MINIROOT to Local Disk Installing the MINIROOT from a remote machine is very similar to copying MINIROOT locally while running MUNIX. The only difference is that you are using a remote command to access the tape device. The first tape from the release set must be loaded on the remote machine. The MINIROOT filesystem is then extracted from the tape, over the network, and directly into the swap area of the local disk.

The hostname of the tapeless machine must be in the tapehost machine's */.rhosts* file. Otherwise, you do not have permission to use the remote tape device. Start the remote copy procedure by logging into the tapehost as "root", supplying a password, and then using the commands shown in Figure 2.32.

Substitute the correct tape device, such as nrst0, where you see an X, and the appropriate disk device, such as rsd0b, where you see DD. When using **dd** be sure to specify partition "b" instead of "a". Copying to partition "a" corrupts the disk label and requires you to run the **format** utility once again to label your disk.

2.4.5.3 Booting MINIROOT from a Tapeless Machine After the copy is complete, you can halt the system and boot the MINIROOT in this fashion. The response to filesystem type and location is different than booting up diskless. You still need to retrieve the boot block over the network. An example is shown in Figure 2.33.

At this point you may enter **suninstall.** Each form can be edited exactly the same as a local install except for two additional fields in the "assign software information" form. The added fields

---

```
tapehost# cat >> /.rhosts
<hostname>          (of tapeless machine being installed)
<Control>-D
tapehost# exit

tapeless#
tapeless# rsh <tapehost> mt -f /dev/nrXtX rew
tapeless# rsh <tapehost> mt -f /dev/nrXtX fsf 3
tapeless# rsh <tapehost> dd if=`/dev/nrXtX bs`=`200b  |  dd of`=`/dev/rDDb
```

FIGURE 2.32. *Remote installation of MINIROOT.*

```
> bie() -asw
Root filesystem type ( 4.2, nfs) 4.2
Root filesystem on ( sd(a-h), xy(a-h), xd(a-h) ): sd0b (depending on disk)
Root on sd0b
Boot: vmunix
123124 + 23421 + 2341
SunOS Release 4.0.3 (GENERIC) #1: Tue Sep 19 09:38:54 PDT 1989
Copyright (c) 1989 by Sun Microsystems, Inc.
mem = 32768K (0x2000000)
avail mem = 31825920
Ethernet address = 8:0:20:6:bf:15
si0 at vme24d16 0x200000 vec 0x40
st0 at si0 slave 32
sd0 at si0 slave 0
sd0: <CDC-WrenIV> cyl 1614 alt 2 hd 15 sec 54>
sd1 at si0 slave 1
sd2 at si0 slave 8
Root filesystem type: 4.2
Root filesystem on: sd0b
Swap filesystem type: spec
Swap on: sd0b
Swapping on root device, is this OK: y
#
```

FIGURE 2.33. *Booting MINIROOT from a tapeless machine.*

prompt for the hostname and IP address of the machine that is acting as the tapehost. Also be sure to add the tapeless machine's hostname to the /.rhosts file on the tapehost if not already done, as in Figure 2-32. After the installation is complete, use the **setup_client** script to remove the diskless support of the tapeless machine. **Setup_client** is discussed at greater length in Chapter 4.

2.5 After suninstall

When **suninstall** is finished, your system will either reboot, or be sitting at the MINIROOT prompt, "#", depending on which selection was chosen in the "assign host information" form. If you choose not to reboot after installation, simply abort the system using the L1-A sequence and issue a **b** at the monitor prompt. The default disk device in the EEPROM is polled and booted. If the default boot device cannot be found, a message is returned and the boot process aborts.

There are a number of reasons why this may occur but the most common is when the primary system disk has changed type or logical identification number. The primary disk is the disk that contains the root filesystem. The default disk is determined by the contents of four EEPROM locations. Some systems may have any one or all of sd0, xd0, xy0, or id000 devices. The EEPROM may be trying to boot from sd0, when you have installed the root filesystem on xd0. If you have installed the root filesystem on a disk other than disk 0, or on a disk type that was not originally connected to the system, you should change the EEPROM. The settings in the EEPROM are much easier to change after the system is running SunOS. The default can be over-ridden at first boot with a manual command as done below.

> bNN()

Substitute NN with "sd" for SCSI disks, "xy" or "xd" for SMD disks, or "id" for IPI disks if the disk type has changed. When the contents of the parentheses are left empty, the system attempts to boot from disk ID zero. If the primary disk ID has changed, say from sd0 to sd1, use a different manual command.

> bsd(,1,)

Once the system has booted, you may define the new primary boot device by using the **eeprom** utility (see eeprom(8S)). After setting the EEPROM, you will not need to enter manual boot commands at the monitor prompt. Other problems that may cause an incomplete boot might be:

- Invalid or mis-spelled YP domain
- Ethernet cable not attached
- Incorrect IP number
- Conflicting hostname

2.5.1 Post-Installation Issues

The majority of post-installation issues concern actions taken on fileservers of some sort. A new YP master cannot boot completely until the YP maps have been made. The server of diskless clients may need to have the diskless clients created if this is not done during **suninstall.** The installation of software on the NFS resource server may begin. All new systems should have a more efficient kernel installed.

2.5.1.1 Booting the YP Master after Installation If you are installing a new YP master machine in a new domain there will be problems achieving a complete boot until YP maps are present. To make the YP maps, you must boot the new YP master into single-user mode, run the **ypinit** command to build the YP database, then continue booting by issuing a control-D or reboot the system. If you have created a separate /var partition, it must be mounted manually before making the maps. Use the commands below to allow a new YP master to complete booting.

```
# domainname < YP domain>
# mount /var
# /usr/etc/yp/ypinit -m
```

It is not necessary that YP datafiles be fully complete at this point. The objective is to create a directory under /var/yp with a name identical to the YP domain name. The files in that directory must have enough data to allow proper function of the database. The **ypinit** utility does this when invoked. As shown above, you must supply the domain name before running **ypinit** in single-user mode. After the system completes booting, the YP datafiles can be edited to suit your needs. See Chapter 3 for more details on YP.

Another post-installation issue may entail editing your */etc/ fstab* so that simultaneous file system checks are done when the system boots. Concurrent filesystem checks can save a great deal of time because serial checking is done by default. When this procedure is done on systems with many filesystems, the system is operational in a shorter amount of time. Simultaneous filesystem checking can be accomplished by changing the **fsck** pass field in the */etc/fstab* file using one simple rule: Filesystems that are on different disks can be checked at the same time.

In Figure 2.34, the last field on each line represents the order to run **fsck,** the file system check. This is the way the file is set up during **suninstall,** in consecutive order. The root filesystem should always be checked first and by itself. No other filesystems should

/dev/sd0a	/	4.2 rw 1	1
/dev/sd2a	/export	4.2 rw 1	3
/dev/sd0h	/home	4.2 rw 1	4
/dev/id000d	/id0d	4.2 rw 1	5
/dev/id000e	/id0e	4.2 rw 1	6
/dev/id000g	/id0g	4.2 rw 1	7
/dev/id000h	/id0h	4.2 rw 1	8
/dev/id001b	/id1b	4.2 rw 1	9
/dev/id001d	/id1d	4.2 rw 1	10
/dev/id001e	/id1e	4.2 rw 1	11
/dev/id001g	/id1g	4.2 rw 1	12
/dev/id001h	/id1h	4.2 rw 1	13
/dev/id000b	/junk	4.2 rw 1	14
/dev/sd2d	/sd2d	4.2 rw 1	15
/dev/sd2e	/sd2e	4.2 rw 1	16
/dev/sd2g	/sd2g	4.2 rw 1	17
/dev/sd2h	/sd2h	4.2 rw 1	18
/dev/sd0d	/tmp	4.2 rw 1	19
/dev/sd0g	/usr	4.2 rw 1	2
/dev/sd0e	/var	4.2 rw 1	20
/dev/id000a	/export/exec	4.2 rw 1	21
/dev/sd2b	/export/root	4.2 rw 1	22
/dev/id001a	/export/swap	4.2 rw 1	23

FIGURE 2.34. *The* /etc/fstab *file before editing.*

be checked at the same time just in case a problem is found and the system reboots. Another filesystem which should be checked by itself is /usr. All other filesystems can be checked simultaneously.

Figure 2.35 illustrates how 23 separate passes of file system checks can be covered in eight. The root filesystem "/", has been left untouched, and is checked first. The /usr filesystem was also left to be checked alone since both of these partitions are vital to your machine's correct operation. The /export, /home, /id0d, and /id1b partitions are all checked at the same time in the third pass. Each of these partitions is located on different disks; /export is on the device /dev/sd2a, /home is on /dev/sd0h, /id0d is on /dev/id000d, and /id1b is on /dev/id001b. Partition names id0d and id1b are being used just for this example. They have no other special meaning. Further examination of Figure 2.35 reveals that

/dev/sd0a	/	4.2 rw 1	1
/dev/sd2a	/export	4.2 rw 1	3
/dev/sd0h	/home	4.2 rw 1	3
/dev/id000d	/id0d	4.2 rw 1	3
/dev/id000e	/id0e	4.2 rw 1	4
/dev/id000g	/id0g	4.2 rw 1	5
/dev/id000h	/id0h	4.2 rw 1	8
/dev/id001b	/id1b	4.2 rw 1	3
/dev/id001d	/id1d	4.2 rw 1	4
/dev/id001e	/id1e	4.2 rw 1	5
/dev/id001g	/id1g	4.2 rw 1	6
/dev/id001h	/id1h	4.2 rw 1	7
/dev/id000b	/junk	4.2 rw 1	7
/dev/sd2d	/sd2d	4.2 rw 1	4
/dev/sd2e	/sd2e	4.2 rw 1	5
/dev/sd2g	/sd2g	4.2 rw 1	6
/dev/sd2h	/sd2h	4.2 rw 1	7
/dev/sd0d	/tmp	4.2 rw 1	4
/dev/sd0g	/usr	4.2 rw 1	2
/dev/sd0e	/var	4.2 rw 1	5
/dev/id000a	/export/exec	4.2 rw 1	6
/dev/sd2b	/export/root	4.2 rw 1	8
/dev/id001a	/export/swap	4.2 rw 1	8

FIGURE 2.35. *The* /etc/fstab *file after editing.*

during the filesystem check pass 4, each partition is also located on different devices.

/dev/id000e	/id0e	4.2 rw 1	4
/dev/id001d	/id1d	4.2 rw 1	4
/dev/sd2d	/sd2d	4.2 rw 1	4
/dev/sd0d	/tmp	4.2 rw 1	4

The same theory applies to the other disk partitions. Because this example has four different disks, only four file system checks should be run during any one pass. If more disks were attached, more concurrent checks could be done.

2.5.2 Trimming the Kernel

When a system has completed the installation, a GENERIC kernel is placed into the root directory for booting. There is no way of knowing which options and devices are connected to a particular system. Consequently the GENERIC kernel is used to cover all possible configurations. The system operates correctly, but for every device or option built into your kernel, a number of memory pages are used. There are options such as system types, and disk and tape devices that are not even connected to your system, and peripherals that may never be connected to your system. Trimming the kernel frees up memory, thus allowing a faster response time overall.

Consider a diskless client that boots a GENERIC kernel. There are options in the GENERIC kernel for every possible disk device, tape device, and display device. A diskless client never uses many of the peripherals that are built into the GENERIC kernel. Response times are slower because of the memory pages taken by these extra devices. The solution is to build a kernel that only contains the minimum necessary devices and options. Memory is thus used more efficiently.

Also consider a standalone machine with a SCSI disk drive and a 1/4″ tape drive. This system could also run much more efficiently if the extra devices were trimmed out of its kernel.

In order to build a new kernel, your system must have the "Sys" category installed. If "Sys" was not selected during **suninstall**, it can be extracted by using the **setup_exec** utility.

Here are the steps needed to create a custom kernel.

1. Gather system and device information.

2. Edit the configuration file.

3. Execute **config**, using the edited file as an argument.

4. Change the working directory to the directory created as a result of **config.**

5. Run **make** to start the build.

6. Copy the new kernel to /, saving the original kernel.

7. Boot the machine with the new kernel.

2.5.2.1 Gathering Device Information You must know your system type as well as which devices are installed on your system so that unneeded devices can be discarded. One way to tell this is to observe the machine while it is booting a GENERIC kernel. As each device is polled, it is displayed to the console. Use the **dmesg** command to view the output of the boot process. The output is different between machines depending on the devices found. Figure 2.36 displays a normal output from **dmesg** on a 3/80 machine.

The line numbers in Figure 2.36 are for discussion only, and are not part of the normal **dmesg** output. Line 1 in Figure 2.36 shows the SunOS release, the name of the kernel, and the date the kernel was built. Line 2 is the copyright message. The next line is

1.) SunOS Release 4.0.3 (GENERIC) #1: Fri Jul 14 11:09:55 PST 1989
2.) Copyright (c) 1989 by Sun Microsystems, Inc.
3.) mem = 16384K (0x1000000)
4.) avail mem = 15114240
5.) Ethernet address = 8:0:20:6:33:6b
6.) sm0 at obio 0x66000000 pri 2
7.) st0 at sm0 slave 32
8.) st1 at sm0 slave 40
9.) sd0 at sm0 slave 0
10.) sd0: <CDC Wren IV 94171-344 cyl 1545 alt 2 hd 9 sec 46>
11.) sd1 at sm0 slave 1
12.) sd2 at sm0 slave 8
13.) sd3 at sm0 slave 9
14.) sd4 at sm0 slave 16
15.) sd4: <Quantum ProDrive 105S cyl 974 alt 2 hd 6 sec 35>
16.) sd6 at sm0 slave 24
17.) sd6: <Quantum ProDrive 105S cyl 974 alt 2 hd 6 sec 35>
18.) fdc0 at obio 0x6e000000 vec 0x5c
19.) fd0 at fdc0 slave 0
20.) zs0 at obio 0x62002000 pri 3
21.) zs1 at obio 0x62000000 pri 3
22.) le0 at obio 0x65002000 pri 3
23.) cgfour0 at obmem 0x50300000 pri 4
24.) bwtwo0 at obmem 0x50300000 pri 4
25.) bwtwo0: resolution 1152 x 900
26.) pp0 at obio 0x6f000000 pri 1
27.) DATE.........
28.) root on sd6a fstype 4.2
29.) swap on sd6b fstype spec size 30765K
30.) dump on sd6b fstype spec size 30736K

FIGURE 2.36. *The output from the **dmesg** command.*

the amount of memory installed in the system, followed on line 4 by the available memory after the kernel has been loaded. The fifth line is the unique Ethernet address for this machine, which is hard coded into a PROM and cannot be changed. The sixth line starts displaying the devices and controllers that are attached to this system. The order that these controllers are displayed in is determined by the order of the controllers in the kernel configuration file. Line 6 shows controller "sm0" at "obio" which means "on-board I/O". On board I/O means that the controller is built into the CPU board. This controller, sm0, is an on board SCSI controller at address 0x66000000, and has an interrupt priority of 2.

The next two lines, 7 and 8, show st0 and st1, SCSI tape 0 and 1. If there is only one 1/4" tape drive on a machine, it is most likely st0. If more than one SCSI tape is installed on your system, then both entries for st0 and st1 need to remain in the configuration file. Since this system is booting a GENERIC kernel, all possible devices that can exist on the "sm0" controller are displayed even if they are not attached to your system. Lines 9–17 are entries for SCSI disks. Of the seven possibilities, three exist on this system: sd0, sd4, and sd6. These are the only disk devices "seen" at boot time on this machine. If a disk device is seen by the system, its label is read and displayed.

After the SCSI devices, are lines 18 and 19, showing the floppy disk controller "fdc0", which is also built into the CPU board. Under the controller is the device fd0 which is floppy disk 0. The next two lines, 20 and 21, are entries for the serial ports, and for the keyboard and mouse. The "zs0" device is for serial ports A and B while "zs1" supports the keyboard and mouse interface. Some new Sun machines, such as the 4/330, have four serial ports built into the CPU board and would support more "zs" devices.

Lines 23, 24, and 25 are display devices. The "cgfour0" entry is a type of color frame buffer while "bwtwo0" is black and white. Line 26 shows the parallel printer port only available on the 3/80 desktop machine. The "pp0" device is also an "on board I/O" device.

The last four lines show the current time and date and where the root, swap, and dump filesystem types are located, as well as their size. The **dmesg** output can be quite helpful in determining which devices to trim out of the configuration file.

2.5.2.2 Editing the Configuration File It is always a good practice to make a copy of the file you wish to edit for safe keeping. Configuration files live in the /usr/kvm/sys/<arch>/conf directory, where <arch> is the kernel architecture of the machine.

```
# ls /usr/kvm/sys/sun3x/conf
```

```
DL470              Makefile.src     XDXT470     files
DL80               GENERIC          README      XYXT470
GENERIC_SMALL                       SDST80      devices
```

The files in capital letters are the configuration files. These can be edited using your favorite editor. The GENERIC configuration file contains information about every system CPU type, device, or option that Sun supports on that kernel architecture. The GENERIC_SMALL file is a somewhat stripped down version of the GENERIC file.

Several template configuration files are also included and differ between architecture and machine type. In this example, the files prefixed with "DL" are configuration files containing the options and devices necessary to build diskless client kernels. There are not any disk or tape devices in these configuration files. SDST files have devices defined for systems with SCSI disks and SCSI tape. The XYXT and XDXT files are for systems with SMD disks and 6250 BPI tape devices.

Each kernel architecture contains a different set of template files. Some options present in the GENERIC configuration file are not in all of the other template files. The SDST and XYXT files may not have all of the pseudo devices and options that are needed by your systems.

Choose the configuration file that resembles the machine you are building the kernel for. In the case of the machine "hal", the SDST80 file will be used since it is a 3/80 machine with SCSI disks and tape devices. Make a copy of the SDST80 file and call it HAL_SDST.

```
# cd /usr/kvm/sys/sun3x/conf
# cp SDST80 HAL_SDST
# chmod +w HAL_SDST
# vi HAL_SDST
```

There are two styles of editing configuration files discussed in this section. One style deletes the unwanted options and devices out of the file. The other, which is preferred, uses the "#" sign to comment out unwanted things. The latter is much easier to correct if problems are encountered. Instead of knowing which lines need to be put back in the file, the comment sign or "#" can be removed. The result is exactly the same.

SunOS 4.0 and 4.0.3 configuration files explain most entries quite well. Even so, there are a number of important items which need attention.

The GENERIC template file for all architectures contains a number of CPU types. You only need to keep the one pertaining to your system.

The Sun-3 GENERIC file has the most different CPU types within a given kernel architecture. When the unwanted CPU type is commented out, any associated device looking for that CPU needs to be commented as well. The first part of the Sun-3 configuration file is shown in Figure 2.37. If any one of the CPU types is commented out, the associated connections must be commented out. Some of these connections are shown in Figure 2.38.

Similarly, any other device associated with the machine type must be removed. Another item to remember when editing the GENERIC configuration file concerns the "mcp" devices and the pseudo-device "mcp64". If you are not using the ALM-2 and you comment out "pseudo-device mcp64", then any other lines referring to the "mcp" devices must be commented out as well.

If the "ident" name is to be called anything other than GENERIC, it should be enclosed between double quotes, "HAL". If this is not done, the kernel build may fail (see Figure 2.39).

machine	"sun3"	
cpu	"SUN3_160"	# Sun-3/75, Sun-3/140, Sun-3/160, or Sun-3/180
cpu	"SUN3_50"	# Sun-3/50
cpu	"SUN3_260"	# Sun-3/260 or Sun-3/280
cpu	"SUN3_110"	# Sun-3/110
cpu	"SUN3_60"	# Sun-3/60
cpu	"SUN3_E"	# Sun-3E (Eurocard VMEbus cpu)

FIGURE 2.37. *CPU types in the Sun-3 GENERIC file.*

```
#
# The following sections describe what kinds of busses each
# cpu type supports. You should never need to change this.
# (The word "nexus" is historical...)

# connections for machine type 1 (SUN3_160)
controller   virtual 1 at nexus?   # virtually addressed devices
controller   obmem 1 at nexus?   # memory-like devices on the cpu board
controller   obio 1 at nexus?   # I/O devices on the cpu board
controller   vme16d16 1 at nexus?   # VME 16 bit address 16 bit data devices
controller   vme24d16 1 at nexus?   # VME 24 bit address 16 bit data devices
controller   vme32d16 1 at nexus?   # VME 32 bit address 16 bit data devices
controller   vme16d32 1 at nexus?   # VME 16 bit address 32 bit data devices
controller   vme24d32 1 at nexus?   # VME 24 bit address 32 bit data devices
controller   vme32d32 1 at nexus?   # VME 32 bit address 32 bit data devices

# connections for machine type 2 (SUN3_50)
controller   virtual 2 at nexus?
controller   obmem 2 at nexus?
controller   obio 2 at nexus?

# connections for machine type 3 (SUN3_260)
controller   virtual 3 at nexus?
controller   obmem 3 at nexus?
controller   obio 3 at nexus?
controller   vme16d16 3 at nexus?
controller   vme24d16 3 at nexus?
controller   vme32d16 3 at nexus?
controller   vme16d32 3 at nexus?
controller   vme24d32 3 at nexus?
controller   vme32d32 3 at nexus?
```

FIGURE 2.38. *Some connections from the Sun-3 GENERIC configuration file.*

The maxusers limit is a definition that is often overlooked. The default number, "8", is a bit low for most systems. If you figure one for each window, most desktop environments surpass this limit very quickly. A good number for a standalone machine is 16. Server machines generally need more while diskless machines need less, but no fewer than eight.

```
#
# Name this kernel "GENERIC".
#
ident        GENERIC
#
# This kernel supports about eight users. Count one
# user for each timesharing serial port, one for each window
# that you typically use, and one for each diskless
# client you serve. This is only an approximation
# used to control the size of various kernel data
# structures, not a hard limit.
#
maxusers     8
```

FIGURE 2.39. *The kernel name and maxusers limit.*

2.5.2.3 Removing Devices

The output from **dmesg** in Figure 2.36 showed that the "sm0" controller has three SCSI disks attached. Observe the number of possible devices available to controller "sm0" by scrolling to "sm0" while editing a copy of the GENERIC Sun3x or SDST80 configuration files, as in Figure 2.40. The "sm0" device is only used in the Sun3x kernel architecture.

Among all of Sun's architectures, there are several different SCSI controllers available. Under each controller type, there are associated disk and tape devices. The "sm0" controller happens to be from a Sun-3/80 machine. Other SCSI controllers might be si0, which is a Sun-3 VME or obio SCSI; the sc0, which is the Sun-2 VME SCSI controller; and sw0, available only on the 4/110. Be sure to choose the correct controller/device(s) for the type of machine you are using.

Once the local devices are known, remove or comment out the disks or tape devices that are not present on this system as well as all the other SCSI controllers and devices. The lines in Figure 2.41 that have the "#" sign in front are ignored when the kernel files are configured. In this case, st1, sd1, sd2, and sd3 are ignored.

Comment out other devices and controllers as needed for your particular system in the same manner. When unneeded devices have been removed, the next step is running **config**.

controller	sm0 at obio? csr 0x66000000 priority 2
tape	st0 at sm0 drive 32 flags 1
tape	st1 at sm0 drive 40 flags 1
disk	sd0 at sm0 drive 0 flags 0
disk	sd1 at sm0 drive 1 flags 0
disk	sd2 at sm0 drive 8 flags 0
disk	sd3 at sm0 drive 9 flags 0
disk	sd4 at sm0 drive 16 flags 0
disk	sd6 at sm0 drive 24 flags 0

FIGURE 2.40. *Devices available to the "sm0" controller.*

2.5.2.4 Running **config** and Building the Kernel The **config** program uses the configuration file to construct a directory filled with object modules and header files. At the same time it creates a *Makefile* that can be used to build a kernel. When running, **config** normally reports only one message:

```
# config HAL
Doing a "make depend"
```

If no errors were reported to the screen, **cd** to the directory just created by **config,** and build the kernel.

```
# cd ../HAL
# make
```

The kernel build produces many pages of output to the screen. The output shown in Figure 2.42 is the tail end of the kernel build.

controller	sm0 at obio? csr 0x66000000 priority 2
tape	st0 at sm0 drive 32 flags 1
#tape	st1 at sm0 drive 40 flags 1
disk	sd0 at sm0 drive 0 flags 0
#disk	sd1 at sm0 drive 1 flags 0
#disk	sd2 at sm0 drive 8 flags 0
#disk	sd3 at sm0 drive 9 flags 0
disk	sd4 at sm0 drive 16 flags 0
disk	sd6 at sm0 drive 24 flags 0

FIGURE 2.41. *Modified configuration file.*

Each "cc" line in the figure is actually one long line. Extra spacing was added to make it more readable.

2.5.2.5 Replacing /vmunix   After the kernel build is complete, the new kernel, called *vmunix,* is put in the same directory where the **make** was executed. Copy the new *vmunix* file to where it is used. If the kernel is used on the local machine, it must be copied to "/". If the kernel will be used somewhere else, you can do a remote copy.

Preserve the current /*vmunix* just in case the new kernel does not boot. A common practice is to move the original /*vmunix* to /*vmunix.orig.* The new kernel can be copied into "/" under an assumed name such as /*vmunix.custom.* Now you have two kernels in /. The plan is to create a link from the new kernel to the real kernel with these commands:

```
# mv /vmunix /vmunix.orig
# n /vmunix.custom /vmunix
```

The link to /*vmunix* must be a hard link. Status programs such as **ps** and **pstat** need the kernel to be called /*vmunix* when running.

2.5.3 Building Diskless Client Kernels

You can build kernels for the diskless clients of like architecture on the server using one of the diskless (DL) templates. Most DL templates contain all the options and devices necessary for diskless clients to operate correctly. It is helpful to include the name of the server in diskless client kernels. If there are ten clients of the server "blue", their kernels can be called "BLUE_CLIENT" to avoid confusion.

The kernel can then be placed in each client's /export/root/ <client> directory to be used when the client boots up. When new clients are added with the **setup_client** utility, by default they are given a GENERIC kernel. A copy of the diskless kernel is kept in /export/exec/kvm/<arch>/boot. The new DL kernel can be copied to this directory for use instead of the GENERIC kernel. After this is done, any new clients created can be given the diskless kernel instead of the GENERIC. Of course, it is always a good idea

```
cc -fsoft -c -O -Dsun3x -DSDST80 -DSUN3X_80 -DCRYPT -DSYSACCT
    -DNFSSERVER -DNFSCLIENT -DUFS -DQUOTA -DINET
    -DKERNEL -I. -I.. -I../.. ../../netinet/in_proto.c
cc -fsoft -c -O -Dsun3x -DSDST80 -DSUN3X_80 -DCRYPT -DSYSACCT
    -DNFSSERVER -DNFSCLIENT -DUFS -DQUOTA -DINET
    -DKERNEL -I. -I.. -I../.. ../../netinet/tcp_debug.c
cc -fsoft -c -g -Dsun3x -DSDST80 -DSUN3X_80 -DCRYPT -DSYSACCT
    -DNFSSERVER -DNFSCLIENT -DUFS -DQUOTA -DINET
    -DKERNEL -I. -I.. -I../.. ../../os/init_dbx.c
cc -fsoft -c -O -Dsun3x -DSDST80 -DSUN3X_80 -DCRYPT -DSYSACCT
    -DNFSSERVER -DNFSCLIENT -DUFS -DQUOTA -DINET
    -DKERNEL -I. -I.. -I../.. ioconf.c
/lib/cpp -undef -Dmc68000 -Dmc68020 -Dsun -DLOCORE -Dsun3x -DSDST80
    -DSUN3X_80 -DCRYPT -DSYSACCT -DNFSSERVER -DNFSCLIENT -DUFS
    -DQUOTA -DINET -DKERNEL -I. -I.. -I../.. mbglue.s >mbglue.pp
as -m68020 -o mbglue.o mbglue.pp
rm -f mbglue.pp
cc -fsoft -I. -c -O -Dsun3x -DSDST80 -DSUN3X_80 -DCRYPT -DSYSACCT
    -DNFSSERVER -DNFSCLIENT -DUFS -DQUOTA -DINET
    -DKERNEL -I. -I.. -I../.. confvmunix.c
loading vmunix
rearranging symbols
text       data       bss        dec        hex
565320     113832     71032      750184     b7268
```

FIGURE 2.42. *Tail end of kernel build.*

to keep a working copy of the GENERIC kernel around for each architecture client that you are serving just in case boot problems arise.

Kernels for each architecture can be created by any machine in that architecture family. A 3/280 server can build kernels for all of its clients that are Sun-3's. A 4/280 server can build kernels for all of its Sun-4 clients, but cannot create Sun-3 kernels. If you have clients on a server that are of a different architecture, there are a few ways that their kernels can be built. Kernels for these diskless clients can be built on a standalone system of the same architecture and copied over the network to the diskless client, or the kernel can be built from the diskless client.

The first option is rather straight forward. Locate a machine on your network that is of the same architecture type as that of the client. Build a kernel using the appropriate DL template. If the machine is a 3/50, use DL50. If the machine is a 4/110, use the DL110 template. After completion, copy the new kernel to tape or over the network and place it in the client's root directory. Reboot the client and the kernel build is complete.

2.5.3.1 Building a Kernel on a Diskless Client   Building a kernel on a diskless client presents you with a small problem in that all clients NFS mount the /usr filesystem with the read-only option. Since all of the kernel configuration files and utilities live under the /usr tree, a small amount of setup is needed. A writable place must be selected with at least enough room to hold a kernel, the configuration file and most of the object modules that are created as a result of the **config.** The kernel itself is over one megabyte in size, so all the other modules and files should be able to fit into a filesystem with five free megabytes available.

A good directory to build a kernel on a diskless client is /tmp. There is usually enough room in /tmp because you are actually using the server's /export/root partition. First, create a directory that contains symbolic links to the files and programs in /usr/sys as shown in Figure 2.43. The diskless client "green" will be used in the next example to build the diskless kernel for Sun-3/50 systems.

Now, remove the link to the architecture type since this is pointing back to the read only filesystem. Then re-link the contents as shown in Figure 2.44. At this point, remove the conf directory because it too is linked to the read only filesystem. Create a writable conf directory to edit the configuration file.

```
green# cd sun3
green# rm conf
green# mkdir conf
green# cd conf
green# ln -s /usr/sys/sun3/conf/* .
```

What is left after all these links is a conf directory in which files can be saved. Select one of the template configuration files and copy it to the present directory.

```
green# cd /tmp
green# mkdir kernel
green# cd kernel
green# ln -s /usr/sys/* .
green# ls -l .
total 23
lrwxrwxrwx  1 root        20 Jan 24 11:34 conf.common -> /usr/sys/
                                             conf.common
lrwxrwxrwx  1 root        14 Jan 24 11:34 debug -> /usr/sys/debug
lrwxrwxrwx  1 root        13 Jan 24 11:34 krpc -> /usr/sys/krpc
lrwxrwxrwx  1 root        13 Jan 24 11:34 lofs -> /usr/sys/lofs
lrwxrwxrwx  1 root        12 Jan 24 11:34 mon -> /usr/sys/mon
lrwxrwxrwx  1 root        12 Jan 24 11:34 net -> /usr/sys/net
lrwxrwxrwx  1 root        15 Jan 24 11:34 netimp -> /usr/sys/netimp
lrwxrwxrwx  1 root        16 Jan 24 11:34 netinet -> /usr/sys/netinet
lrwxrwxrwx  1 root        12 Jan 24 11:34 nfs -> /usr/sys/nfs
lrwxrwxrwx  1 root        11 Jan 24 11:34 os -> /usr/sys/os
lrwxrwxrwx  1 root        12 Jan 24 11:34 rpc -> /usr/sys/rpc
lrwxrwxrwx  1 root        16 Jan 24 11:34 sbusdev -> /usr/sys/sbusdev
lrwxrwxrwx  1 root        13 Jan 24 11:34 scsi -> /usr/sys/scsi
lrwxrwxrwx  1 root        14 Jan 24 11:34 sparc -> /usr/sys/sparc
lrwxrwxrwx  1 root        15 Jan 24 11:34 specfs -> /usr/sys/specfs
lrwxrwxrwx  1 root        12 Jan 24 11:34 sun -> /usr/sys/sun
lrwxrwxrwx  1 root        13 Jan 24 11:34 sun4 -> /usr/sys/sun4
lrwxrwxrwx  1 root        14 Jan 24 11:34 sun3 -> /usr/sys/sun3
lrwxrwxrwx  1 root        15 Jan 24 11:34 sundev -> /usr/sys/sundev
lrwxrwxrwx  1 root        14 Jan 24 11:34 sunif -> /usr/sys/sunif
lrwxrwxrwx  1 root        12 Jan 24 11:34 sys -> /usr/sys/sys
lrwxrwxrwx  1 root        12 Jan 24 11:34 ufs -> /usr/sys/ufs
lrwxrwxrwx  1 root        11 Jan 24 11:34 vm -> /usr/sys/vm
```

FIGURE 2.43. *Linking directories necessary to make a kernel.*

```
green# cp DL60 BLUE_CLIENT
green# vi BLUE_CLIENT
green# config BLUE_CLIENT
Doing a "make depend"
green#
green# cd ../BLUE_CLIENT
green# make
```

When you have finished editing the configuration file, run **config** using the edited file as the argument. Change your working

```
green# arch -k
sun3
green# rm sun3
green# mkdir sun3
green# cd sun3
green# ln -s /usr/sys/sun3/* .
green# ls -l
lrwxrwxrwx  1 root    21 Jan 24 11:39 a.out.h -> /usr/sys/sun3/a.out.h
lrwxrwxrwx  1 root    27 Jan 24 11:39 asm_linkage.h -> /usr/sys/sun3/asm_linkage.h
lrwxrwxrwx  1 root    22 Jan 24 11:39 buserr.h -> /usr/sys/sun3/buserr.h
lrwxrwxrwx  1 root    21 Jan 24 11:39 clock.h -> /usr/sys/sun3/clock.h
lrwxrwxrwx  1 root    18 Jan 24 11:39 conf -> /usr/sys/sun3/conf
lrwxrwxrwx  1 root    19 Jan 24 11:39 cpu.h -> /usr/sys/sun3/cpu.h
lrwxrwxrwx  1 root    27 Jan 24 11:39 dbx_machdep.c -> /usr/sys/sun3/dbx_machdep.c
lrwxrwxrwx  1 root    20 Jan 24 11:39 diag.h -> /usr/sys/sun3/diag.h
lrwxrwxrwx  1 root    22 Jan 24 11:39 eccreg.h -> /usr/sys/sun3/eccreg.h
lrwxrwxrwx  1 root    22 Jan 24 11:39 eeprom.h -> /usr/sys/sun3/eeprom.h
lrwxrwxrwx  1 root    22 Jan 24 11:39 enable.h -> /usr/sys/sun3/enable.h
lrwxrwxrwx  1 root    21 Jan 24 11:39 frame.h -> /usr/sys/sun3/frame.h
lrwxrwxrwx  1 root    22 Jan 24 11:39 intreg.h -> /usr/sys/sun3/intreg.h
lrwxrwxrwx  1 root    23 Jan 24 11:39 iocache.h -> /usr/sys/sun3/iocache.h
lrwxrwxrwx  1 root    21 Jan 24 11:39 machine -> /usr/sys/sun3/machine
lrwxrwxrwx  1 root    22 Jan 24 11:39 memerr.h -> /usr/sys/sun3/memerr.h
lrwxrwxrwx  1 root    19 Jan 24 11:39 mmu.h -> /usr/sys/sun3/mmu.h
lrwxrwxrwx  1 root    21 Jan 24 11:39 param.h -> /usr/sys/sun3/param.h
lrwxrwxrwx  1 root    19 Jan 24 11:39 pcb.h -> /usr/sys/sun3/pcb.h
lrwxrwxrwx  1 root    19 Jan 24 11:39 psl.h -> /usr/sys/sun3/psl.h
lrwxrwxrwx  1 root    19 Jan 24 11:39 pte.h -> /usr/sys/sun3/pte.h
lrwxrwxrwx  1 root    19 Jan 24 11:39 reg.h -> /usr/sys/sun3/reg.h
lrwxrwxrwx  1 root    19 Jan 24 11:39 scb.h -> /usr/sys/sun3/scb.h
lrwxrwxrwx  1 root    24 Jan 24 11:39 seg_kmem.h -> /usr/sys/sun3/seg_kmem.h
lrwxrwxrwx  1 root    21 Jan 24 11:39 seg_u.h -> /usr/sys/sun3/seg_u.h
lrwxrwxrwx  1 root    22 Jan 24 11:39 setjmp.h -> /usr/sys/sun3/setjmp.h
lrwxrwxrwx  1 root    27 Jan 24 11:39 swapgeneric.c -> /usr/sys/sun3/swapgeneric.c
lrwxrwxrwx  1 root    20 Jan 24 11:39 trap.h -> /usr/sys/sun3/trap.h
lrwxrwxrwx  1 root    22 Jan 24 11:39 vm_hat.h -> /usr/sys/sun3/vm_hat.h
lrwxrwxrwx  1 root    23 Jan 24 11:39 vmparam.h -> /usr/sys/sun3/vmparam.h
```

FIGURE 2.44. *More links for kernel build.*

directory to ../BLUE_CLIENT and run **make** to start building the kernel.

The new kernel can now be placed in the client's root directory with the **mv** or **cp** commands. Use the procedure described earlier to save the original kernel in the event that problems arise. Clean up the files and directories left behind by this kernel build. This is easily done with the **rm** command.

```
green# cd /tmp
green# rm -rf kernel
green#
```

The diskless system must be rebooted with the new kernel for the changes to take effect.

2.5.3.2 Diskless Kernel Script
If you are creating many client kernels, a script would be handy. The script in Figure 2.45 can be used to do just that. It is executed from the client in an area that is writable by root. *Do not run this script on a server.*

Invoke the script by using this command line, assuming that you call the script **build_kernel:**

```
# build_kernel <hostname>
```

2.5.4 Pre-Installed Systems

As with any installation, you should know what the hostname, Internet Protocol number, and YP domain are before starting. Some desktop machines are shipped with a pre-installed operating system loaded on their internal disk. The idea behind this is to allow you to unpack the system, power it up and answer a few questions relating to its environment and have it immediately running on your network. No lengthy installation procedure is necessary.

2.5.4.1 Boot and Configure
Upon powering up the pre-installed system, it boots up into single-user mode and begin its query session. You are first prompted for a terminal type. This is most likely the Sun bit-mapped display. Next, choose the appropriate time zone and local time. Once these questions have been an-

```
#!/bin/sh
#
# Create a new kernel for diskless and dataless clients
#
if [ $# -ne 1 ]; then
echo "$0 hostname"
exit 0
fi
#
# Set architecture
#
ARCH = 'arch -k'
#
# This template entry can be changed to reflect the template
# file you wish to use when building your kernel.
#
TEMPLATE = DL50
#
# Begin creating the directory tree of symbolic links.
#
mkdir /tmp/$1
cd /tmp/$1
ln -s /usr/sys/* .
rm $ARCH
mkdir $ARCH
cd $ARCH
ln -s /usr/sys/$ARCH/* .
#
# Create the conf directory.
#
rm conf
mkdir conf
cd conf
ln -s /usr/sys/$ARCH/conf/* .
#
# Copy the file defined as the TEMPLATE above to the machine name.
#
cp $TEMPLATE $1
chmod +w $1
#
# Invoke the "vi" editor on the configuration file.
#
vi $1                                                    (continued)
```

FIGURE 2.45. *Diskless kernel build script.*

```
#
# You must write the file out even if no changes were made.
#
echo -n "Continue if vi found template (y/n)"
read ans

case $ans in
        [Nn]*) exit 0;;
        [Yy]*) continue;;
esac
#
# Start the config.
#
echo "Running configuration"
config $1
#
# Start the "make"
#
cd ../$1
echo "Changing directory to ../$1, starting make"
make
#
# Move the original vmunix to vmunix.orig, copy the new kernel to /.
#
echo "Moving original kernel to vmunix.orig"
echo "Moving new kernel to /vmunix"
mv /vmunix /vmunix.orig
cp vmunix /vmunix
#
# Remove the mess left behind.
#
echo "Cleanup"
rm -rf /tmp/$1
```

FIGURE 2.45. (*continued*).

swered, clear the "noname" with a Control-U, and enter the host-name making sure that it is not already used in your local net. If so, your network will not operate properly. After entering the selected hostname, you are asked if the system is attached to a network. If so, enter "y", then enter the IP address or host number of this machine. Do not use the default. The next screen asks if this machine is joining a YP domain; if so, enter the domain name and the system should finish booting. Make sure you enter the correct YP domain because once again, misspelled domain names cause the system to look for a non-existent domain.

Once the system has reached the login prompt, login as the user "root" and create a password. One of the very first procedures that should be done on a pre-installed system is a full backup of everything. Pre-installed systems do not come with any release tapes unless specifically ordered. Even if you backup everything, you are not able to install the system from the backup tapes. If at all possible, acquire a set of SunOS release tapes.

One of the last steps to do now is create a user account for the machine which is best done on the YP master (if using YP). See Chapter 4 for details concerning the addition of user accounts.

2.5.4.2 Unconfiguring the Pre-Installed System
If you wish to "unconfigure" a pre-installed system and re-name it, or bring it back to the original pre-installed state, the **sys-unconfig** utility can be used. This un-does everything that was done when the system was first brought up. Certain files and directories are preserved when running **sys-unconfig** such as /home/hostname and /etc/ hosts, but one cannot be sure that the file you need is saved. Always backup anything you wish to keep before performing a **sys-unconfig.**

2.5.5 Adding More Software
There are a number of software categories not included on the pre-installed system. Most of these categories can be NFS mounted from a server which supports the correct architecture. If you find the need to take more bundled software from the release tape, it can be extracted with the **setup_exec** utility. There is not enough free disk space in the /usr partition to extract everything, but if a second disk is available, partitions and mount points can be created to support such a task.

2.5.5.1 Running **setup_exec**
There are a number of uses for the **setup_exec** program. It can be used to extract bundled SunOS software from release tapes. **Setup_exec** can also be used to add

system executables for clients of unlike architecture. (This is how it gets the name **setup_exec**.) You may also use **setup_exec** to convert a standalone machine into a server of diskless clients.

setup_exec lives in the /usr/etc/install/script directory and must be run as root. Three command line arguments are needed to bring up the software form: the architecture you are installing, a path to where the executables reside, and the path in which the kvm files are loaded. The option, -o, overwrites the existing files if so desired. This is dangerous to do if extracting the "/usr" category for the architecture of your machine. Certain executable files such as **tar** are overwritten while they are being used. This causes **setup_exec** to abort in the middle. Then you are stuck with no way to "tar" files from the tape.

The normal path for executables to reside in is the /usr directory on a standalone machine, and in the /export/exec directory on a server of multiple architectures. The normal path for the kvm files on a standalone machine is /usr/kvm, while the kvm path for unlike architectures is /export/exec/kvm. Both of these paths can be altered when running **setup_exec.** If any paths are changed from their default values, then some additional modifications must be made to both server and client files. Among these files on the server side are the */etc/exports* and the */etc/bootparams* file. The client's */export/root/<client>/etc/fstab* also needs its mount paths changed so that the correct directory is mounted.

A standalone system can be easily converted to a server of diskless clients by running the **setup_exec** program. If an /export directory exists, this program extracts the files needed from the release tape as well as makes all the necessary links and edits the */etc/exports* file. If an /export directory does not exist, **setup_exec** creates one in your root partition. You will most likely run out of disk space in root if an /export partition has not been designated. If you are planning to convert a standalone machine into a server, make sure the filesystem that contains /export is large enough to hold a client's root, swap, and /usr files.

Start **setup_exec** by changing your working directory to /usr/etc/install. Executing **setup_exec** with no arguments displays a usage message detailing what it expects as an argument (see Figure 2.46).

The correct command for extracting the Sun-4c executables

```
# cd /usr/etc/install/script
# setup_exec

Usage: setup_exec arch execpath kvmpath [-o]

where arch  = sun2, sun3, sun3x, sun4, or sun4c
execpath    = full pathname of executables
              (e.g. /export/exec/sun3 )
kvmpath     = full pathname of sub-arch executables
              (e.g. /export/exec/kvm/sun3x )
-o          = override software selection protection
```

FIGURE 2.46. *Usage for the setup_exec utility*

from 4.0.3 would look like the command below. In SunOS 4.0, only two arguments were needed as there is no "kvmpath".

setup_exec sun4c /export/exec/sun4c /export/exec/kvm/sun4c

After entering the correct command line arguments a form is displayed which is similar to Figure 2.47. This is the same program

```
SOFTWARE FROM [DEL=erase one char of input data] [RET=end of input data]
Architecture Information :
 Type: [sun2] [sun3] [sun3x] [sun4] x[sun4c]
 Path where executables reside: /export/exec/sun4c
 Path were sub-arch dependent executables resdie: /export/exec/kvm/sun4c
Media Information :
 Device Type: [st0] [st1] [st2] [ar0] [mt0] [xt0]
 Drive Type:  [local] [remote]

Choice : [all] [default] [own choice] [required] [quit]



Are you finished with this form [y/n] ?
[x/X=select choice] [space=next choice] [^B/^P=backward] [^F/^N=forward]
```

FIGURE 2.47. *The setup_exec form.*

```
SOFTWARE FORM [DEL=erase one char of input data] [RET=end of input data]

Architecture Information :
 Type: [sun2] [sun3] [sun3x] [sun4] x[sun4c]
 Path where executables reside: /export/exec/sun4c
 Path were sub-arch dependent executables reside: /export/exec/kvm/sun4c
Media Information :
 Device Type: [st0] [st1] [st2] [ar0] [mt0] x[xt0]
 Drive Type:  x[local] [remote]

Choice : [all] [default] [own choice] [required] [quit]

Extractlist:

usr
Kvm
Install
Sun-4c_Usr
Sys
Networking
Debugging
SunView_Users
SunView_Programmers
SunView_Demo
Text


Are you finished with this form [y/n] ?
[x/X=select choice] [space=next choice] [^B/^P=backward] [^F/^N=forward]
```

FIGURE 2.48. *The completed setup_exec form.*

used by the "assign software information" form in **suninstall** to extract bundled SunOS categories from the release tape.

Insert the release tape for the architecture you wish to add and select the appropriate tape device. It takes a little time to position the tape and read the table of contents. Once this is complete, the cursor is positioned on one of the choice selections. In this example, the default categories for the 4c architecture will be selected. Move the cursor in front of the [default] selection and type "x". The tape starts moving, and then the query session begins.

You have to answer "y" or "n" for the rest of the categories, depending on what you want available to diskless clients of this architecture. When your selections have been made, the extract list is displayed, as in Figure 2.48.

If the list is acceptable, answer "y" and the installation begins. If you would like to change the categories selected, answer "n" to begin again.

2.5.5.2 Special Considerations

There are some special considerations concerning **setup_exec,** the Sun-4, and Sun-4c architectures. If you have a server that supports both the Sun-4 and Sun-4c architectures, you must make certain that when more software categories are installed from the release tape, the Sun-4c architecture tape must be the last one installed.

Several libraries were revised in between the 4.0.3 and the 4.0.3c release. The Sun-4 machines may use the same libraries on the 4.0.3c tapes, but the Sun-4c machines cannot use libraries from the 4.0.3 Sun-4 release tapes. These libraries do not "know" about the Sun-4c kernel architecture, so always make certain that if you want to add more bundled OS software categories, then use the 4.0.3c tapes last. This will overlay the Sun-4 libraries with the later versions.

YP

3

3.1 What is YP?

What follows is a quick description of YP. Use it as an introduction before reading the later sections of this chapter. YP often seems very confusing to a new Systems Administrator, but there really is no magic involved and it simplifies your job immensely!

Please note that with the release of SunOS 4.1, this service will no longer be called YP. The new name is NIS, which stands for Network Information Service. Only the name for the service was changed. The commands will still be called "ypthis" and "ypthat", and the maps will still be stored in /var/yp, but the maps will be known as NIS maps instead of YP maps and the service will be called NIS rather than YP. The information presented here will remain valid and useful.

YP is a database for centralized systems administration of the files that are needed to make your Sun network operational. YP has many ways of looking up or using this data during normal operation of your network. Before YP, cumbersome processes that copied password, hosts, and other files around the network were necessary to keep a large network synchronized. Almost all of the files that are edited to add a machine or a user to the network, or to establish connections to other networks, can be managed from one server when YP is implemented. This one server is known as the YP master. It has the master copy of the ASCII datafiles that are manipulated to create the database that can be referenced by all the computers in your YP domain. There should be only one YP master server for each YP domain.

A YP domain can be described as a group of database files that contain information for a specific group of systems. These files are all located in /var/yp/'domainname' on the YP master (domainname is the name of your local YP domain). The YP domain can be spread over mutiple networks or can exist on one network with several other YP domains. The latter condition often needs some special attention (see the Advanced Topics section).

To change the database on the YP master, first edit the ASCII datafile or datafiles that need to be changed, and then run **make** in./var/yp. The commands in */var/yp/Makefile* will massage the data in the ASCII datafile and turn it into one or more database files. The database files are known as YP maps, which are described in more detail later in this chapter.

To make the database accessible over many nets, and to provide a backup for your YP master, you will need to establish at least one YP slave. The slave servers will not have the datafiles that exist on the YP master, but they will hold copies of all the YP maps that are created on the YP master. Part of the process that creates the database on the YP master will transfer all modified maps to the slave servers. If you have installed YP slaves, YP will continue to process requests even if the master server goes down. Without any slave servers, if your master goes down, all requests that depend on the YP maps will be unanswered. Slave servers also make it possible for the YP domain to exist over multiple networks.

It is wise to always have at least one copy of all of the ASCII files that are the basis for your YP maps and the YP makefile on another server. One of your slave servers would be a good choice. Store these files in a special directory (such as /var/yp/ypmaps) so that the maps do not accidentally get made on this system. If the YP master should go down when you need full YP service, you could easily move the files to their appropriate positions and turn the slave into the master until the old master is fixed (see the Advanced Topics section). Make sure that you only have one YP master for each domain at a time.

Both the master and slave servers are called YP servers. They will respond to requests for information from all other systems in the YP domain. Since the YP maps are distributed across all the YP servers within the domain, it does not matter which server you get a response from. In particular, when you run **login** on a system running YP, the maps on a YP server will be consulted to determine if you are a valid user, if the password you entered is right,

where your home directory is and which shell or program to run.
This process is standard any time you run **login,** but with YP it will
not matter which system in your YP domain you log in to, since
every system on the network will be able to get this information
through the YP service.

Figure 3.1 is a picture of a fictitious network that will be
discussed in the following sections. Please note that this network
is made up of three networks and there are three gateway systems.
The hostnames of the gateways are red, yellow, and north. These
systems will have direct access to two networks.

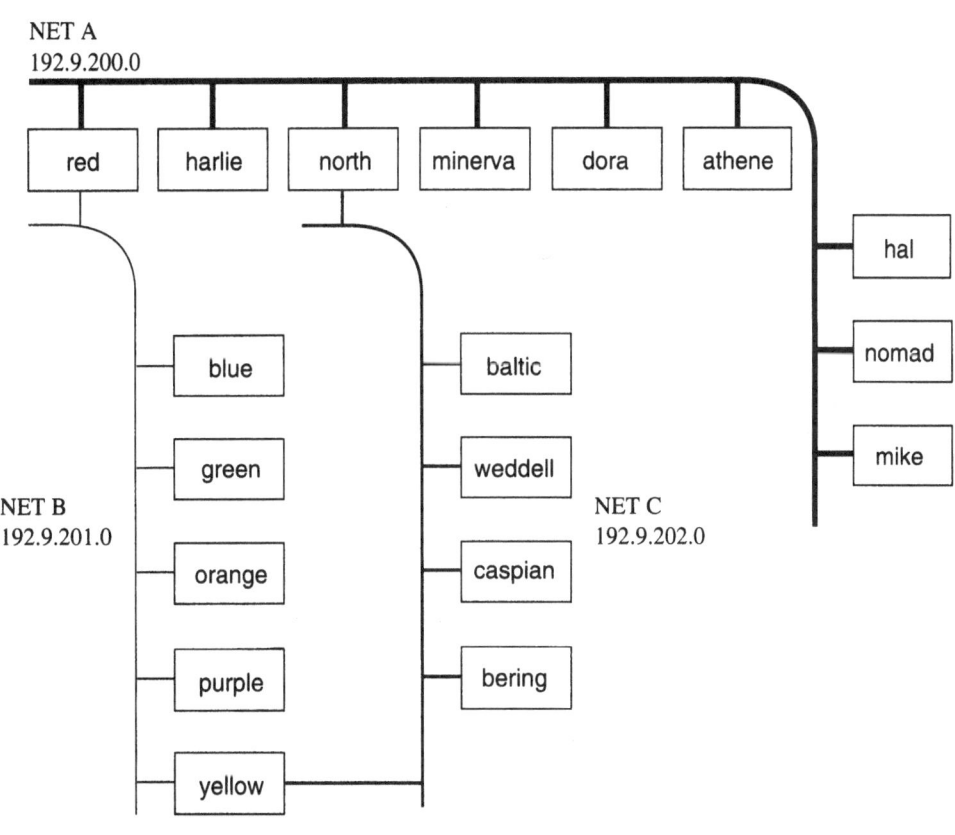

FIGURE 3.1. *Local network.*

3.2 YP Maps and YP Makefile

In this section all of the standard YP maps and their datafiles will be discussed. Since some of these maps are almost never touched, the more "popular" ones are presented first. Each map discussion will have a general description of what function the map is used for, what the datafile should look like, a sample datafile and a description of what is done to make the actual maps. In all cases, the portion that discusses the actual making of the maps depends on some knowledge of the **make** command (see make(1)), but a complete understanding of the command is not necessary.

Each ASCII datafile is manipulated by the commands in the YP makefile, named */var/yp/Makefile*, to create at least one YP map. The data portion of the YP map is stored in a file called <map>.pag. The other half of each YP map is a file called <map>.dir. These files are created by the **makedbm** command (see makedbm(8)).

Most maps have a key and an associated value. The key is a piece of data that can uniquely identify an entry within a map. The value is the data associated with that key. The key for the map called hosts.byname would be a hostname, while the key for hosts.byaddr would be the host's address. Both YP maps contain the same information, a hostname and its address, but the key you include to request the information is different. The example below illustrates this:

```
harlie% ypmatch harlie hosts.byname
192.9.200.1   harlie loghost
harlie% ypmatch 192.9.200.1 hosts.byaddr
192.9.200.1   harlie loghost
```

The **ypmatch** command is discussed in detail in the next section, but in general, if you give it a key and the YP map that you want it to search, it will print the value associated with the key. In this case the value is the same for each key.

The formatting of the ASCII datafiles is very critical in some cases. The "#" sign indicates a comment. A comment is normally ignored by any of the process checking the data in the YP maps. Comments are usually included to add extra information or to make the file easier to support. The comments can either be placed on a single line or included on the same line as the data. The single line comments can also be called full line comments. Some datafiles can include either of these types of comments while others cannot include any at all. Please read the discussion of each map carefully to determine if you can use either full line comments or comments at the end of each entry. A "\" can be included to spread one record over several lines. This character must be the last one on the line, if the record is to continue over several lines. Use of these special characters or blank lines is not allowed in some of the ASCII datafiles. The map discussions below include the particulars for each datafile.

All of the standard YP maps can be made using the makefile found in /var/yp. If you are not familiar with the **make** command, just think of it as a specialized shell script. The commands in this makefile invoke regular UNIX commands like **awk** and **sed** to format the data. Some familiarity with these commands will be helpful while reading the following sections (see sed(1) and awk(1)).

Figure 3.2 shows an example of a typical entry in the YP makefile. In this example, and in all of those that follow, the line numbers are included to make identifying each line easier. They have no other significance, and do not appear in the standard makefile.

In the YP makefile the following values are standard:

```
DIR = /etc
DOM = 'domainname'
YPDIR = /usr/etc/yp
YPDBDIR = /var/yp
YPPUSH = $(YPDIR)/yppush
MAKEDBM = $(YPDIR)/makedbm
```

The first line in the makefile example determines if the date of the $(DIR)/file is more recent than the date of file.time. File.time is a timestamp used to mark when the last update took place. If the date of $(DIR)/file is more recent, then it has been changed since the last make, so the map needs to be re-made. Line two checks to make sure that the datafile exists. If not, an error message is printed (see line 15). Formatting of the ASCII file is done in line 3. The output from the formatting commands is then piped into the **makedbm** program which creates the actual YP map files. For each entry in the datafile, **makedbm** uses up to the first white space (tab or

```
1) file.time: $(DIR)/file
2)    -@if [ -f $(DIR)/file ]; then \
3)       awk 'BEGIN { OFS=" "; } $$1 !~ /^#/ { print $$2, $$0 }' \
4)          $(DIR)/file | $(MAKEDBM) - $(YPDBDIR)/$(DOM)/file.byname; \
5)       touch file.time; \
6)       echo "updated file"; \
7)       if [ ! $(NOPUSH) ]; then \
8)          $(YPPUSH) file.byname; \
9)          echo "pushed file"; \
11)      else \
12)         :; \
13)      fi \
14)    else \
15)       echo "couldn't find $(DIR)/file"; \
16)    fi
   .
   .
80) file: file.time
81) $(DIR)/file:
```

FIGURE 3.2. *Makefile sample.*

space character) as the key. The rest of the entry is data associated with that key. After the map has been created, the date on file.time is updated (line 5). The command on line 7 checks to see if the NOPUSH variable has been set. If the **make** is run with the NO-PUSH variable, then the map is only updated locally, otherwise it is also pushed to all of the YP slaves. Normally this is done without the NOPUSH variable, since you want to update the data on all of your YP slaves. A more specific discussion of the make command for YP and the **makedbm** command is included in the section on the YP commands.

If you need to edit this file make sure that you indent the text with tab characters instead of spaces. This is the most common mistake that people make when they first work with any type of makefile.

All sections of the YP makefile follow this same standard layout. Normally, the only thing that changes is the way that the data is formatted and the name of the map that is being created.

The following discussions of each datafile and/or YP map will only point out differences from this standard structure.

3.2.1 Aliases

The alias maps are checked by **sendmail** to route mail within your local net. The default file name is */etc/aliases*. The alias file should contain one entry for each user and one entry for whatever departmental or group aliases are necessary. Each alias must be unique. Each entry can take any of the following forms:

```
username:       username@system
usergroup:      list_of_usernames
everyone:       list_of_usergroup_aliases
personal list:  :include:fullpath_for_my_list
```

Full line comments and blank lines can be included in the datafile to make it more readable and easier to maintain, but do not add any text or comments after each entry. Also, each entry must be one continuous line; you may not use the "\" character to spread the list for one alias over several lines. Some type of sorting should be done to make this file manageable. Alphabetical sorting by alias will probably work best under most situations. This makes it very easy to check for duplicate aliases or alias names that have too much in common. It is best to only include lower case letters in the alias file. Figure 3.3 is a sample alias datafile.

You may wish to set an alias for root and/or for postmaster in the YP alias file. This alias should route mail to the individual or individuals that are doing system administration for that network. If root is aliased, then the postmaster's mail will also be rerouted since postmaster in the standard alias file is aliased to root. This will provide a quick way to check on any problem mail that any of the systems in your network are generating. Sometimes getting mail for both root and postmaster for all of the systems that are in your YP domain can be too much for one person to handle; but in most situations, the mail for postmaster should be rerouted to a central point so that someone is notified when mail is not functioning properly.

The alias for "all" includes aliases for the programming and marketing groups. Nesting aliases like this can make it very easy to add new employees to all of the appropriate aliases; however, if

```
#
# YP aliases file for domain sunnet
#

# Following alias is required by the mail protocol, RFC 822
# Set it to the address of a HUMAN who deals with this system's mail problems.
Postmaster: root

# Alias for mailer daemon; returned messages from our MAILER-DAEMON
# should be routed to our local Postmaster.
MAILER-DAEMON: postmaster

# Aliases to handle mail to programs or files, eg news or vacation
decode: " | /usr/bin/uudecode"
nobody: /dev/null

# Individual aliases

curly:      curly@baltic
dick:       dick@blue
harry:      harry@blue
larry:      larry@baltic
moe:        moe@blue
tom:        tom@baltic

# group aliases by department

programmers: larry, moe, curly
marketing: tom, dick, harry

# group aliases by interest

graphics-users: larry, harry

# special aliases

root: curly
all: programmers,marketing
```

FIGURE 3.3. *Sample alias file.*

you have many aliases, making sure that each person only receives one piece of mail can be difficult. Multiple levels of nesting can make the administration of an alias file very complex.

The permissions on the file */etc/aliases* is set to 666. You will probably want to change this to 644 at your earliest convenience, to keep unauthorized people from making changes to the file. If you do not do this then any user who can login onto your YP master could make changes to this file.

Note that you can include mail lists in this file, but it is not advisable to include this type of alias entry in the YP alias file since it is unlikely that all of your systems will have the list available locally. If you want to have a mailing list that exists outside of YP, then the YP alias should look like:

```
hiking:        hiking@blue
```

and the alias entry in */etc/aliases* on blue should look like:

```
hiking: :include:/home/blue/tom/mail.list
```

The file called mail.list should be an ASCII file that contains a list of mail recipients. This will provide the user with the ability to make changes to the list without having to get you involved. The other option available is to not include the hiking alias in the YP file and to require that everyone send mail to hiking@blue. Both of these options will work. The one that is "right" depends on the circumstances.

The ASCII file for aliases is turned into two maps. One map has the mail alias as the key and the email address as the value; this YP map is called mail.aliases. The other is called mail.byaddr and the email address is the key with the alias as the value. Located below are the non-standard parts of the YP makefile that creates these maps:

```
1) ALIASES=/etc/aliases
2) MKALIAS=$(YPDIR)/mkalias
   .
   .
3) cp $(ALIASES) $(YPDBDIR)/$(DOM)/mail.aliases; \
4) /usr/lib/sendmail -bi -oA$(YPDBDIR)/$(DOM)/mail.aliases; \
5) $(MKALIAS) $(YPDBDIR)/$(DOM)/mail.aliases $(YPDBDIR)/$(DOM)/
mail.byaddr; \
```

6) rm $(YPDBDIR)/$(DOM)/mail.aliases; \

.

.

7) $(ALIASES):

The third line copies the alias datafile and the fourth invokes **sendmail** using this file as the standard mail alias file (see sendmail(8)). Line 5 calls a command named **mkalias** rather than the standard **makedbm** command. The command removes blank lines and comments and also reformats the data. It is not documented.

On the YP master, the YP alias file and the local alias file should not be the same file. In order to do this, copy */etc/aliases* to */etc/aliases.yp* and change line 1 in the section of the YP makefile to:

ALIASES=/etc/aliases.yp

Sendmail will automatically search for an alias in the local alias file, */etc/aliases*, and then will check the YP map if it exists. This means that the YP master will not need the YP aliases in its local alias file. Also, leaving the YP datafile as */etc/aliases* will make the "newaliases" process unnecessarily long on your server. At first the two aliases files will be identical, but as you add more users the YP alias file will become much larger than */etc/aliases*. When you make the changes to the YP makefile you should also comment out or remove line 4 in the portion of the YP makefile shown above. **Sendmail** should continue to use */etc/aliases* as the local alias file on the YP master.

3.2.2 Group

The purpose of the group file is to provide access to files for a specific group of users. Each user is assigned to a group when they are included in the passwd file, but if they need access to other groups, their login name will need to be added to the appropriate record in the the group file. The following is an example of the format of each entry in */etc/group:*

grpname:*:num:user1,user2

where grpname is the name of the group; * is either left alone or is an encrypted password; num is the group number (gid); and the rest is a list of all of the users who should be in this group. Each group entry should be one continuous line. The group name should be no more than eight characters. The group number and the group name must be unique. If the group name is not unique, the first one in the datafile will be the only one in the YP map. Any duplicated names will not be included. The datafile should not contain any comments or blank lines.

The wheel group, gid zero, can be used to control the ability of users to use the **su** command to become root (see su(1)). If any users are listed in the wheel group, only these users will be allowed to **su** as root. Any user will still be able to **login** or **rlogin** as root, however, if they know the root password. This only restricts the user's ability to become root, because the user can still run **su** to become other users.

Start numbering the local groups at 100. This should reserve a sufficient buffer area so new packages or programs that require a group number will not conflict with the entries that you have already made.

This file can be a problem if you have too many users that want access to one group. There is a limit of 1024 characters that can be entered in one group entry. The make process will fail if the line is too long with the following error:

```
awk: string users      users:*:100:us . . . too long to print
record number 12
entry too big
```

When this happens the group entry with the error (in this case users) is removed from the YP map and the only way to get it back in again is to shorten the group listing and remake the maps. Please note that this is well over 12 lines in your standard 80 character **SunView** window. If your groups grow to this size, find some way to do what you need with two groups.

There is no easy way to split one group into two groups. You can get around this by not including a list for a large group. Every user is set up in a group with their password entry. In a standard environment you would include an entry in the group file for the group listed in the passwd file and one for each additional group that the user needs to be in. In the Sun environment, gid's that are included for each user in the passwd map do not have to be included in the group file. So for groups that are too large to fit in the group file, you should use the group number in the passwd file and not list the individuals in the group file.

This file is made into two YP maps. One is group.bygid and has the gid as the key; the second map is group.byname and has the group name as the key.

The contents of this file can be checked using the **grpck** command (see grpck(8)). In particular, it will check the */etc/passwd* file (including the yp entries if there is a + in the bottom of the file) to verify that all of the users are in the passwd file. This can be very useful for checking for typing errors or for keeping the file current if it or the passwd file changes frequently.

3.2.3 Hosts

This file should contain one entry for each Ethernet interface on your network. This is the file that is checked for most of the communications between systems. Each entry can be of the form:

```
IP_number    hostname      # comment
```

The IP number should be entered as "x.x.x.x", where x is a number between 0 and 255. You can choose these numbers yourself (if you aren't going to be connected to the Internet), but if you wish to connect you must request a network number (see Chapter 5). In many situations, you will eventually want to connect to the Internet. If you have any doubts at all go through the process to get a "real" network number. Revamping all of your host's entries at a later date is a very large, tedious, and involved job.

Make sure that the host number consists of four numbers separated by three periods. Too many or too few numbers or periods will skew the YP map and will prevent your network from functioning properly.

All hostnames must start with a lower case alphabetic character and should not be more than ten characters in length. The hostname may not contain capital letters or spaces, but after the first letter it can contain numbers. The hyphen character can be included to join two words into one hostname (the-beach, for example). The ten character limit is not a hard limit, but because some commands truncate the name to ten characters, it is a good idea to limit the length of the hostname. There is no real minimum number of characters for a hostname, but three characters is the normal lower limit. The comment is optional, but it is often useful to add something for each entry, such as the name of the user who works on this system or some notation about how this system is being used. Earlier versions of Sun OS (before 4.0) needed some sort of white-space after the hostname for everything to work properly. This bug has been fixed in the latest releases. Figure 3.4 is a sample host file.

It is helpful if the hostnames for gateways indicate both the system that they are on and the network that the gateway is accessing (such as server hostname: harlie, gateway hostname: harlie-bnet). Under this sort of naming convention it can often make sense to have gateway hostnames that are over ten characters, but make sure that the first ten characters are significant so that you can always tell which gateway you are working with, especially if you have multiple gateways on one system. Study the example below:

```
harlie% netstat -i
Name  Mtu   Net/Dest    Address     Ipkts       Ierrs  Opkts     Oerrs  Collis   Queue
ie0   1500  sun-ether   harlie      135505501   0      50501583  0      810037   0
ie1   1500  sun-ether   harlie-net  43668060    1789   12670176  0      701204   0
ie2   1500  sun-ether   harlie-net  38226265    1646   33132983  0      403678   0
lo0   1536  loopback    localhost   822282      0      822282    0      0        0

harlie% netstat -i
Name  Mtu   Net/Dest    Address     Ipkts       Ierrs  Opkts     Oerrs  Collis   Queue
ie0   1500  sun-ether   harlie      135505501   0      50501583  0      810037   0
ie1   1500  sun-ether   harlie-bne  43668060    1789   12670176  0      701204   0
ie2   1500  sun-ether   harlie-cne  38226265    1646   33132983  0      403678   0
lo0   1536  loopback    localhost   822282      0      822282    0      0        0
```

In the first case, the hostnames for the gateways were harlie-netb and harlie-netc, but it is difficult to tell them apart from each other from the output. In the second set, the hostnames were set to harlie-bnet and harlie-cnet. You can immediately tell the gateways apart.

The hostfile is easier to manage if the entries are sorted numerically and if each network is separated by comments from the others. Also, do not add extra zeros to the host numbers. For example, the host number for harlie should be entered as 192.9.200.1 and not as 192.009.200.001. Padding entries will cause interesting

```
#
# YP hosts file for domain sunnet
#

127.0.0.1        localhost
#
# Main net
#
192.9.200.0      sunnet neta        # sunnet network
192.9.200.1      harlie ypmaster    # YP master
192.9.200.2      minerva            # print server
192.9.200.3      dora               # resource server
192.9.200.4      athene             # modem server
192.9.200.5      hal                # source machine
192.9.200.6      nomad              # backup server
192.9.200.7      mike               # YP slave
192.9.200.8      red-gtw            # gateway to netb
192.9.200.9      north-gtw          # gateway to netc
#
# Marketing net
#
192.9.201.0      netb               # marketing network
192.9.201.1      red                # gateway & slave server
192.9.201.2      blue               # netb client server
192.9.201.3      green              # blue client
192.9.201.4      yellow             # gateway & slave server
192.9.201.5      orange             # blue client
192.9.201.6      purple             # blue client
#
# Programmers net
#
192.9.202.0      netc               # programmers network
192.9.202.1      north              # gateway & slave server
192.9.202.2      baltic             # netc client server
192.9.202.3      weddell            # baltic client
192.9.202.4      caspian            # baltic client
192.9.202.5      bering             # baltic client
192.9.202.6      yellow-gtw         # gateway to netb
```

FIGURE 3.4. *Sample hosts file.*

problems because host addresses that have preceding zeros are turned into octal numbers during the process that makes the maps (see inet(3N)).

The first valid host number is "#.#.#.1". The "0" address can not be used for your first host. This address can be included to identify your local network (see Figure 3.4). This can be very useful in an environment with several dozens of networks and multiple groups supporting them.

More than one hostname can be included with each IP address. This is known as aliasing or nicknaming and is used to define special hostnames such as datehost, mailhost and loghost. The first name listed in the host entry is the name that will be used when identifying any outgoing communication, however, any incoming communications can go to either hostname.

```
192.9.200.1    harlie ypmaster
```

In this example, harlie is being aliased as ypmaster. The "ypmaster" nickname can be transferred to another host entry if the YP master function needs to be moved. Any requests made to the "ypmaster" hostname will always find the right server. This is often much easier than renaming a host. This aliasing mechanism can also be useful when changing the hostname on a system. Using the old name as a hostname alias will allow mail to be delivered to the old name so that you do not disrupt service. The old name can be removed later when all mail aliases have been updated.

The */etc/hosts* datafile is used to create two maps, hosts-.byaddr and hosts.byname. As usual, hosts.byaddr uses the IP number as a key, and hosts.byname uses the hostname as the key. Included below is the non-standard part of the makefile that creates these maps:

```
1) STDHOSTS=$(YPDIR)/stdhosts
    .
    .
2) sed -e "/^#/d" -e s/#.*$$// $(DIR)/hosts | $(STDHOSTS) \
3)    | awk '{for (i = 2; i <= NF; i++) print $$i, $$0}' \
4)    | $(MAKEDBM) - $(YPDBDIR)/$(DOM)/hosts.byname; \
5) $(STDHOSTS) $(DIR)/hosts | \
6)    awk 'BEGIN { OFS = " "; } $$1 !~ /^#/ { print $$1, $$0 }' \
7)    | $(MAKEDBM) - $(YPDBDIR)/$(DOM)/hosts.byaddr; \
```

The **stdhost** command in line 1 is another undocumented command. It removes blank lines and lines that start with a "#", but does not remove comments at the end of a line. The third line includes a loop which will create additional entries in the hosts.byname YP map for each alias that is included for that IP number, allowing you to find matches for all of the aliases included in the host file. The fifth line again invokes **stdhost** to start the formatting for the hosts.byaddr YP map.

3.2.4 Passwd

The **passwd** file contains all the pertinent data needed to establish a login session for your users. This is the format of each entry:

    username:encrypted_passwd:uid:gid:real_name:home_dir:cmd_to_run

where username is the login for each user; encrypted_passwd is the encrypted password for that user; uid is the user's ID number (badge or employee number + a constant is a good rule for determining this, but the number cannot exceed 32000); gid is the group ID number from the group file; real_name is the user's real name (this is used by **sendmail**); home_dir is the path for the user's home directory; and cmd_to_run is the first command executed after login (usually /bin/csh). It is best to start the uids for your network at either 100 or 1000 so that you do not have conflicts with accounts for different software packages.

The passwd map should contain one entry for each user/login in your local net. Each username cannot be longer than eight characters. If you attempt to add more characters, you will find that the user cannot login successfully. There is no minimum number of characters, but three characters are the normal lower limit.

You should comment out the root password in the password ASCII datafile used to create your YP maps:

    root:*:0:1:Operator:/:/bin/csh

and add a real password entry for root to each /etc/passwd on every system in your network. This will prevent anyone from becoming root on any system unless they know the local password. You can also remove this entry altogether from the datafile.

If you want the ability to login across all machine boundaries as root, add an entry like the following to your passwd file:

netroot:ksjdfhw0ue:0:1:Network Root:/:/bin/csh

This will give you root access to every system in your domain that is running YP and has a "+" in their passwd file. You will not be conflicting with or replacing the local root password. This access can be misused if someone else gets the password, so you should be very careful. It can be useful when you have users who want to have their own root password on their own systems, but expect you to take care of everything when they have forgotten their root password. Since you are in effect allowing anyone who knows the netroot password access to all systems in your network, this should be implemented and monitored carefully.

Entries with the same uid can be used if you need to change a user's login. In this case the first entry in the file is the new name and below it is the old one.

curly:jsd37642bas:1004:100:Ted Washington:/home/blue/curly:/bin/csh
tedw:weuor2784:1004:100:Ted Washington:/home/blue/curly:/bin/csh

In order for this example to work, you would need to move the old home directory /home/blue/tedw to /home/blue/curly. This will let your user get his mail with both names until everyone learns to use the new name. Make sure to remove the old entry after people stop using it. The mail issue can also be resolved by setting an alias on the system receiving the mail. The best method depends on your environment.

Every entry should normally have an encrypted password in order to prevent unauthorized use. The character "*" is often used in cases when you need to reserve a uid but you do not want anyone logging in using that name. The only case in which you would not want an encrypted password or a "*" is when you have an entry to run **sync**. It is often very convenient to be able to use the command without having to go through the complete user login sequence. The normal entry in *etc/passwd* is:

sync::1:1::/:/bin/sync

This will run the **sync** command as the user daemon, but will do nothing else. Other good choices for this sort of entry are:

```
date::1:1::/:/bin/date
tty::1:1::/:/bin/tty
```

The **tty** command is especially useful if you have many terminals attached to one workstation and you need to know which port a terminal is connected to.

Make sure that no extra characters, including spaces, are added to the end of each entry. If you happen to include a space you will get the following error when your new user tries to login:

```
/bin/csh : No such file or directory
No shell
Connection closed.
```

This error can be very disconcerting to a new user!

The */etc/passwd* file is manipulated into two YP files, passwd.byname and passwd.byuid. The first uses the login name as the key and the second uses the uid.

On the YP master, the YP passwd file and the local passwd file should not be the same file. In order to do this, copy */etc/passwd* to */etc/yp.passwd* and change all entries in the */var/yp/Makefile* from ($DIR)/passwd to ($DIR)/yp.passwd. Figure 3.5 marks all lines that need to be changed with a preceding "*". Leaving the file as */etc/passwd* will give all the users in your network the ability to login on your master server. When you add new users, you will need to put the new information in */etc/yp.passwd*. This file should grow much larger than the */etc/passwd* file. Also, remove the "+" from the bottom of */etc/passwd* if you are restricting login access to the YP master.

There is a command called **pwck** which checks your password file (see pwck(8)). This command is of limited use since it verifies that the home directory in the password entry is locally available. This would create an error for any user who does not have a home directory mounted on the system upon which you are running the command. See the Problems section in this chapter for another way of checking this file.

3.2.5 Bootparams

The bootparams map is used by diskless clients to mount the correct root and swap filesystems. Other filesystems, such as usr,

```
* passwd.time: $(DIR)/passwd
*  -@if [ -f $(DIR)/passwd ]; then \
   awk 'BEGIN { FS = ":"; OFS = " "; } / [a-zA-Z0-9_]/ { print $$1, $$0 }' \
*    $(DIR)/passwd  |  $(MAKEDBM) - $(YPDBDIR)/$(DOM)/passwd.byname; \
   awk 'BEGIN { FS = ":"; OFS = '"'; } /[a-zA-Z0-9_]/ { print $$3, $$0 }' \
*    $(DIR)/passwd  |  $(MAKEDBM) - $(YPDBDIR)/$(DOM)/passwd.byuid; \
   touch passwd.time; \
   echo "updated passwd"; \
   if [ ! $(NOPUSH) ]; then \
    $(YPPUSH) passwd.byname; \
    $(YPPUSH) passwd.byuid; \
    echo "pushed passwd"; \
   else \
    : ; \
   fi \
   else \
*   echo "couldn't find $(DIR)/passwd"; \
   fi


* netid.time: $(DIR)/passwd $(DIR)/group $(DIR)/hosts $(DIR)/netid
*  @$(MKNETID) -q -p $(DIR)/passwd -g $(DIR)/group -h $(DIR)/hosts \
   -m $(DIR)/netid > .ypjunk; \
   $(MAKEDBM) .ypjunk $(YPDBDIR)/$(DOM)/netid.byname; \


* $(DIR)/passwd:
```

FIGURE 3.5. *Passwd portion of the YP makefile.*

crash, and dump can also be mounted using the bootparams entry, but these should be mounted through */etc/fstab* in most cases. The root and swap filesystems must be defined in bootparams for a diskless client to boot. There should be one entry for each client. The data that you need will be put in the server's */etc/bootparams* file when you do the client install (see Chapter 4). This data can then be easily added to the */etc/bootparams* file on the YP master.

Below is a sample entry for the bootparams file:

```
client    root=server:/export/root/client \
          swap=server:/export/swap/client
```

The syntax lists the hostname of the client first, followed by information about the location of the root and swap filesystems. This information includes the name of the filesystem, the name of the clientserver, and the path for the filesystem that is to be mounted. Be sure to include the "\" as the last character on the line if the entry continues over more than one line. Each entry is read as one line, even though it is easier for us to read and administer each entry on several lines. Full line comments can be used, but do not add comments at the end of a data line. Blank lines should not be included in this datafile. Grouping the clients by server and then sorting the entries alphabetically is very useful for large sites. Figure 3.6 shows a sample bootparams datafile.

There is only one YP map made from this file. The key for this file is the client name and the value includes the client name and all of the filesystems that are necessary for the client to boot. The YP map is called bootparams.

```
#
# bootparams file for sunnet
#
# diskless clients of blue
#
green        root=blue:/export/root/green \
             swap=blue:/export/swap/green
orange       root=blue:/export/root/orange \
             swap=blue:/export/swap/orange
purple       root=blue:/export/root/purple \
             swap=blue:/export/swap/purple
#
# diskless clients of baltic
#
weddell      root=baltic:/home/root/weddell \
             swap=baltic:/home/swap/weddell \
             usr=baltic:/home/exec/sun386.sunos4.0.1
caspian      root=baltic:/home/root/caspian \
             swap=baltic:/home/swap/caspian
bering       root=baltic:/home/root/bering \
             swap=baltic:/home/swap/bering
```

FIGURE 3.6. *Sample bootparams file.*

3.2.6 Ethers

Each diskless client needs an entry in the ethers YP maps. The Ethernet address for each system is displayed on the console when the system is turned on. The output of **dmesg** can also include the Ethernet address for the local system:

```
harlie% dmesg | grep Ether
Ethernet address = 8:0:20:0:a6:3d
```

The format for each entry is:

```
Ethernet_address    hostname
```

The ASCII file can include comments on whole lines or at the end of a line. You may also add blank lines if desired. Dividing the data by server for the diskless clients or by CPU type for the standalone systems is a good idea when the file gets large. It would be best to keep the file in order by sorting using either the Ethernet addresses or the hostname, at a minimum. Large ethers files without any order can be very hard to maintain.

Keeping the ethers YP maps up-to-date and including all systems in the maps, even those which are not diskless clients, can help in resolving "duplicate IP address sent from Ethernet #:#:#:#:#:#" messages. This message most often occurs when someone has accidentally installed a system with an IP address that is being used by another host. This message will show up on both systems that are trying to use the one IP address. If you have the Ethernet address for both systems in your ethers file and an up-to-date hosts file, you should be able to decide quickly which system should be running with that IP address and also correct the IP address for the other system. Unfortunately both systems must be rebooted once this message has occurred. A sample ethers file is included in Figure 3.7.

The Makefile allows for aliasing much like the hosts file. You can add a entry like:

```
8:0:20:0:34:9f   harlie ypmaster
```

Usually, this is not useful and just gives you more to administer.

Two maps are created from this datafile. Both maps include the same values, but ethers.byaddr has the Ethernet address as the key and ethers.byname has the hostname as the key. The following

```
#
# ethers file for sunnet
#
# diskless clients
#
# blue
#
8:0:20:1:d8:4f    blue
8:0:20:0:30:5e    green
8:0:20:0:30:5f    orange
8:0:20:0:30:5g    purple
#
# baltic
#
8:0:20:7:6a:18    baltic
8:0:20:2:18:da    weddell
8:0:20:2:18:db    caspian
8:0:20:2:18:dc    bering
#
# standalone systems
#
# sun3
#
8:0:20:0:34:9f    harlie
8:0:20:6:da:77    minerva
8:0:20:7:6a:18    dora
```

FIGURE 3.7. *Sample ethers file.*

text shows the special commands in */var/yp/Makefile* which are used to create these maps:

```
1) STDETHERS = $(YPDIR)/stdethers
   .
   .
2) ethers.time: $(DIR)/ethers
3) -@if [ -f $(DIR)/ethers ]; then \
4)   $(STDETHERS) $(DIR)/ethers \
5)   ¦ awk '{print $$1, $$0; for (i = 3;i <= NF;i++) print $$i,$$0}' \
6)   ¦ $(MAKEDBM) - $(YPDBDIR)/$(DOM)/ethers.byaddr; \
7)   awk 'BEGIN { OFS = " ";} $$1 !/^#/ { print $$2, $$0 }' \
```

```
8)      $(DIR)/ethers ¦ \
9)      $(MAKEDBM) - $(YPDBDIR)/$(DOM)/ethers.byname; \
```

Again, it is the formatting of the data that is different for this map. The **stdethers** command on line 4 is an undocumented command. It removes all the blank lines and comments from the ASCII datafile. The command also strips preceding 0's from ether numbers. It is only run when making the ethers.byaddr map, however, so the ethers datafile should not include any padded numbers (see the text below for a further discussion). Padding the Ethernet address will prevent your diskless clients from booting.

Adding the extra zeros can make the datafile easier to manage. For instance, it is very easy to find errors if you pad the entries since all the numbers will line up in the datafile. In order to be able to pad the Ethernet address, change line 7 and 8 in the above example to:

```
$(STDETHERS) $(DIR)/ethers \
¦ awk 'BEGIN { OFS = " "; } $$1 !˜/ˆ#/ { print $$2, $$0 }' ¦ \
```

Since **stdethers** will strip the extra zeros, this change will allow you to pad the numbers.

3.2.7 Netgroup

This map is often confused with the group map. The group map controls access to files or directories, while the netgroup file controls NFS mount and remote access. Each entry in the netgroup datafile can follow these two forms:

```
biggroup source finance other
source (hostname, username, domainname)
```

The first line is a way to join two or more netgroups into one hierarchy. A good example of this would be if you had one group that was doing programming and another doing finance. You would want both of these groups to be able to get to general access files such as the manual pages, but you do not want to give them access to each other's files. In this case, you would give access to the man pages to netgroup biggroup, but would want to restrict the home directories or general purpose directories to either source or finance.

The second entry shows a triplet. The triplet includes three pieces of information for each entry. Any information that you want can be left out of the triplet, but the more that you put in the more secure your network will be. You can enter just the hostnames while leaving the other fields blank. Make sure to leave the commas and the parantheses as they are shown in the example. The triplets are used to make individual entries for each system in the network.

You can include full line comments and blank lines in this file, but do not put comments on the lines with the data. Also, do not mix triplets and netgroup names within one netgroup entry. Each netgroup can be made up of individual host entries or of netgroup names but you can not combine the two in one netgroup. You may split out the host entries into a separate netgroup and include that name in the larger netgroup.

There is a limit to the number of characters that can be included in each netgroup. You will get an "entry too big" error when you try to make the map if you have exceeded the maximum number of characters. The limit is over 1100 characters per entry. If you go over this limit, then split the netgroup into two or more pieces.

Figure 3.8 shows sample netgroup file. Notice that it has one large netgroup named "everybody", which includes the netgroups named "market", "source", and "servers".

In some situations you may want to include an entry for each host in your network and then only include the netgroup alias in the bigger netgroups. This is illustrated in Figure 3.9.

This sort of organization can make the file easier to maintain, since you will not need to move triplets around if a machine needs to be added to a different group. In most situations, however, this is a large amount of "extra" data that you might not need.

The */etc/netgroup* file is turned into three maps. The first is named netgroup and uses the netgroup name as the key and the list of triplets or other netgroups as the values. The second map is netgroup.byuser. It uses the user name as the key and the netgroup name as the value. The last map is netgroup.byhost. The value for this map is the netgroup name and the key is the hostname.

You can add one machine to several netgroups if necessary. If you have several groups that partially overlap, you will probably

```
#
# netgroup file for sunnet
#
everybody \
    market \
    source \
    servers
market \
    (green,,sunnet) \
    (orange,,sunnet) \
    (purple,,sunnet)
source \
    (bering,,sunnet) \
    (caspian,,sunnet) \
    (weddell,,sunnet)
servers \
    (athene,,sunnet) \
    (baltic,,sunnet) \
    (blue,,sunnet) \
    (dora,,sunnet) \
    (hal,,sunnet) \
    (harlie,,sunnet) \
    (mike,,sunnet) \
    (minerva,,sunnet) \
    (nomad,,sunnet) \
    (north,,sunnet) \
    (red,,sunnet) \
    (yellow,,sunnet)
```

FIGURE 3.8. *Sample netgroup file.*

need to do this. In this case, creating one netgroup for each machine can make this file much easier to maintain.

Listed below are the special lines in */var/yp/Makefile* that help create the netgroup maps.

1) REVNETGROUP = $(YPDIR)/revnetgroup

   .
   .

2) $(MAKEDBM) $(DIR)/netgroup $(YPDBDIR)/$(DOM)/netgroup; \
3) $(REVNETGROUP) -u ¦ $(MAKEDBM) - $(YPDBDIR)/$(DOM)/netgroup.byuser; \
4) $(REVNETGROUP) -h ¦ $(MAKEDBM) - $(YPDBDIR)/$(DOM)/netgroup.byhost; \

```
#
# netgroup file for sunnet
#

everybody \
                market \
                source

market \
                green \
                orange \
                purple

source \
                bering \
                caspian \
                weddell

bering          (bering,,sunnet)
caspian         (caspian,,sunnet)
green           (green,,sunnet)
orange          (orange,,sunnet)
purple          (purple,,sunnet)
weddell         (weddell,,sunnet)
```

FIGURE 3.9. *Short sample netgroup file.*

The **revnetgroup** command is used to manipulate the data so that it can be made into maps using the hostname or the username as a key. This is another undocumented command, but this is the only place that it should be used.

To make life easier, try to create different names for your groups, netgroups, and aliases. It can be very confusing when a user asks to be added to the "source group". This wording has been used to refer to any one or a combination of these files. Keeping the names separate will make your job much more simple.

3.2.8 Netmasks

This file is used when subnets have been established on your network. If you are using standard subnets you should not have to add anything to this file. Each entry in */etc/netmasks* should be of the form:

    network_number   netmask

This file may contain full line comments, but no blank lines or comments at the end of data lines are allowed.

There is only one map made from this file. It is called net-masks.byaddr. During the "make" process the parts to this map have the permissions lowered to 600. This seems to be an error and the command lines that do this can be removed if you wish. Leaving the lines in will not break anything, it is just inconsistent with the rest of the files.

3.2.9 Networks

Each entry in */etc/networks* should contain the name and number for each network. You may also include an alias name or several aliases with each entry, but it is optional. The form of each line should be:

    network_name   network_number   alias

Make sure never to remove the loopback network entry. You can include full line comments, but should not include blank lines or end of line comments. The field separator in each line must be one or more tab characters.

This ASCII datafile is turned into two YP maps. One is called networks.byname. The key for this map is the network name. One entry for each network and for each alias name is included in this YP map. The second YP map is called networks.byaddr. It uses the network number as the key and only has one entry for each network.

3.2.10 Protocols

This datafile lists all of the protocols used in the Internet. Protocols are simply a set of rules or standards that explain how software and hardware should work together over the network. This file is very seldom changed. Each entry is of the form:

    protocol_name   protocol_number   alias   # comments

Each field should be separated by one or more tabs. Do not include blank lines in the file. Full line comments and in-line comments for each entry are allowed in */etc/protocols*.

The first map that is made is protocols.bynumber. This map includes one entry for each protocol, with the protocol number as the key. The second map is called protocols.byname. This map creates maps with both the protocol name and any aliases as a key, so that you can have multiple entries for each protocol.

3.2.11 Rpc

The */etc/rpc* datafile lists all of the remote procedure calls. These are all processes that are services that are run on remote systems in your network. Many of the YP process, such as **ypserv**, **ypbind** and **yppasswdd** are listed in this file. The format of each entry is:

remote_procedure   port_number   alias

The alias can be one or more names. Each port_number must be unique for things to work properly. Full line comments can be included, but do not include blank lines or comments after an entry. The fields should be separated by tabs.

This file is massaged into one map called rpc.bynumber. The map has the portnumber as the key and all of the other information as the value.

3.2.12 Services

All of the available Internet services are listed in */etc/ services*. Each entry includes:

service_name   port/protocol_name   aliases

Each port/protocol_name pair must be unique. The protocol must be listed in */etc/protocols*. Comments can be placed on a full line or after the alias for a service, but in the latter case, the comment is retained in the YP map. Do not include blank lines. The fields should be separated by tabs.

One YP map called services.byname is generated from the /etc/services datafile. The expected key for this map is the service name, however, the actual key is the port/protocol_name value which is the second field in the datafile. Since most incoming network transactions are identified by the port number and protocol, having a map generated that uses these values as the key is expedient. This will be the format that the computer will want to see the data in; however, this can be a little confusing to the programmer who wants to know the port number that **tftp** is running on. You can get around this problem by using the following command syntax to extract the information that you want:

```
harlie% ypcat services ¦ grep tftp
tftp        69/udp
```

The **ypcat** command is discussed in much more detail later in this chapter. If you do not want the information for **tftp**, substitute "tftp" for whatever service you are looking up the port number and protocol name for.

3.2.13 Publickey

The data in */etc/publickey* is consulted when running secure networking (see the discussion in Chapter 5). The ASCII data is in the form of username followed by the user's publickey and then the user's secret key. The last two values are separated by a colon. This file should not be edited by hand unless you are deleting an entry. This file can be changed using **chkey** or **newkey**.

The map that is created is called publickey.byname. The key for this YP map is the username or the hostname and the values are the public and secret key for that account.

3.2.14 Netid

This map is also used for secure networking. There is almost no documentation on this file. It is created using data from */etc/passwd, /etc/group,* and */etc/hosts.* If any of these files are changed, the netid YP map will be re-created. Do not attempt to create a */etc/netid* file by hand.

The YP map is called netid.byname. Its key is an entry of the form unix.hostname@domainname for root accounts or unix.uid@domainname for other accounts. The value for this key is the user ID and the group ID for that user.

Netid is only consulted if you are running secure networking.

To disable this map, edit the makefile and add the line indicated with a "*".

```
netid.time: $(DIR)/yp.passwd $(DIR)/group $(DIR)/hosts $(DIR)/netid
*   -@if [ -f $(YPDBDIR)/$(DOM)/publickey.byname ]; then \
    @$(MKNETID) -q -p $(DIR)/yp.passwd -g $(DIR)/group \
        -h $(DIR)/hosts -m $(DIR)/netid > .ypjunk; \
    $(MAKEDBM) .ypjunk $(YPDBDIR)/$(DOM)/netid.byname; \
    rm -f .ypjunk; \
    touch netid.time; \
    echo "updated netid"; \
    if [ ! $(NOPUSH) ]; then \
        $(YPPUSH) netid.byname; \
        echo "pushed netid"; \
    else \
        : ; \
    fi \
    else \
        echo "not making netid"; \
    fi
```

This will prevent the netid map from being created until it is needed. The last echo command should be displayed each time the YP maps are made, unless the publickey YP map has been created.

3.2.15 C2secure

These are a collection of maps that are required for C2 security to work. C2 security is just a package of software that will increase the level of security available. The two maps are called passwd.adjunct.byname and group.adjunct.byname. When C2 security is running, these two maps will contain the passwords that are normally placed in the passwd and group files.

In the first file, /etc/security/passwd.adjunct, each entry should be of the form:

```
name:passwd:min:max:default:always:never
```

in which name is the user's login (this entry should also be in the passwd file); passwd is the user's encrypted password; min is the lowest security level for this user; max is the maximum security level for this user; default is the security level that the user will get when they login in unless they have selected a different one;

always is a list of flags that indicate which events should be audited; and never is a list of flags that indicate events that should never be audited.

The format of the second file, */etc/security/group.adjunct*, is:

group:passwd

in which group is the name of the group and passwd is the encrypted password for this group.

The makefile does not work as it comes originally. To fix the file make the changes on the lines indicated with a "*" shown in Figure 3.10. These changes will make sure that the maps are not pushed to any of the slave servers after the maps are updated. These maps should only exist on the YP master.

3.2.16 Ypservers

The ypservers map is a list of all of the YP servers in the domain. This map needs to be changed everytime you add or delete any YP server. The map is originally created when you run **ypinit** on the YP master, although no datafile is created. In order to change this file on a standard YP master, you must run the following commands:

```
# cd /var/yp/domain_name
# /usr/etc/yp/makedbm -u ypservers > /tmp/ypservers
# vi /tmp/ypservers
# /usr/etc/yp/makedbm /tmp/ypservers ypservers
```

The **makedbm** command in the second line makes a datafile, */tmp/ ypservers*, from the existing map. You then edit this file to add/ change/delete whatever is necessary and then recreate the map using this new datafile. This does not push the map however, so if you want the map to be available to more than your YP master you will need to push it (see the section on the **yppush** command).

In sites that change this file often, it would probably be best to do the following on your master server. Use the **makedbm** -u command from above but redirect the output to a file called */etc/ ypservers*. Use the chmod command to set the permissions on the file to 644. Then add this map to the YP makefile by adding ypservers to the all list at the beginning of the file and adding the

```
c2secure:
  -@if [ -f $(DIR)/security/passwd.adjunct ]; then \
*       make passwd.adjunct.time; \
*       make group.adjunct.time; \
  fi


passwd.adjunct.time: $(DIR)/security/passwd.adjunct
  -@if [ -f $(DIR)/security/passwd.adjunct ]; then \
      awk 'BEGIN { FS = ":"; OFS = " "; } /^[a-zA-Z0-9_]/ { print $$1,
  $$0 }' \
      $(DIR)/security/passwd.adjunct ¦ \
      $(MAKEDBM) -s - $(YPDBDIR)/$(DOM)/passwd.adjunct.byname;
  \
      chmod 600 $(YPDBDIR)/$(DOM)/passwd.adjunct.byname.dir; \
      chmod 600 $(YPDBDIR)/$(DOM)/passwd.adjunct.byname.pag; \
      touch passwd.adjunct.time; \
      echo "updated passwd.adjunct"; \
*#    if [ ! $(NOPUSH) ]; then \
*#        $(YPPUSH) passwd.adjunct.byname; \
*#        echo "pushed passwd.adjunct"; \
*#    else \
*#        : ; \
*#    fi \
  else \
      echo "couldn't find $(DIR)/security/passwd.adjunct"; \
  fi


group.adjunct.time: $(DIR)/security/group.adjunct
  -@if [ -f $(DIR)/security/group.adjunct ]; then \
      awk 'BEGIN { FS = ":"; OFS = '"; } /^[a-zA-Z0-9_]/ { print $$1, $$0 }' \
      $(DIR)/security/group.adjunct ¦ \
      $(MAKEDBM) -s - $(YPDBDIR)/$(DOM)/group.adjunct.byname; \
      chmod 600 $(YPDBDIR)/$(DOM)/group.adjunct.byname.dir; \
      chmod 600 $(YPDBDIR)/$(DOM)/group.adjunct.byname.pag; \
      touch group.adjunct.time; \
      echo "updated group.adjunct"; \
*#    if [ ! $(NOPUSH) ]; then \
*#        $(YPPUSH) group.adjunct.byname; \
*#        echo "pushed group.adjunct"; \
*#    else \
*#        : ; \
*#    fi \
  else \
      echo "couldn't find $(DIR)/security/group.adjunct"; \
  fi
```

FIGURE 3.10. *C2 security makefile changes.*

following lines after the netmasks.time entry:

```
ypservers.time: $(DIR)/ypservers
   -@if [ -f $(DIR)/ypservers ]; then \
      $(MAKEDBM) $(DIR)/ypservers $(YPDBDIR)/$(DOM)/ypservers;\
      touch ypservers.time \
      echo "updated ypservers"; \
      if [ ! $(NOPUSH) ]; then \
         $(YPPUSH) ypservers; \
         echo "pushed ypservers"; \
      fi \
   else \
      echo "couldn't find $(DIR)/ypservers"; \
   fi
ypservers: ypservers.time
$(DIR)/ypservers
```

3.3 YP Commands

The following section will present a short description of what each YP command will do and how it might be used. In all cases, further reading of the associated manual pages is suggested.

3.3.1 Ypserv

Ypserv is the process that looks up information in the YP maps (see ypserv(8)). It should be running on all YP servers. The process looks in /var/yp for a directory called "domainname" and if it exists it will attempt to lookup data in the YP maps for that domain. Since this command does no other checking, an empty directory in /var/yp will be enough to start **ypserv,** but will completely block the booting of any client that binds to this server. Once **ypserv** has started there is no error checking to see if a map or a file is missing. This scenario is further discussed in the Troubleshooting section.

3.3.2 Ypbind

Ypbind is a process which "remembers" where a local YP server is and how to contact it (see ypbind(8)). It will also request the name of a new YP server if the server that is currently bound

crashes. All client systems and anyone wanting to access the YP database must run **ypbind.** This process broadcasts a request for a YP server that has the appropriate /var/yp/"domainname" directory. The first YP server that responds to this request is the system that you are bound to. The name of the server that you are bound to can be checked using the **ypwhich** command. **Ypbind** can be run with the -ypset option which will allow anyone who is root on any system in the network to set which server the current machine should be bound to. This is a very insecure option and should not be used if at all possible. In Sun OS 4.0.3, a -ypsetme option is included. This option will only allow root on the local machine to run the **ypset** command. This is much more secure and should be used in situations when one slave server is on a different network and needs to bind to itself or to ensure that the YP master always binds to itself. Both of these situations will work best if **ypbind** is run with the -ypsetme option and if **ypset** is run (see below).

3.3.3 Ypset

The **ypset** command can be used to select which YP server to which your system will attempt to bind (see ypset(8)). The command requires a server name or a server IP address. Since this command is often used before **ypbind** has completed binding (so there are no YP maps to look up the data in) it is best to use the command with the server IP address. In 4.0.3 and newer versions of SunOS, **ypbind** must be started with the -ypset or -ypsetme options in order for the **ypset** command to work.

There is also a -hhost option which will allow you to run **ypset** on a remote system. This practice is not something that you would want to use in a production environment; however, in some test environments this option could be useful.

3.3.4 Ypinit

This command is used to set up a YP database on any of the YP servers (see ypinit(8)). The -m option sets up the local system as a YP master, while the -s option is used to initialize the YP data base on a slave server. The -s option also requires a hostname. It is probably best to use the name of your YP master in all cases. If for

some reason you cannot use the YP master, make sure that the files on the YP slave that you use are up-to-date. How to employ **ypinit** is described in the sections about initializing YP masters and YP slaves.

3.3.5 Ypmake

This is not really a command, but a series of two commands. This process is important enough to warrant its own manual page (see ypmake(8)). The two commands are:

```
harlie# cd /var/yp
harlie# make
```

The **make** command will use the makefile, */var/yp/Makefile*, to update all out-of-date YP maps. It should be run any time one of the ASCII datafiles is changed. Including a datafile name after the make command will make the YP maps that are based on that datafile. For example, "make hosts" will make hosts.byaddr and hosts.byname but will not make netid or any other map that is out-of-date. This can be used to force the update of one specific map before some others. Using **make** without any map names can be used to find un-authorized changes to the YP maps. For instance, if you have just made changes to */etc/hosts*, and the YP make process starts creating a new map for password, you will probably want to find out what has changed and who has done it.

To test the makefile, **make** can be run with the "-n" option (see make(1)). All of the commands that the **make** should do will be displayed, but they will not be executed. This is a good way to verify any changes that have been made to the makefile without accidentally destroying the YP datafiles.

The makefile includes three variables that can be set from the command line. The -DIR=/newpath option will change the directory that the datafile is in. This is normally /etc and is set in the makefile. For instance, if you decided to move all of the datafiles to a special directory, such as /var/yp/mydatafiles, then you could do either of the two following steps to update your YP maps after they are edited:

```
harlie# cd /var/yp
harlie# make -DIR=/var/yp/mydatafiles
```

or edit */var/yp/Makefile* and change the fourth line to say:

DIR=/var/yp/mydatafiles

The next option, -NOPUSH=0, can be used to inhibit the **yppush** of the maps after they are made on the master. You might use this to check out a new map before you push it out to the YP slaves. The "0" can be any string that you would like as long as it is not a null-string.

The -DOM=otherdomain option can be used to create maps for other YP domains. One YP server can serve for multiple domains. However, it can make administering both domains very complicated. Please read the section on "Several domains on one ypserver" before attempting this.

3.3.6 Makedbm

This command makes all the YP maps (see makedbm(8)). It creates the *.pag and *.dir files. In each datafile, "\" will be interpreted to mean that the data is continued on the next line, but any comments are included in the maps. This is why the YP makefile often includes commands that strip the comments from the data before **makedbm** is run.

The following command will reconstruct the hosts file from one of the host YP maps:

```
harlie# /usr/etc/yp/makedbm -u hosts.byaddr > /tmp/hosts
YP_LAST_MODIFIED 0639602950
YP_MASTER_NAME harlie
192.9.200.1 192.9.200.1 harlie loghost      # sunnet YP master
127.0.0.1 127.0.0.1 localhost
```

This command can be used as the last step in trying to recreate a corrupted datafile. The output will not include any comments that might have been in the original datafile, unless the comments were part of the value. It will not preserve any special formatting that made the datafile more manageable. Also, extra information, such as the key and other values that makedbm adds, must be deleted before the datafile can be used to create a YP map. It would be best to use backups instead of the datafile if at all possible.

3.3.7 **Yppush**

The **yppush** is used in the YP makefile to transfer YP maps to the slave servers (see yppush(8)). This command is also located in /usr/etc/yp, so it is not part of your default search path. Normally, no one would use this command since it is part of the make process and is called from the YP makefile. In most of the situations that require this process to be run, it is best to restart the YP make process. You might run this command to force the transfer of a map if something happened during the normal make process. This command includes a -v option that supplies extra debugging information. Normally this command will display error messages if something goes wrong during the transfer.

3.3.8 **Ypxfr**

Ypxfr is used to pull a map from another YP server to the local system (see ypxfr(8)). It should be used if you have problems completing a successful **yppush** from the YP master.

Also, included in /usr/etc/yp are three scripts: ypxfr_1perday, ypxfr_2perday, and ypxfr_1perhour. The scripts are identical except for the list of maps that are pulled. It would be best to change the scripts to pull the maps using the -f option, thus forcing the transfer even if the local version of the map is newer than the one on the master server. If you are having problems with the normal push of the YP maps then you will probably want to run one or more of these scripts through **cron** to update the local maps.

If **ypxfr** is called from cron and if the file */var/yp/ypxfr.log* exists then all output from the transfer will be appended to the end of the ypxfr.log. This can give you a good record of the transfers that have occurred.

3.3.9 **Yppoll**

Yppoll can be used to determine if a particular map is supported in your YP domain (see yppoll(8)). This command is located in /usr/etc/yp so is not part of the normal search path. It will also tell you the order number and which host is the YP master. You must use a complete map name; no nicknames are supported:

```
harlie% /usr/etc/yp/yppoll hosts
Can't get any map parameter information.
Can't get order number for map hosts.
    Reason: no such map in server's domain
Can't get master for map hosts.
    Reason: no such map in server's domain
harlie% /usr/etc/yp/yppoll hosts.byname
Domain sunnet is supported.
Map hosts.byname has order number 639604088.
The master server is harlie.
```

The order number is the system time in seconds when the map was built on the YP master. This data could be used to make sure that the maps were up-to-date or the command could be used to see if a special or "home-grown" YP map is supported in the local domain.

3.3.10 Ypwhich

The **ypwhich** command without any arguments will report back the name of your YP server (see ypwhich(1) and ypwhich(8)). The -m option will list all of the YP maps for your current domain and the name of the YP master for each map. Using this option can be very useful if someone has run a **make** on a slave server by accident. The following command can be run to verify that the master for all of the YP files is harlie:

```
north% ypwhich -m ¦grep -v harlie
```

Any maps that are displayed are maps that have most likely been made by accident on a YP slave. These maps should be removed from the slave and maps should be transferred from the master to the slave using **ypxfr.**

On occasion, if you have just restarted **ypbind,** you will need to run **ypwhich** twice to get the expected response. The bind process can take longer than it takes for the system to return a prompt, so the first try will respond with a "not bound" error message. The second try should display the right message.

If a hostname is included with the **ypwhich** command, the YP master for that host will be shown. This could be used to test if a client is in the correct domain or is bound to the correct ypserver.

3.3.11 Ypcat

The command **ypcat** is used to print out values in the YP database (see ypcat(1)). It will print out the whole YP map, but is often used with **grep** to be able to find the information that is not in any of the YP maps as a key. For instance,

harlie% **ypcat** passwd ¦ grep ":0:"

will find all of the entries in the passwd file that have root privileges or a group ID of 0.

In this case, **ypcat** has been used with a map nickname, "passwd". There is no YP map called passwd, but the system is set up with several nicknames which can be seen by using the following command:

harlie% **ypcat** -x
Use "passwd" for map "passwd.byname"
Use "group" for map "group.byname"
Use "networks" for map "networks.byaddr"
Use "hosts" for map "hosts.byaddr"
Use "protocols" for map "protocols.bynumber"
Use "services" for map "services.byname"
Use "aliases" for map "mail.aliases"
Use "ethers" for map "ethers.byname"

So the "**ypcat** passwd" command really executed a "**ypcat** passwd.byname". This list of nicknames just shortens the amount of typing that you would need to do under most circumstances. The -k option displays both the keys and the values. This is useful for looking at maps such as ypservers, which is just a list of keys.

harlie% **ypcat** ypservers

harlie% **ypcat** -k ypservers
harlie

The first command only prints out one blank line for each YP server. The second command actually displays the important information.

3.3.12 Ypmatch

Ypmatch, also, is used to print out values in the YP database, but it will print only one entry for each key you give it (see ypmatch(1)). You can enter many keys in one command line, but no wild card characters are allowed.

```
harlie% ypmatch harry harri passwd.byname
harry:soNr2Cb3P8jOg:1001:10::/home/baltic/harry:/bin/csh
Can't match key harri in map passwd.byname. Reason: no such key in
map.
```

Every key that you include should produce some sort of output, even if it just tells you that you are having problems typing.

This command supports a -x option which prints out all of the map nicknames like the ypcat command. It also has a "-k" option which prints out the key, a colon and then the value associated with the key.

```
harlie% ypmatch -k localhost hosts
localhost: 127.0.0.1 localhost
```

3.3.13 Yppasswdd

This is a daemon process that will make changes to the datafile that the passwd YP maps are made from (see yppasswdd(8C)). Once the changes are made, this command will also run a "ypmake" to propagate the changes. This command should be started from the */etc/rc.local* script on your YP master. To do this add the following lines to */etc/rc.local* after the entry for **ypupdated**:

```
if [ -f /usr/etc/rpc.yppasswd d-a -d /var/yp/'domainname' ]; then
    /usr/etc/rpc.yppasswdd /etc/yp.passwd
fi
```

This example will work when the datafile for the passwd maps have been changed as described in the end of section on the passwd datafile. The arguments to this command include the filename of the YP datafile, */etc/yp.passwd* in this case. This can be changed to */etc/passwd* or any other filename that is being used as the datafile for the passwd maps. There is also a -m option which will pass options to the **make** command after the datafile has been changed (see the previous section on ypmake). This process must be running on the YP master in order for users to be able to change their YP passwords.

3.3.14 **Yppasswd**

This command is used to change a user's password in the passwd YP map (see yppasswd(1)). You must know the old password in order to make the change. The command will ask for the old password and then the new password. Like the **passwd** command, you will be requested to type in the new password twice to prevent mistakes. If the user has forgotten his or her YP password another mechanism discussed in the Troubleshooting section must be used to remedy the problem. The **yppasswdd** server must be running on the YP master for this command to work (see the section above).

You can add a YP password for a user by running the following command as root:

harlie# **yppasswd** username

This will only succeed if you know the user's old password or if the password has been removed.

This command is often confused with **passwd. Yppasswd** will only make changes in the YP maps, while the **passwd** command will only make changes in the local */etc/passwd* file. In a standard environment a user would use **passwd** to change their root password on their own system, but would use **yppasswd** to change the password for their login account, which should be included in YP. If there is an entry in the local passwd file, then either the **passwd** command must be used or the entry must be deleted.

3.4 YP Master Server Initialization

Figure 3.11 shows a sample of how to set up a YP master. The server must be in single user mode and the domainname must be set. The **ypinit** command establishes all of the YP maps. You will be asked to supply the hostnames for all YP servers in the YP domain that you are creating. This data is used to create the ypservers YP map. Once this map has been established, the rest of the maps are created. The last message warns that if you are re-establishing a new YP master for some reason on an already active YP domain, then you will need to run **yppush** to update the maps on the old YP servers, so that the maps will remain synchronized.

```
harlie# cd /var/yp
harlie# ls
Makefile   binding      updaters
harlie# /usr/etc/yp/ypinit -m
```
Installing the yp data base will require that you answer a few questions.
Questions will all be asked at the beginning of the procedure.

Do you want this procedure to quit on non-fatal errors? [y/n: n] **n**
OK, please remember to go back and redo manually whatever fails. If
you don't, some part of the system (perhaps the yp itself) won't work.

At this point, we have to construct a list of the hosts which will run yp
servers. harlie is in the list of yp server hosts. Please continue to add the
names for the other hosts, one per line. When you are done with the list,
type a <control D>.
    next host to add: **harlie**
next host to add: ^**D**
The current list of yp servers looks like this:

harlie
Is this correct? [y/n: y] **y**
There will be no further questions. The remainder of the procedure
should take
5 to 10 minutes.
Building /var/yp/sunnet/ypservers. . . .
Running /var/yp/Makefile. . . .
updated passwd

   .

   .

updated netmasks

harlie has been set up as a yp master server without any errors.

If there are running slave yp servers, run yppush now for any data bases
which have been changed. If there are no running slaves, run ypinit on
those hosts which are to be slave servers.

FIGURE 3.11. *Initiating a YP master.*

After running the **ypinit** command, make sure that the following lines in */etc/rc.local* are uncommented:

```
#if [ -f /usr/etc/ypserv -a -d /var/yp/'domainname' ]; then
#   ypserv;     (echo -n ' ypserv')   > /dev/console
#fi
```

This will cause **ypserv** to be started on this server each time it reboots. At this point you can either reboot the system, or start **ypserv** and **ypbind** by hand:

```
harlie# /usr/etc/ypserv
harlie# /usr/etc/ypbind
```

These commands will make your new YP master fully functional. The last thing you will need to do is to start **yppasswdd**.

3.5 YP Slave Server Initialization

To start the process of initiating a YP slave server you must first make sure that your server is running **ypbind. Ypwhich** will tell you if the current server is bound and which system it is bound to. Next, run "**/usr/etc/yp/ypinit** -s master" on the new slave server. "Master" is the hostname for either the YP master or any other slave that is known to be stable. This process will transfer the YP maps to this new server.

In order for YP to be usable on the local system, the following files might need to be edited: aliases, ethers, group, hosts, netgroup, netmasks, networks, passwd, protocols, services, hosts.equiv and /.rhosts. All of these files are found in /etc except for the last one. The files for ethers, netgroup, networks, protocols and services do not need to be present on any YP client or YP slaves. They only need to be present on the YP master.

The alias file does not require any special editing since **sendmail** will check the YP alias map after the local file. For YP passwords to function, you will need to make sure that there is a "+" at the bottom of */etc/passwd*.

The group file can consist of one entry:

```
+:
```

This entry will use only the YP maps to determine the names of any groups. You may also add local groups if you enter the data before the "+". It is recommended that you try to keep all of the groups in the YP maps.

The hosts file must always contain an entry for the local hostname and for the localhost or loopback host entry (see example below):

```
#
# If the yellow pages is running, this file is only consulted when booting
```

```
#
# These lines added by the Suninstall Program
#
192.9.200.1    harlie loghost        # sunnet YP master

127.0.0.1 localhost
#
# End of lines added by the Suninstall Program
#
```

These entries are used when the local host is in single user mode and any other time that the network is down or YP is not available.

The hosts.equiv file is not part of the YP database, but you can use entries from the netgroup YP maps. A single "+" in this file will give any user login access to the local server without requiring a password once they are logged in somewhere on the net. This situation can cause security problems. Since this only controls whether users will need to include a password when they rlogin across the network, it is better to leave this file empty. This will require all users to enter a password to get in (see section in Chapter 6 about the hosts.equiv file). The file that is installed during **suninstall** has a "+" in it, which you will probably want to remove.

/.rhosts is similar to hosts.equiv except that it controls root access to the local server. In almost all cases this file should be empty. Any host that is listed in this file will be able to become root on the local host without supplying a root password.

The next step in initializing a YP slave server is to start **ypserv**:

```
harlie# /usr/etc/ypserv
```

You will also want to make sure that the following lines in /etc/ rc.local are uncommented:

```
if [ -f /usr/etc/ypserv -a -d /var/yp/'domainname' ]; then
    ypserv;      (echo -n ' ypserv')   > /dev/console
fi
```

The final step is to add the local host to the ypservers map on the YP master. You may do this in either of two ways depending on how you decided to maintain the ypservers map (see the discussion in this chapter on the ypservers datafile). Installing an ASCII datafile on the master server is much easier than running the manual process if you change the list of slave servers often.

Always remove or rename the YP makefile (/var/yp/Makefile)

on slave servers so that the YP make doesn't accidentally get run on the slave servers. If this happens, the slave server will be master for whatever new maps are created. These YP maps will then not be updated when the YP master datafile is changed. **Ypwhich** -m will display the name of the YP master for each file. If a YP slave has become a master, then it is best to remove the effected maps and use **ypxfr** to get the correct maps in place. Make sure to remove or rename the makefile if this happens.

3.6 YP Clients

The easiest way to install a YP client is to indicate that the system is a YP client in the **suninstall** process (see Chapter 2). If this is not possible, then a manual process can be used.

First, make sure that the domainname is set properly in */etc/ rc.local* for the new client. Edit */etc/passwd, /etc/hosts* and */etc/ group* as you would for a slave server (see previous discussion). You do not need the networks, protocols, ethers, services, and netgroup files on YP clients. Finally check to see if **ypbind** is running. If it is not, start it with the following command:

```
mike# /usr/etc/ypbind
```

Also make sure that the following lines are uncommented in */etc/ rc.local:*

```
if [ -f /usr/etc/ypbind ]; then
   if [ -f /etc/security/passwd.adjunct ]; then
      ypbind -s;   (echo -n ' ypbind')   > /dev/console
   else
      ypbind;      (echo -n ' ypbind')   > /dev/console
   fi
fi
```

Also make sure that the lines that start **ypserv** are commented out in */etc/rc.local*. This will prevent anyone from accidentally becoming a YP slave.

3.7 Problems

The following section deals with some of the most common problems when using YP. In general, try not to make big changes any more than is absolutely necessary. The more you change, the more likely there will be a mistake. Also, become accustomed to using the "set list" option in **vi** when checking your work (see vi(1)). This will display all normal and special characters and can help you locate problems before you make the YP maps. If you change a map and everything goes haywire, try to check the YP maps that were made to find the error. If all else fails, find someone else to look at it, even if you must explain everything to them. Another set of eyes often will find errors quickly.

Always double check the formatting of the ASCII files. A space after a password entry or an extra "." in the host file can cause all sorts of problems.

3.7.1 Yppasswd Not Working

If you have problems with a large group of people not being able to change their password or login you should run the following command:

awk -F: 'NF \!= 7 {print $0}' */etc/passwd*

This commands checks to make sure that there are the proper number of colons on each line in your passwd file. It will print out any lines with the improper number of fields. This error condition only occurs after someone has manually entered or deleted data from the passwd file. The file must be fixed in order for the commands which access the passwd file to work properly.

3.7.2 YP Slave is Master

Sometimes when the Makefile in /var/yp is not renamed or moved, a **make** will accidentally be run on a YP slave. You can check for this by running "**ypwhich** -m" on any clients of the YP slave. If this command indicates that the master server for any of the maps is a YP slave, then the map.dir and map.pag files should be removed from the /var/yp/'**domainname**' directory and **ypxfr** should be run using the YP master as the host to get new copies of these files. This error can cause all sorts of problems, so an occasional check of your YP slaves is probably a good idea.

3.7.3 Forgotten YP Password

The best way to fix a forgotten YP password is to become root on the YP master, edit the passwd ASCII datafile, and remove the encrypted password. Next make the YP maps. Finally either have users reset their password themselves or do it for them as root by using the **yppasswd** command.

3.7.4 Client Hung in Boot Process

When a diskless client system boots it will display the local Ethernet address, the host number in hexidecimal characters for the YP server that is answering the request, and the host number for the client. If the client is not booting properly check this information carefully. Make sure that the host number that is given for the YP server is valid. If your standalones are allowed root access, you can end up with accidental YP servers. If this happens, you should kill **ypserv** on the extra YP server, remove the /var/yp/ 'domainname' directory, and reboot the client.

3.8 Advanced Topics

This final section includes discussion of some of the more advanced YP concepts. Become comfortable with the earlier concepts before you attempt to use the following procedures.

3.8.1 Automatic Updating of YP Maps

The scripts called ypxfr_1perday, ypxfr_1perhour, and ypxfr_2perday, located in /usr/etc/yp, can be used to force an update of the YP maps on a slave server (see the section on the command **ypxfr**). This situation is often necessary if you have a slave server that is on a very busy network or is experiencing some other type of communication problem, such that the YP maps do not always successfully transfer from the YP master. You can use these scripts as a basic template to create your own ypxfr scripts that you can tailor to your specific needs.

3.8.2 One YP Domain on Many Nets

If you have one YP domain spread over many nets, it is a good idea to have two YP slaves for this domain on each net. These servers should be bound to themselves or to each other. This will keep a local network running even if a gateway between the YP master and the YP slaves goes down.

3.8.3 Many YP Domains on One Net

Try to avoid this scenario if you can, but sometimes it is not possible. If you must do this make sure that the hosts files between the two domains are identical. This will allow YP servers for each domain to give a diskless client its proper host address, when the client first comes up. If they are not identical, a client may not boot depending on which YP server it gets its host address from.

Make sure to remove old information when a user moves from one YP domain to another. Duplicate bootparams entries can cause the client to not boot if the rest of the information has been updated.

3.8.4 Several Domains on One Ypserver

If you need to have one or more YP domains on the same network, it is often useful to let your YP slaves serve both domains. You can only have one YP master for each domain, but **ypserv** only depends on the existence of the appropriate /var/yp/'domainname' directory, so a slave server can serve two or more domains if it is convenient. For instance one YP slave could have YP maps in /var/yp/sunnet and /var/yp/testnet. A YP server only needs to have one copy of **ypserv** running, even if it is serving multiple domains. Make sure that you have allowed space in the /var for the new domain YP maps if you are going to do this.

3.8.5 Changing a YP Slave into a YP Master

If you have hardware problems on your YP master or if you simply want to upgrade your YP master to a new release without having several hours of down time you may wish to change one of your YP slaves into a YP master. In any case, you need to deactivate the old YP master, and start a new one.

The first step should be to install all of the ASCII datafiles and the YP makefile on your new YP master. A YP slave that has backup copies of the datafiles, would probably be the quickest system to change. If you do not save copies on another system and if this is a hardware emergency then you will have to go through the process of restoring all of the datafiles and the YP makefile from backups.

Next you should kill **ypbind** on your new YP master and

remove /var/yp/'domainname'. Also, if the old YP master is still running, you should make sure to kill **ypserv** and remove /var/yp/' domainname' on the old server. This will halt all processes that use YP until you are done creating your new YP master, so make sure that the network is quiet.

The last step is to run "**ypinit** -m" on your new YP master to establish it as the YP master for your domain. The new YP master will need to be rebooted or have **ypserv** and **ypbind** started. You will most likely need to reinitialize the YP slaves as well. This is a time-consuming process but is much better than the alternatives.

3.8.6 Adding Your Own YP Maps

You may maintain your own YP map by either creating your own additional makefile in /var/yp or by adding your new map to the existing one. Be sure that you save a copy of the original makefile before you make any additions to it! The spacing in any makefile is critical and often requires some special editing before it can replace the old file. The tabs in the makefile should not be substituted with spaces, so be careful.

To establish a YP map that contained employee names and home phone numbers, first you would need to create the ASCII datafile. For this example, the file will be called */etc/homephone*. Listed below is the contents of the file:

Tom Jones	415-555-1212
Dick Henry	415-555-1313
Harry Smith	415-555-1414

In order for this map to be supported like all of the others it should be added to */var/yp/Makefile*. The first thing to be done is to add the new map to the "all" list in the makefile.

```
all: passwd group hosts ethers networks rpc services protocols \
    netgroup bootparams aliases publickey netid c2secure netmasks \
    homephone
```

Make sure that the "\" is at the end of the line (with no spaces after it) and that the character before the data on the second and third lines is a tab, not a bunch of spaces. This is very important because **make** will not run properly without the correct formatting.

Next create an entry for the homephone YP map. It should

```
#!/bin/csh
#
if ( -f /tmp/yplock) then
    echo " someone else is editing the YP maps"
    echo " try back later"
    exit 0
endif
touch /tmp/yplock
clear
while ( ! $?exit )
echo " "
cat << MENU
        YP Datafiles Edit Script

    1) aliases

    2) bootparams

    q) Done with editing

MENU
    echo ";;
    echo -n "      which file would you like to edit? "
    set afile = $<
    switch ($afile)
      case '1':
        vi /etc/aliases
        breaksw
      case '2':
        vi /etc/bootparams
        breaksw
      case [Qq]:
        set exit = yes
        breaksw
      default:
        echo ' "'
        echo " $afile is not allowed."
        continue
        breaksw
    endsw
end
```

FIGURE 3.12. *YP master script.*

```
onceagain:
    echo ' ""
    echo -n "     should make be run?"
    set amake = $<
    switch ($amake)
        case [yY]:
            cd /var/yp;make
            breaksw
        case [nN]:
            echo -n "     are you sure that you"
            echo -n " do not want to run the make?"
            set amake2 = $<
            if ( $amake2 == y) then
                echo ' ""
                echo " This can cause problems with YP."
                echo " You should manually run a YP make"
                echo " as soon as possible."
            else
                echo -n " "
                goto onceagain
            endif
            breaksw
        default:
            echo " answer y or n please"
            continue
            breaksw
    endsw
rm /tmp/yplock
```

FIGURE 3.12. *(continued).*

look something like:

```
homephone.time: $(DIR)/homephone
    -@if [ -f $(DIR)/homephone ]; then \
        awk 'BEGIN { FS = " " } { print $$1, $$0 }' \
        $(DIR)/homephone : $(MAKEDBM) - $(YPDBDIR)/$(DOM)/
        homephone; \
    touch homephone.time; \
    echo "updated homephone"; \
    if [ ! $(NOPUSH) ]; then \
        $(YPPUSH) homephone; \
        echo "pushed homephone"; \
    else \
```

```
            : ; \
        fi \
    else \
        echo "couldn't find $(DIR)/homephone"; \
    fi

homephone: homephone.time
$(DIR)/homephone:
```

This YP map will echo back the full name and phone number for an individual if you give it the person's first name as a key. Two maps could have been made; the first keyed by first name and the second by last name.

3.8.7 Race Conditions

Since the updating of the date stamp file occurs after the map is made, if someone updates the datafile while the map is being made, then you won't know exactly what is in the map. It is best to have only one person at a time editing and making the maps. A good example of this problem is netid. If someone has edited one of the files that netid is dependent on before your make gets to the netid make, then the data in the netid make would be different than your other maps.

The shell script in Figure 3.12 will help with this problem. It will function as it is, but since only aliases and bootparams have been included as datafiles to be edited, the script will need some work to make it useful. The script is intended to restrict write access to the datafiles to the first person who runs the script. No one will be able to edit the files until this person is done, if everyone is utilizing the script. This technique is not intended to provide security, just to keep things clean.

Administering a Network of Sun Systems

4

Isolating one single item in Sun systems administration is difficult. All parts are interrelated. As a Sun administrator, your main responsibility is to support systems and user accounts on the network. You maintain the systems and accounts when problems arise. These responsibilities mean you must know how to use YP. To understand YP, you must become acquainted with how systems and user accounts are added or removed from a network. A working knowledge of the Network File System and its relationship with YP will aid in the management of systems and resources.

Your other functions include the installation and maintenance of application software. Applications must be installed in a manner that allows only the machines with a password or license for that application to use them. Legal problems are possible if a certain level of security is not maintained. Much of the application-level security is provided by the vendor in the application. You can lock down your applications further from unauthorized use by instigating additional security measures.

Peripheral installation and maintenance also falls under the jurisdiction of the system administrator. A basic understanding of printers, disks, and tape devices is necessary to configure and use these peripherals. In effect, as a Sun systems administrator, you are required to know how to maintain each aspect of system and network administration.

The procedures to add systems to your network are slightly different for each system type. When adding any new machine, you need to give it a hostname and assign it a host number or IP address on the YP master server. When adding a standalone workstation, you need to assign an IP address, a hostname, and probably create a login or user account for the person that uses the machine. When adding a diskless client, you need to obtain the diskless machine's Ethernet address and assign to it an IP address and hostname. Once this has been done, locate a server for the client's architecture, run **setup_client** on that server, and, finally, create a login account for whoever will be using the system. Server systems are rarely assigned a specific login account, while most workstations have at least one main user, and sometimes many different users.

Removing systems from the network is generally done by deleting the IP address from the hosts file on the YP master, and powering down the machine. Removing user accounts is done by deleting the login entry from the YP or local password file and mail aliases, then removing the home directory. Removing diskless machines is accomplished by running the **setup_client** script on the server of that client.

Understanding how all these steps fit together is best shown by starting from the ground floor and building up. In the next few pages, you will learn how to install a small network of Sun machines. This hypothetical network contains a YP master server, a diskless client server for several diskless clients, and a number of other machines from standalone systems to an NFS resource server. This example presents the basic idea showing how Sun workstations and servers operate together.

This chapter has two major parts: server administration and workstation administration. The server administration section covers what needs to be done to set up the fileservers on your network, such as the YP master, NFS resource server, diskless client servers, and print servers. The workstation administration section covers administrative steps that must be performed on individual workstations for proper communication within the network. Some working examples of how workstations can use fileservers are provided.

4.1 Server Administration

Starting a network from scratch begins with securing a network number, before the physical network is installed. Some foresight in the growth of your network can help you determine which network class is appropriate for your site. (See Chapter 5 for instructions on how to obtain a registered network.)

Small installations of Sun workstations may have one or two

desktop machines loaded with options and disk space to act as servers for other machines in the network. A network of this size can use a class C address, allowing a maximum of 254 nodes or systems before another network is needed.

A medium sized installation may have some high-end deskside systems acting as fileservers, or may have a single server-sized system in a closet or back room. If more than one floor in a building is used, two separate class C addresses may be necessary. This configuration allows up to 508 separate nodes.

Larger installations of Sun machines often have designated computer rooms constructed specifically for the fileservers. Often the computer rooms themselves have a separate network installed. An installation such as this may have many class C networks, all connected together through a maze of routers and gateways. If you expect to use more than 100 different networks, a class B network address is worth consideration.

4.1.1 Server Room Set Up

An environmentally controlled server room with an uninterruptible power source and HALON fire protection is good investment. A raised floor hides network cables and other essential wiring while providing the most efficient air-flow to all machines.

When considering the installation of specialized computer room for your site, the three most important issues are power, cooling, and cable routing. Always try to have enough power available to completely fill the room with systems. Each system should have its own separate circuit with the correct amperage and voltage. The server systems also require special power connectors.

A good cooling system can extend the life of your servers, while filtering dust and other contaminants out of the air. The ambient temperature of a server room is normally set at 70 degrees Fahrenheit, and the relative humidity at 50 percent. The systems, disk drives especially, start to shut themselves down if the temperature rises over 95 degrees F. If you line up three or four server systems next to each other, they become quite warm if some kind of cooling system is not used. Consider that the internal temperature of the card cage is much hotter than the temperature of the room.

Cabling can be quite bothersome. Every machine must have some kind of console device whether it be an ASCII terminal or a Sun monitor. There is less cabling to deal with when you use ASCII terminals. Sun monitors each need at least one cable, but you also need to connect a Sun keyboard, which entails one more cable.

You also must run a transceiver cable to each machine for the network connection. Each of the transceiver cables must be tapped directly into the thick-net cable or connected to a multiplexor box. Some multiplexor boxes can fit under a raised floor, some cannot.

In a server room, ASCII terminals are preferred as system consoles. It is not an economical use of space or money to connect bit-mapped display monitors to server systems unless they are absolutely necessary. A possible alternative to using bit-mapped displays or ASCII terminals is to dedicate one machine to be a console server. A console server needs to have a number of tty ports. Each port is connected to a different server system as its console device. To access any of the system consoles attached to the console server, you can use your workstation to **rlogin** to the console server, and then use **tip** to connect the system of your choice. A small amount of setup is needed, but this procedure can really save space and money.

Once you have obtained your IP address and had your network installed, you can begin installing the support systems, starting with the YP master server.

4.1.2 The YP Master Server

It is suggested that you use the YP database for your administrative functions because it simplifies your job greatly. The YP master must be installed first on a network that is using YP. Every other machine that is added to your network is dependent on this system for inter-network communication and user-account information. Install the YP master using **suninstall** as detailed in Chapter 2. Once installed, each system on the network is added to the YP master's hosts datafile whether it is a standalone, server, or a diskless client.

The YP master need not be a large rack-mounted server machine. It should be one of your faster systems, preferably a Sun-4, so YP requests are given prompt attention. Remember, when installing a YP master to reserve enough disk space in the /var directory because this is where the maps reside. A common practice is to create a separate partition for /var. Again, you do not need a massive amount of disk space for the YP master server. The size of your YP database can vary greatly. Datafiles that have been converted into YP database maps are not equal in size. Creating a 40 MB /var partition will ensure enough free disk space for future growth.

Once the YP master has been installed, follow the special boot procedure to initialize the database. After the database has been initialized, you may let the YP master finish booting.

Begin populating the *letc/hosts* datafile with the Internet Protocol addresses and hostnames of the systems that belong to the network. Use your favorite text editor to edit the *letc/hosts* file on the YP master and add the IP addresses and hostnames. Be sure to use the Tab key between each address and the hostname when editing this file. Problems occur when spaces are used instead of tabs.

The YP master's *letc/hosts* file contains only itself and its localhost address after a fresh installation. To add more hosts to the network, decide the names and addresses of the other machines that are to be installed. The systems that are usually installed soon after the YP master are other servers, used to support the diskless and standalone machines. You may wish to add the names and addresses of your workstations to the hosts file at this time, if you have chosen their hostnames.

Some administrators choose to reserve the lower addresses of the network for server systems, while using the upper addresses for workstations. This type of arrangement allows new servers to be added to the network easily. The host number of a machine has no effect on its speed or ability to communicate. When a number of different network addresses are used, the hosts file on the YP master server may be similar to Figure 4.1.

Figure 4.1 is the hosts file for the domain sunnet, containing systems that will soon be attached to the network. Each entry has a comment to explain its purpose. Because these are the first names and numbers to be added to the domain, finding a free IP address is painless. New systems can be added in any order. The IP ad-

```
#
# YP hosts file for domain sunnet
#
127.0.0.1  localhost
#
# Main net
#
192.9.200.0     sunnet neta           # sunnet network
192.9.200.1     harlie ypmaster       # YP master
192.9.200.2     minerva               # print server
192.9.200.3     dora                  # resource server
192.9.200.4     athene                # modem server
192.9.200.5     hal                   # source machine
192.9.200.6     nomad                 # backup server
192.9.200.7     mike                  # YP slave
192.9.200.8     red-gtw               # gateway to netb
192.9.200.9     north-gtw             # gateway to netc
#
# Marketing net
#
192.9.201.0     netb                  # marketing network
192.9.201.1     red                   # gateway & slave server
192.9.201.2     blue                  # netb client server
192.9.201.3     green                 # blue client
192.9.201.4     yellow                # gateway & slave server
192.9.201.5     orange                # blue client
192.9.201.6     purple                # blue client
#
# Programmers net
#
192.9.202.0     netc                  # programmers network
192.9.202.1     north                 # gateway & slave server
192.9.202.2     baltic                # netc client server
192.9.202.3     weddell               # baltic client
192.9.202.4     caspian               # baltic client
192.9.202.5     bering                # baltic client
192.9.202.6     yellow-gtw            # gateway to netb
```

FIGURE 4.1. *Sample* /etc/hosts *file.*

dresses used throughout this chapter are class C addresses. This network address is the default number shown during the installation. Do not use this address for your network if you plan on connecting to the Internet; use a unique number. The only way you can guarantee a unique Internet address is to request one.

The first and last entry in each network address is reserved for the broadcast address. You should never assign either address to one machine. The numbers zero and 255 are used when networks need to talk to other networks.

When you have completed the additions to the */etc/hosts* file, you may wish to create a netgroups map. The sorting of machines into different groups can be used to grant or deny NFS mount access to selected machines. It can also be used to grant or deny login access if the netgroup is included in */etc/hosts.equiv* or */.rhosts* (See Chapter 6). The sample */etc/netgroups* file from Chapter 3 serves as a good example. Netgroups are not a requirement, but do aid in administration.

The sunnet domain (shown in Figure 4.2) is divided into four separate netgroups: everybody, market, source, and servers. The everybody netgroup contains other netgroup names while the market, source, and servers netgroups contain system names, which is the preferred method of arranging netgroups.

Once all the changes have been made to the YP datafiles, the database must be updated. This is done by executing **make** while in the /var/yp directory.

```
# cd /var/yp
# make hosts netgroups
updated hosts

pushed hosts

updated netgroups

pushed netgroups
```

After the YP make procedure is complete, the domain is operational. When additional machines join the domain, be sure to keep your YP master current by adding them to both the hosts and netgroups datafiles. The section below explains how to setup the NFS resource server.

```
#
# netgroup file for sunnet
#

everybody \
                market \
                source \
                servers

market \
                (green,,sunnet) \
                (orange,,sunnet) \
                (purple,,sunnet)

source \
                (bering,,sunnet) \
                (caspian,,sunnet) \
                (weddell,,sunnet)

servers \
                (athene,,sunnet) \
                (baltic,,sunnet) \
                (blue,,sunnet) \
                (dora,,sunnet) \
                (hal,,sunnet) \
                (harlie,,sunnet) \
                (mike,,sunnet) \
                (minerva,,sunnet) \
                (nomad,,sunnet) \
                (north,,sunnet) \
                (red,,sunnet) \
                (yellow,,sunnet)
```

FIGURE 4.2. *Sample /etc/netgroups file.*

4.1.3 NFS Resource Server

Although not a requirement, the second machine often in-stalled on a new Sun network is the NFS resource server. Some sites do not have the luxury of such a machine, but it helps to improve network resource management. The resource server should not be the same machine as the YP master or diskless client server if at all possible. Alternatives to a single resource server might be configuring a few of the standalone machines to offer a single resource such as the manual pages, demos, games, or application software. It is more difficult to keep track of NFS resources that are spread out among many different machines.

The function of an NFS resource server is to act as an extension of a local disk to networked clients. Other systems can greatly expand their access to many utilities by way of the resource server without using any local disk space. Diskless systems may also tap into the services offered by an NFS resource server by simply mounting them over the network.

NFS mount access is controlled by the */etc/exports* file in conjunction with the YP netgroups map. Systems that are NFS servers are normally configured to have eight **nfsd** processes, and one **rpc.mountd** process running to handle the NFS mount requests. These background processes or daemons are started during the execution of the */etc/rc.local* script, but only when the */etc/exports* file exists. The */etc/exports* file is created during installation on all servers of diskless clients. It does not exist by default on standalone machines. Simply creating the */etc/exports* file on a standalone machine and rebooting starts the daemons necessary to become an NFS server.

Use the **suninstall** program to install the resource server, reserving filesystems for resources. After the installation is complete, unbundled products and other shared resources can be loaded and prepared for exporting. One common shared resource is the on-line manual pages. Software that is resident on a SunOS release tape is considered a "bundled" product, while software that lives on its own release media is usually "unbundled". The on-line manual pages are considered "bundled" since they can be extracted from the SunOS release tape.

Before exporting the manual pages, run the **catman** utility (see catman(8)). **Catman** reads each manual page file and creates a "cat" file so that you will not need to wait for pages to be formatted every time a **man** request is made. The files created by **catman** take up another eight megabytes of disk space. Be sure there is enough room in your /usr or /usr/share partition.

Unbundled Sun applications are installed by using the **extract_unbundled** script. Installing non-Sun applications is generally done with instructions that are provided by the vendor of that application. While an application is being installed, a directory or directories containing executables for a specific architecture are created. If the same application is used by two different architectures, it is best to keep the executables in separate directories unless they are specifically configured in one. To do this, create a master share directory on your NFS resource server called /export/local. In it create sub-directories for each of the different architectures such as /export/local/sun4 and /export/local/sun3. (Remember that both Sun-3 and Sun-3x systems can share programs in the /export/local/sun3 directory and Sun-4 and Sun-4c clients share the /export/local/sun4 executables.)

In this example, the NFS server supports three different applications. Each application is used by a different department within the company. The marketing people use a new-fangled package called "whizbang" for their presentations. This has been installed into the /export/whizbang directory. The programmers opt to use a different compiler than provided in the operating system. The new compiler and all of its attendant programs have been installed in the directory /export/newcomp. Finally, the OpenWindows windowing system has been installed on the NFS server in the /export/local/sun[3,4]/openwin directory. OpenWindows is used by both departments.

When the applications have been installed, their directories can be added to the */etc/exports* file to make them available on the network as an NFS resource. Entries in the */etc/exports* file take the format of:

> directory   options

where the directory is the name of the directory you want to export, and the options are any options associated with mounting that directory (see exports(8)). In this example, each directory has been exported with the read-only option. Remote systems that mount any of these directories must specify the read-only option during the **mount** operation. If no specific options are given during a **mount** operation, NFS defaults to read-write.

It is best to export shared resources using the read-only option to ensure their contents from being changed by any clients. If read-only is not specified, directories are exported read-write. Other options that can be included in the */etc/exports* file are shown in Figure 4.3.

Option	Description
ro	# Read-only to all machines.
rw=hostname:hostname2	# Read-only to machines not included in this list.
anon=uid	# Requests from unknown users get the uid specified
	# setting anon=−1 disables anonymous access.
root=hostname:hostname2	# Allow the superuser root to write over the
	# NFS mount only for the machines specified.
access=client:client2	# Allow mount access to specified clients
	# clients can be a hostname or a netgroup.
secure	# Only used with secure networking.

FIGURE 4.3. *Options for exporting an NFS resource.*

The most common option used in the exports file is setting a resource to be read-only, followed by the *access* option, which limits mount access to specific machines. Access is only allowed if the specified host or netgroup is already known in the local YP domain. A more practical use of mount access can be seen in Figure 4.4.

The exports file in Figure 4.4 allows any machine to mount the /usr/share/man, /export/local/sun3, and /export/local/sun4 directories. The last two entries can only be mounted by the specified netgroup. The /export/whizbang directory is restricted to machines in the netgroup "market". The /export/newcomp directory is limited to machines that belong to the "source" netgroup. There is a limit on the number of hostnames that can follow each entry in the */etc/exports* file. This is a big reason to use a netgroup instead of simply listing every machine. Netgroups are also easier to maintain, and can be used to control other activities besides NFS mount access.

After the */etc/exports* file has been edited, execute **exportfs**, which makes the resources available. **Exportfs**, when used with the "-a" option, reads the contents of the */etc/exports* file to determine which directories are to be exported. All entries present are exported. You may also use **exportfs -u** to unexport all or indicated pathnames. Other arguments to **exportfs** include the same options included in the */etc/exports* file. These options can be specified on

```
#
# Exports file for dora
#
/usr/share/man          -ro
/export/local/sun4      -ro
/export/local/sun3      -ro
/export/whizbang        -ro, access=market
/export/newcomp         -ro, access=source
```

FIGURE 4.4. *The /etc/exports file for sunnet.*

a single command line to make directories available without adding them to the */etc/exports* file. Finally, **exportfs** without arguments reports the NFS resources that are currently exported.

After the directories have been exported, the resource server waits idle until a network client is installed. Little maintenance is needed on the resource server, unless new applications arrive, or a new utility is developed. In larger installations, each network may have their own local NFS resource server. Some type of scheme should be devised to propagate the resources throughout the entire installation so that utilities are identical from network to network. This is best done by using a model that is similar to the YP master and slave setup. One of the NFS resource servers "owns" the master files and distributes them to specified slave servers, who then pass the files down to other slaves. This type of constant updating is necessary to insure congruency, and can be accomplished by initiating **rdist** from the master server (see rdist(1)).

4.1.4 Additional NFS Information

NFS is a most valuable tool for all who use it. One of its minor limitations is the way sub-directories of exported resources are handled. When a parent directory is exported, any sub-directory of that parent is mountable, inheriting the same export options as the parent, unless the sub-directory lies on a different disk partition. For example, in Figure 4.5, the /export/newcomp resource has two sub-directories: black and white. The black directory is located on the same disk partition as its parent, /export/newcomp. The /export/newcomp/white directory is a mount point for a separate

```
dora# exportfs
/usr/share/man -ro
/export/local/sun3 -ro
/export/local/sun4 -ro
/export/whizbang -ro, access=market
/export/newcomp -ro, access=source
```

FIGURE 4.5. *Exported resources on the server dora.*

disk partition. When the parent directory, /export/newcomp, is mounted by a remote machine, the contents of /export/newcomp/black are a usable part of the resource while the /export/newcomp/white directory is empty. Sub-directories of NFS resources located on different disk partitions must be exported separately.

Under normal circumstances, the superuser, root, cannot write on NFS mounted resources. You may override this option by including the specific hostname for root access in the /etc/exports file, or by using the "anon=0" option, which allows root access for all. The "anon=0" option should be avoided as it opens a very large security hole.

4.1.5 Print Servers

Print servers are a luxury item. If you can afford to dedicate one machine to do nothing but spool and maintain print jobs then do it, especially if your users print large jobs. Print servers do not have to be machines with local disks, although it is preferred because the network can be unreliable. When installing a print server, remember that it does not need a place for user files such as a home directory. The disk space that would normally be used in this partition can be added to the partition where the spooling occurs. In SunOS 4.0 and higher, all spooling is done in /var. Reserve enough disk space in /var so that many print jobs can be spooled at the same time.

One of the most common printer types used in Sun networks is the LaserWriter(TM). The laserwriter understands the Post-Script™ language developed by Adobe Systems. The standard

SunOS does not include any PostScript tools or programs. You need the TranScript software. The TranScript™ software is an unbundled Sun package that is installed with the **extract_unbundled** utility. During the installation, a number of questions are asked concerning the printer's name and the device to which it is attached so that proper setup can be achieved.

Installing a printer on any UNIX machine entails editing the */etc/printcap* file to describe special characteristics used by that printer. The TranScript installation provides a number of prototype printcap files so that very little editing is necessary. The file you choose depends on the responses given during the execution of **extract_unbundled**. The script takes a snapshot of your existing */etc/printcap* file, and appends the entry of the new printer onto it.

The first line of an entry indicates the printer's primary name and each of its nicknames, separated by the delimiting character "¦", also called a pipe (see Figure 4.6). The default printer name is "lp". Some of the other printer names are needed by certain applications which look for the keywords "lw" or "postscript" in the printcap file when printing jobs. The printer name you choose during the installation of the TranScript software is placed after the second pipe. In this case, the printer name is "printer1". Most printcap options are explained further in the printcap manual page (see printcap(5)).

Printcap entries are seldom changed once the printer is installed. One change that can be made without much risk is moving the printer to a different serial port. If you would like to have the

```
lp¦lw¦printer1¦ps¦postscript¦PostScript:\
    :lp=/dev/ttyb:\
    :af=/var/adm/lw.acct:\
    †tn;=/usr/spool/printer1:\
    :lf=/usr/spool/printer1/printer1-log:\
    :br#9600:rw:fc#0000374:fs#0000003:xc#0:xs#0040040:mx#0:sf:sb:\
    :if=/usr/tran/sparc/lib/psif:\
    :of=/usr/tran/sparc/lib/psof:gf=/usr/tran/sparc/lib/psgf:\
    :nf=/usr/tran/sparc/lib/psnf:tf=/usr/tran/sparc/lib/pstf:\
    :rf=/usr/tran/sparc/lib/psrf:vf=/usr/tran/sparc/lib/psvf:\
    :cf=/usr/tran/sparc/lib/pscf:df=/usr/tran/sparc/lib/psdf:\
```

FIGURE 4.6. *Entry for laserwriter in /etc/printcap.*

option of changing serial ports, change the ":lp=/dev/ttyb" entry to a non-existent device in /dev, such as /dev/lw. The TranScript installation script creates a link to the printer name entered during the installation. If you wanted to change the printer to a different port, just remove the */dev/lw* link, and link it to the different port.

The creation of spooling directories is done during the installation of the TranScript package as well. This is where queued jobs live until they are sent to the printer. Each printer should have its own spooling directory located in the /var/spool directory. The spooling directories must be owned by the user daemon and group daemon if they are to function properly. The directory permissions and ownership are also set during the installation script for devices that are attached to the local machine. You must make the directories and change ownership manually on every remote system that plans on using a non-local printer.

The accounting (:af=) and log file (:lf=) entries specified in the printcap file grow during normal operation of the printer. The */var/spool/<printer>/<printer-log>* file accepts error and status information whenever a print job is executed. The */var/adm/lw.acct* file keeps track of who is using the printer and how many pages were printed during each job. Most of the time, this is not of much use to you unless you want to check error conditions or monitor who is using all the paper. If you do not care to keep accounting information, or error logs, use a symlink between the filename shown in the printcap file, and */dev/null*. All data directed to the file will be thrown away. If the printer begins to develop problems, the symlink can be removed, and the errors re-captured.

If it is necessary to maintain some of these logs, you will need to monitor the growth of the files and determine when to remove the data. Depending on the size of the /var partition and how fast the log files grow you may be able to remove these files once a week or possibly once a month. The files can be removed by **cron** (see Chapter 9 for more help with this command). A crontab entry like:

```
2 1 * * * 0 cp /dev/null /var/spool/<printer>/log
```

will remove the contents of log file on Sunday morning at 1:02 AM.

4.1.5.1 The lpc Utility   The line printer control program, **lpc,** controls the operation of printers listed in the */etc/printcap* file (see lpc(8)). Use this command to start, stop, enable, or disable a printer, or to rearrange the order of the print queue. **Lpc** is not limited to systems with local printers. It is used to start and stop the spooling on remote printers too. The **lpc** utility can be executed by any user for status information. Changes can only be made when executed by root because most of its operation is done on the line printer daemon, **lpd.**

The stop option only stops the printing on the printer, it does not stop the queuing of new jobs on the print server. The start option works in the same mode as the stop. It does not affect the queuing of new jobs. Enable and disable only affect the queuing of print jobs in the spool area. The disable option is used to prevent any further queuing of jobs, and is helpful if you are having a problem with the printer, or if you have a large job in the queue that you need to clear before any other jobs can enter. Always make sure to enable the queue later. There is more information about resolving printer problems in Chapter 8.

There are two way of using **lpc.** You can enter the complete command with options from the command line, or enter a "subshell" by typing **lpc** without arguments. Doing the latter returns the "lpc>" prompt. From this prompt you may directly enter **lpc** commands.

4.1.5.2 Non PostScript Printers   If you choose not to use a PostScript type printer, simply attach the device to one of the serial ports on the back of the system and edit the */etc/printcap* file to inform the system about the new device. The default */etc/printcap* file contains a number of examples for common printer and plotter types that can be used on Sun systems. Creating your own filters for devices not shown here is possible, but not within the scope of this book.

4.1.5.3 Controlling Printer Access   When a printer is installed, access is automatically granted to any other system known on the network. Remote hosts may add known printers to their local */etc/ printcap* file and make the necessary spooling directories. It is up to the print server to grant or deny print requests from remote machines. To deny access for certain hosts, first remove the "+"

```
minerva# lpc
lpc> ?
Commands may be abbreviated.
Commands are:
abort     enable    disable   help   restart   status   topq   ?
clean     exit      down      quit   start     stop     up
lpc>stat lp
lp:
    queuing is enabled
    printing is enabled
    no entries
    no daemon present
```

FIGURE 4.7. *The lpc subshell.*

entry from the */etc/hosts.equiv* file to disallow access for all known systems. Then, add the hostnames of selected systems to a file called */etc/hosts.lpd*. Hostnames included in this file are given access to print. Any time a new host or netgroup is added to the */etc/hosts.lpd* file, you must re-start **lpd.**

Once the print server is installed, little maintenance is needed except for the occasional recycling of daemons and queues, often caused by a novice user sending an unprintable file to the printer. (See Chapter 8 for details on how to correct this situation.)

4.1.6 The Client Server

There is no mystery behind a server of diskless clients. Think of this system as a big NFS server that exports SunOS as its resources instead of applications. Each diskless machine that boots from this server owns a separate root directory and swap file. All other resources are shared.

When adding a client server to your network, assign it an IP address and hostname. Update the YP master's hosts datafile with this information and re-build the maps. Use **suninstall** to install the base SunOS and to create the diskless clients if you wish. Chapter 2 explains how to do this. The next section explains how to add more diskless clients to the server after the system is up and running.

4.1.6.1 Adding Clients Select the diskless machines, noting their kernel and application architecture type. Gather the Ethernet addresses by powering on each system and writing down the six field number displayed in the banner information (such as 8:0:20:20:12:a). Ethernet addresses cannot be edited. They are unique to every machine. Abort the diskless machines, using the L1-A sequence, or turn them off after you have gathered this information. Machines that try to boot over the network before they are configured cause a fair amount of unnecessary network traffic.

Add the list of Ethernet numbers to the */etc/ethers* datafile on the YP master, assigning each a hostname. The hostname must also be assigned an IP address and added to the */etc/hosts* datafile on the YP master. Re-build the YP database on the YP master. In Figure 4.1, the server blue, and its clients, green, orange, and purple have been added to the hosts maps. The corresponding ethers datafile is similar to Figure 4.8 below. It is necessary to add the client machine's IP address, hostname, and Ethernet address before running **setup_client**.

If you are not using YP, you must use a different procedure before running **setup_client**. Instead of adding the hostname and ethers information to the YP database, add the addresses directly to the */etc/hosts* and */etc/ethers* files on the client server, making sure that the hostname and IP address are not already in use.

4.1.6.2 Setup_Client The **setup_client** script adds and deletes diskless clients from a server. There are several command-line arguments given in order for **setup_client** to execute. Most of these arguments remain constant, depending on where the executables reside and the path to the client's root, swap, and home directories. When **setup_client** is invoked with an incorrect number of arguments or without any arguments, a usage message is displayed along with examples of what it expects the command line arguments to be (see sample in Figure 4.9).

Setup_client lives in the /usr/etc/install/script directory, which is not in the default search path. If you are doing a large amount of adding and removing diskless clients, you may want to add this path to the server's */.cshrc* file.

This technique allows you to execute **setup_client** from any current working directory. If you choose not to do this, you must

```
# ethers file for sunnet
#
# diskless clients
#
# blue
#
8:0:20:1:d8:4f  blue
8:0:20:0:30:5e  green
8:0:20:0:30:5f  orange
8:0:20:0:30:5g  purple
```

FIGURE 4.8. *Sample /etc/ethers file.*

change your working directory to /usr/etc/install/script before executing **setup_client,** or type in the full path. Because the command line is already long, the chances of a typing error are increased if the latter method is used.

The first argument to **setup_client** is "add" or "remove", depending on whether you want to install or delete a diskless client. The second argument is the client's hostname. The hostname and IP address must already exist in the local */etc/hosts* file or in the YP hosts map. A message is reported if this information cannot be found.

Can't match key green in map hosts.byname. Reason: no such key in map.
setup_client: can't obtain ip address from YP for 'green'!

If you see this message, update the YP master's hosts datafile and re-build the map. The third argument to **setup_client** is the YP type. The most common YP type for a diskless machine is a YP "client". This allows the diskless machine to use the YP maps within the domain for network and user account information. Do not set up a diskless machine to be a YP master or slave server. The other choice for the YP type argument is "none" or do not use YP. If you are not using the YP database, each client's */etc/hosts* file must be kept current so that it knows about the other machines on your network. This includes resource servers and print servers. In order for your diskless machine to NFS mount the resource server, it must be added to the client's local */etc/hosts* file. Repeating the

```
blue# setup_client -x
setup_client: incorrect number of arguments.
usage:
setup_client op clientname yptype size rootpath swappath homepath execpath kvmpath arch
where:
op                = "add" or "remove"
clientname        = name of the client machine
yptype            = "master" or "slave" or "client" or "none"
size              = size for swap
                    (e.g. 16M or 16m ==> 16777216 bytes
                    16000K or 16000k ==> 16384000 bytes
                    31250B or 31250b ==> 31250 blocks)
rootpath          = parent pathname of client root (e.g. /export/root)
swappath          = parent pathname of client swap (e.g. /export/swap)
homepath          = parent pathname of client home (e.g. /home, remotehost:/home)
execpath          = full pathname of executables
                    (e.g. /export/exec/sun2, /export/exec/sun3, etc)
kvmpath           = full pathname of sub-arch executables
                    (e.g. /export/exec/kvm/sun3x)
arch              = "sun2" or "sun3" or "sun3x"
                    or "sun4" or "sun4c"
```

FIGURE 4.9. *Usage message for setup_client.*

procedure on every diskless machine can become quite impossible on larger networks given that most administrators enjoy precious little free time.

The next command line argument used by **setup_client** sets the size of the client's swap file. A normal client swap file is 16 megabytes. The size can be specified in megabytes, kilobytes, or blocks. The most common choice is megabytes. If you don't know how much memory is installed on your diskless machine, look at the banner information of the machine when it is first powered up. It displays the amount of memory that is seen by the boot PROM. Double that number and enter it as the swap argument, appending an "M" or "m" to indicate the size in megabytes. If a client machine has only four megabytes of memory installed, this argument should be no less than "8m".

The "rootpath" and "swappath" arguments are used first to

create the client's root directory and swap file, then these two arguments are added to the */etc/bootparams* file so that when the client is booting, it may find the path to its root and swap mounts. The normal path to a diskless client's root files is /export/root. The normal path to a diskless client's swap file is /export/swap. You may use alternate directory paths if you find there is not enough disk space remaining for either of these directories.

The homepath argument is the path to the home directory. If another server is to be used for this client's user account, enter it here. If not, just enter /home and the client will use the server's /home/<server> directory. If you want to use a non-standard home directory, such as /home/blue2, *you can enter it here, but it won't work*. To get around this, edit the client's */export/root/ <client>/etc/fstab* file after it has been created and change the server:/home/<server> entry to server:/home/<server>2 before booting the client. After doing this, the client mounts the proper alternate home directory when booting. Be sure that the alternate home directory is exported.

The "execpath" and "kvmpath" arguments are similar to the command-line arguments used in the **setup_exec** script. You may use a different execpath if you installed the system executables in a directory other than /export/exec. Sun-3 and Sun-3x diskless clients normally use the /export/exec/sun3 path, while Sun-4 and Sun-4c architecture clients can share the /export/exec/sun4 path.

The last argument to **setup_client** is the kernel architecture of the client which is one of: sun2, sun3, sun3x, sun4, or sun4c. This argument is used to locate the correct files in the /export/exec/kvm and /tftpboot directories.

When all command line arguments are input correctly, **setup_client** begins making the client. Each client takes approximately four or five minutes to build, depending on the architecture of the server machine. The normal screen output from a successful execution of **setup_client** is similar to Figure 4.10.

In Figure 4.10, the diskless client "green" has been added to the server "blue". "Green" is a SPARCstation 1 machine, Sun-4c architecture type. It has been set up as a YP client in the domain "sunnet", which is the same YP domain as its server. There has been 16 megabytes of swap created for this client. The path to its root files is the normal /export/root. The path to its swap file is also

```
blue# setup_client add green client 16m /export/root /export/swap \
    /home /export/exec/sun4 /export/exec/kvm/sun4c sun4c

Start creating sun4c client "green" :
Creating root for client "green".
Creating 16m bytes of swap for client "green".
Updating /etc/exports to export "green" info.
Completed creating sun4c client "green".
blue#
```

FIGURE 4.10. *Output from a successful setup_client.*

normal, /export/swap. This client uses the home directory path of its server, /home/blue. The path to its executables is /export/exec/ sun4 since the 4c architecture is able to share the same binaries as sun4 machines. The path to the kernel specific files cannot be shared between systems of different kernel architecture. This path should be /export/exec/kvm/sun4c. The final argument specifies that the kernel architecture of the client being added is sun4c.

After the **setup_client** script is complete, there are a number of other steps which must be carried out before the client is able to boot. One of these steps is adding the new boot parameters, created by the addition of the client, into the YP bootparams map.

4.1.6.3 Bootparams If you are using your YP master also as a server of diskless clients, any changed YP datafiles are automatically re-made when **setup_client** is executed. Using one system for both server types is generally frowned upon, but can be done. When adding diskless clients to a server that is not a YP master, other information must be added to the YP database after the client is made. Specifically, the information from the local server's */etc/ bootparams* file needs to be placed in the YP bootparams map, and the map re-made. Login to the YP master as root and add the new boot parameters to the */etc/bootparams* file, for each client created in the YP domain, as in Figure 4.11 below.

Be sure to use the TAB key between the hostname and the root path, and as the first character on the continuation line, or else the entry will fail. When the maps have pushed, verify the entry using **ypmatch** or **ypcat**.

From the diskless client server:

```
blue# cat /etc/bootparams
green    root=blue:/export/root/green \
         swap=blue:/export/swap/green
blue# rlogin harlie -l root
blue# logout
Connection closed

harlie# cat >> /etc/bootparams
green    root=blue:/export/root/green \
         swap=blue:/export/swap/green
 ^D

harlie# cd /var/yp;make bootparams
updated bootparams

pushed bootparams
```

FIGURE 4.11. *Updating the bootparams information.*

Other administrative functions done to new diskless clients
are: editing the */etc/fstab* to add mounts for NFS resource servers,
editing the */etc/printcap* file to add references to any network
printers, and making the spooling directories for those network
printers. If you are using netgroups, you must add this new system
to the */etc/netgroups* file on the YP master as well so that NFS
mounts can occur. A good habit to develop is to create a root
password for each client. This can be done after the system has
booted, or from the server using the "-F" option to the **passwd**
command (see passwd(1)).

Once these steps have been completed, you can boot the
diskless client. A discussion of booting diskless clients follows the
setup_client shell script examples below.

4.1.6.4 Creating Your Own setup_client Script The command line
for **setup_client** can be quite cumbersome. Typing errors seem to
happen quite often with a command line of this length. It is less
frustrating to incorporate a shell script for adding and removing
clients. Most of the arguments to **setup_exec** are constant, except

for the client's name and architecture type. The script in Figure
4.12 takes only two command line arguments: the client name and
the architecture. All other arguments are defaults such as the root
path and swap path. If you have set up non-standard paths to the
client's root and swap directories, they can be put into this script so
that files are put in the correct directories.

Two major assumptions in this script are that all diskless
clients added are YP clients in the same domain as the server
running this script, and that all clients have a 16 megabyte swap
file created as their swap space. The swap file may be too little or
too big depending on resources available. Using the script from
Figure 4.12, the following command adds the Sun-4c client
"green" to the server "blue".

> blue# **add_client** green sun4c

4.1.6.5 Removing Diskless Clients Deleting diskless clients from a
server uses all but one of the same command-line arguments as
adding. Rather than using "add" as the second argument to **setup_
client** use "remove". This will remove the client's /export/root/
<client-name> directory and swap file as well as the tftpboot link.
The normal screen output while removing a diskless client is
shown in Figure 4.13.

After removing the client, delete the entry in the YP master's
/etc/hosts, /etc/ethers, and the */etc/bootparams* files that refer-

---

```
#!/bin/sh
# Script to add a diskless client
#
# Usage must be "add_client [name] [architecture]"
#
if [ $# -ne 2 ]; then
echo "usage:"
echo "$0 hostname architecture"
exit 0
fi
setup_client add $1 client 16m /export/root /export/swap /home \
/export/exec/$2 /export/exec/kvm/$2 $2
```

FIGURE 4.12. A *setup_client* shell script.

blue# **setup_client** remove green client 16m /export/root /export/swap \
/home /export/exec/sun4 /export/exec/sun4c/kvm sun4c

Start removing sun4c client "green":

Removing root for client "green".

Removing swap for client "green".

Completed removing sun4c client "green".

FIGURE 4.13. *Removing a diskless client with* **setup_client.**

ence the client. Then, re-make the YP map so the changed parameters are known by all machines in the YP domain.

Because the command line for removing diskless clients is the same as for adding, a script can be created in the same fashion as **add_client** above. This script combines the features of **add_client** but allows you to add or remove clients without typing such a long command line.

When the script in Figure 4.14 is employed, only three arguments are needed to add or remove a diskless client.

blue# **client_script** add green sun4c

```
#!/bin/sh
# Script to add or remove a diskless client
#
# Usage: " client_script [add,remove] [hostname] [architecture]"
#
if [ $# -ne 3 ]; then
echo "usage:"
echo "$0 [add,remove] hostname architecture"
exit 0
fi
setup_client $1 $2 client 16m /export/root /export/swap /home \
/export/exec/$3 /export/exec/kvm/$3 $3
```

FIGURE 4.14. *Script to add or remove a diskless client.*

or

    blue# **client_script** remove green sun4c

As each client is created, a root directory is made in */export/root* for the client, and a swap file is created in */export/swap*. The */export/root* and */export/swap* directories for the server blue would be similar to Figure 4.15 after the clients green, orange, and purple have been created:

    Always try to keep enough free space on your servers so you can add one more client. Scores of problems can be corrected on diskfull machines by booting them diskless and surveying the disk. Running diskless is preferred to booting and loading from tape because it is faster, and the full SunOS utilities are available to you, rather than only a subset of commands as in MUNIX or MINIROOT. Remember that booting over the network can be a most useful tool when determining system problems.

4.1.6.5 Booting Diskless Clients Booting diskless clients is
straightforward once you understand the process. The first steps in booting a diskless client are making sure the client is properly set up on a server and then powering the system on. Most workstations have a parameter set in their EEPROM to poll for boot devices when first powered up. This parameter can be negated by using some cryptic commands from the PROM monitor, or by using the **eeprom** command after booting SunOS (see eeprom(8s)).

    When the poll flag is on, devices are polled in a non-selectable sequence, beginning with SCSI devices. If a SCSI peripheral is

---

```
blue# ls -l /export/root
drwxr-sr-x  1 root    512           Jul 20 22:51 green
drwxr-sr-x  1 root    512           Jul 20 22:55 orange
drwxr-sr-x  1 root    512           Jul 20 22:59 purple
blue#blue# ls -l /export/swap
-rw------T   1 root    16777216  Jul 20 22:51 green
-rw------T   1 root    16777216  Jul 20 22:55 orange
-rw------T   1 root    16777216  Jul 20 22:59 purple
blue#
```

FIGURE 4.15. *Contents of /export/root and /export/swap.*

attached to the system, a boot is attempted on that device, even if no power is supplied. If the boot fails, the system returns to the monitor prompt. The same situation occurs with other local disk devices, such as xy0, or id000. The polling order checks local disk devices before any network interfaces, unless specifically told otherwise. Clients without attached peripherals end up attempting to boot from the network if not interrupted.

When a system begins to boot over the network, it broadcasts its Ethernet address out the Ethernet port, hoping that another system can translate that address into an IP number. The first machine that translates this address replies back to the booting machine, giving it its IP number. This type of communication is known as RARP, Reverse Address Resolution Protocol. Only the systems running the **rarpd** process can reply to a message initiated in this protocol. The **rarpd** process is automatically started on systems that have a /tftpboot directory. The /tftpboot directory is only present on systems that are servers of diskless clients. The **rarpd** gets its information from the local */etc/ethers* file on the server or from the YP ethers map. If there is no ethers or hosts entry for the booting machine, a message similar to Figure 4.16 is displayed on the console of the diskless machine when attempting to boot.

If you see this message, check the Ethernet cable connection of the booting system, or the */etc/ethers* and */etc/hosts* entry on the YP master. This message says that the client is broadcasting its Ethernet address, but is getting no replies. Once the Ethernet address has been found and translated, the IP number is used to obtain a boot block. The boot block for each diskless client is stored in the server's /tftpboot directory. A different boot file is necessary for each architecture that is supported on the diskless client server. When diskless clients are added to a server, a symbolic link is made to the boot file of the architecture that is speci-

---

```
Requesting Internet Address for 8:0:20:0:12:3
Requesting Internet Address for 8:0:20:0:12:3
Requesting Internet Address for 8:0:20:0:12:3
```

FIGURE 4.16. *Diskless boot failure message.*

fied in **setup_client.** The link is named the hexadecimal representation of the client's IP address. The client "green" has an IP address of 192.9.201.3. This address converted to hexadecimal is C009C903. The server's /tftpboot directory is shown in Figure 4.17. The figure illustrates how the symbolic link is used to point at the correct architecture boot file, using C009C903 as part of the link name. The other part of the link name is the kernel architecture of the client. If more than one diskless machine were configured to this server, similar links would be resident in this directory, also pointing to the client's architecture boot file.

When a match to a client's request is found in this directory, the server contacts the TFTP daemon, **tftpd,** and transfers the boot file to the client. After the client receives the boot program, it begins looking for a program to load, typically */vmunix,* which lives in the /export/root/<client> directory. Before the client can locate its root directory path, another RARP broadcast is done to obtain its hostname. Then, the hostname is used as a key to obtain the server name and the full pathname to the root directory from the **bootparamd** daemon. Once the server and pathname are found, the root directory is mounted and */vmunix* is read and loaded.

After the kernel has been loaded, some housekeeping is done, device drivers are loaded and buffers are allocated. The swap daemon, swapper, is started so that processes can be swapped in and out. Next */etc/init* is started, which in turn executes the */etc/rc* scripts.

The first rc script to execute is */etc/rc.boot.* It begins by establishing a search path for commands that are executed within this

```
lrwxrwxrwx  1 root        10  Apr 29  11:13  C009C903.SUN4C ->boot.sun4c
-rwxr-xr-x  1 root    179568  Apr 29  1989   boot.sun4
-rwxr-xr-x  1 root    121352  Apr 26  14:02  boot.sun4c
lrwxrwxrwx  1 root         1  Apr 29  1989   tftpboot -> .
-rwxr-xr-x  1 root     43240  Apr 29  1989   tpboot.sun4
-rwxr-xr-x  1 root     42928  Apr 26  14:02  tpboot.sun4c
```

FIGURE 4.17 *A client's tftpboot link.*

script, then setting the hostname of the system. Next, the appropriate Ethernet device is turned on using the **ifconfig** command with the hostname as an argument. This seems inappropriate on diskless machines since the system has been using the Ethernet interface to get this far. It is necessary because the protocols used to obtain the hostname and IP address, could not save the data for use by the kernel.

Finally, rc.boot checks to see if a filesystem check should be run. Normally, on a diskfull system, filesystem checks are executed on all filesystems listed in the */etc/fstab* file. Filesystem checks are never done from diskless clients. Maintaining filesystem consistency is the responsibility of the system that mounts the disk device. Filesystem integrity is maintained by the server system. Since all mounts on diskless clients are of the NFS type, no filesystem checking is done. The boot process on diskfull and diskless machines is similar after this point except for the way filesystems are mounted. The call to mount local filesystems is done from the */etc/rc* script, which is executed after */etc/rc.boot*, once the filesystems have been given a clean bill of health. The call to mount all NFS type filesystems is done in */etc/rc.local*, which is started by the */etc/rc* script. This is done to insure that certain network daemons, such as **portmap, in.routed,** and **ypbind,** are started before the **mount** -vat nfs line is executed. Systems are not network functional until the network daemons have been successfully started. The */etc/rc.local* script also sets the YP domain name which must be done before **ypbind** is started.

You can compare how mounting is done between diskless and diskfull machines by simply viewing the filesystem table, */etc/fstab*, residing on every system. When a system is diskfull, the */etc/fstab* file contains entries for mounts that are of type 4.2 (local mounts). The mount entries have a local disk device, accessed through an entry in the /dev directory; a mount point, which is a directory that the disk partition is mounted on; which type of mount it is; the mount options for that partition; the interval between dumps; and the order in which the **fsck** is run during boot time. The */etc/fstab* from a standalone system may be similar to Figure 4.18.

The disk partition sd0a is mounted on /. It is a 4.2 mount, with

/dev/sd0a	/	4.2 rw 1 1
/dev/sd0f	/home	4.2 rw 1 4
/dev/sd0g	/usr	4.2 rw 1 2
/dev/sd0h	/var	4.2 rw 1 3

FIGURE 4.18. *Diskfull /etc/fstab file.*

read-write permissions. The dump interval is one and it is the first filesystem checked by **fsck** when booting. The disk partition /dev/ sd0f is mounted on the directory */home*. It also is a 4.2 mount, with read write permissions, and a dump interval of 1. This disk parti- tion is the fourth filesystem to be checked. The third and fourth entries in this file follow the same pattern, the major difference being the device used, the mount point, and the pass in which **fsck** is executed.

The fstab of a diskless client is similar to the diskfull system except there are no local devices to mount. Instead these are NFS mounts. The local device/partition entry is replaced by the syntax <server:mount path> as in Figure 4.19.

The diskless client server "blue" holds the root files for the client "green" in the /export/root/green path. This directory is mounted on the client's / directory. It is an NFS type mount, with read and write permissions. The dump interval is zero, because dumps are done on the server. The **fsck** pass is zero, since consis- tency checking is also done on the server.

The server "blue" also contains the /usr files for this client in the directory /export/exec/sun4. They are NFS mounted on the client's /usr directory. The mount for /usr is a read-only mount. It is done this way to prevent diskless clients from modifying the /usr files on the server since /usr may be shared by multiple clients. If this were a homogeneous server, the /export/exec/sun4 directory would be a symbolic link to the server's /usr directory.

The /usr/kvm mount is a directory that contains the kernel files specific to that particular CPU. This directory is where the configuration files are kept when you want to build a new kernel. Other kernel-specific files and programs reside here such as **ps**,

blue:/export/root/green	/ nfs rw 0 0
blue:/export/exec/sun4	/usr nfs ro 0 0
blue:/export/exec/kvm/sun4c	/usr/kvm nfs ro 0 0
blue:/home/blue	/home/blue nfs rw 0 0

FIGURE 4.19. *Diskless /etc/fstab file.*

and **pstat.** The path for these files on the server is in the /export/exec/kvm/sun4c directory.

After all mounts have occurred, a number of other system and network daemons are started such as **biod,** the block I/O daemon, which allows I/O to NFS mounted filesystems. Next, checking is done for certain non-standard devices so that special daemons related to those devices can be started. An example of one non-standard daemon is the **dbconfig** command which is started if the file */dev/dialbox* exists. The dialbox is a device that can be attached to a serial port and allows the manipulation of graphical images.

After checking for special devices some local daemons are started such as **sendmail, rpc.statd,** and **rpc.lockd.** The **sendmail** daemon is for electronic mail, while **rpc.statd** and **rpc.lockd** interact to provide crash and recovery services for NFS.

Once the */etc/rc.local* script is finished, the remaining lines in */etc/rc* are executed. Some of these lines start standard daemons, such as */usr/lib/lpd,* and re-initialize the **uucp** facility, when configured. After the rc scripts are complete, the login prompt is displayed. The system has finished booting and is waiting for a user to login.

4.1.7 Home Directories

In the Sun environment, each user has a login account. User accounts are assigned a home directory in the YP passwd map. A home directory is the location in the filesystem hierarchy where a user is placed upon a successful login to their account. The Sun convention is that user accounts are placed in the /home/<hostname>/<login> directory path. Because a large amount of user accounts are mounted by diskless client machines, the path to each home directory includes the server name. Diskless clients from the machine "blue" NFS mount blue's /home/blue directory. This naming convention is used so that administrators know exactly where a home directory is located. If all diskless clients were to use the convention of /home/(user account), it would be difficult to determine where the user account was without looking in the local *etc/fstab* file for a mount path to a remote machine. It also complicates mounting of home directories from different servers at the same time.

There are a number of different ways in which user accounts can be administered. One idea is to have a machine or two dedicated to nothing but serving user accounts. A home directory server is a great idea, but it has a few drawbacks. It allows for a single point of failure for every user whose account lives on this server. If the home directory server develops a problem and goes down, users mounting it won't be able to access their files. That can mean many down user accounts. Another problem with a single home directory server is that the network traffic in and out of this machine can become quite intense, possibly slowing performance for all.

A positive aspect of a home directory server is knowing that user account files are always located on one or two machines. Instead of backing up ten machines with five users each day, you only need to backup one machine with all fifty users on it.

The most common convention concerning home directories is to set up the diskless client server to contain the home directory accounts for each system it serves. This technique is preferred although it is more bothersome in the backup department. Two hundred users may be affected during a home directory system malfunction. A maximum of 20 are affected using the common convention.

4.1.7.1 Adding New Accounts

A number of steps are involved in adding user accounts. First, a login entry must be created in the password file either on the local machine or the YP master server. Account names cannot be longer than eight characters and must be unique. Next, the home directory must be created on the server or local machine. Finally, prototype login files that are executed upon login are copied to the new home directory. Some file permissions and ownerships need adjusting so that other users are not able to read the new account's files.

Before adding a new account, it is a common practice to have the new user provide some necessary information such as their preferred login name, their full name, and some kind of unique number to be used as a user identification number, or uid. Some naming convention is necessary so that accounts that currently exist either in the local domain or in another YP domain are not duplicated.

Other files can be set up to provide all users with a common starting point. Sun provides prototype login initialization files in the /usr/lib directory. The files needed depend on the login shell. Accounts using the **csh** execute the *.cshrc* and *.login* files each time a login occurs. In /usr/lib, these files are named *Login* and *Cshrc*. In the Bourne shell, **sh,** the *.profile* file is read when a login occurs. A prototype *.profile* file is not provided in /usr/lib, however. Other prototype files that may be of interest to you are the *Mailrc* which sets up local parameters for electronic mail, and *Exrc*, used to initialize some common editor parameters.

Choose the prototype files needed and copy them to a common directory such as /home/<server-name>/proto. Be sure to change the filenames, such as *Login* to *.login*, and *Cshrc* to *.cshrc*, and so on. You may edit cach file to better suit your environment. When adding new user accounts, copy the files to each new home directory. This procedure insures a common starting point for all users.

When working with a large number of user accounts, you must have some way of verifying that the new account name does not conflict with any existing accounts. It is in these instances that the YP database becomes most useful. A number of YP commands can be used to verify the existence or non-existence of user accounts and user ID's. Before adding a new user, use the **ypcat** or **ypmatch** as shown in Figure 4.20 to check for any occurrences of the new account that you wish to add.

If the response to **ypmatch** is similar to that of Figure 4.20, the username is not known and can be used. The next step is to locate a unique user identification number (uid). The easiest way to find an unused uid is to use the next sequential number available from the

```
harlie# ypmatch laura passwd
Can't match key laura in map passwd.byname.
Reason: no such key in map.

harlie# ypcat passwd | grep 103
harlie#
```

FIGURE 4.20. *Using **ypmatch** and **ypcat** before adding account.*

YP master's password file. If the last user account added owns uid 102, then the next account can use number 103. If your password file is not sorted by sequential uid, then other steps can be taken. At your earliest convenience, arrange the password file in sequential order. Use the following command to list the all uid's in ascending order:

> **awk** -F: '{print $3}' /etc/passwd | **sort** -n

Another way to check for a free uid is using the **ypcat** command as in Figure 4.20. If no match is found, the prompt returns without a message, indicating uid number 103 is not currently used in the domain. The technique of selecting random user identification numbers should be avoided.

A group identification number (gid) must also be assigned for each user account. Groups are listed in the */etc/group* file. You may add your own group by making an entry in this file and using the new entry as the gid in the password file.

4.1.7.2 Editing the Password File

Once you have the user's login name, uid, and gid, you can edit the YP password datafile. Each account entry contains seven fields separated by a single colon, ":", as in the line below.

> login:encrypted password:uid:gid:description:home directory:login shell

You must supply the information needed in each of these fields. The encrypted password field should be left empty as it is set up using the **yppasswd** command. The gid field should exist in the */etc/group* file. The account description is usually the user's full name. **Sendmail** uses this field when sending out mail to identify the sender. The home directory path is where the user is placed upon a successful login, and the login shell is the program that should be run once the login has completed. The login shell most often used on Sun systems is the **csh,** which resides in /bin. Another shell sometimes used is the Bourne shell, **sh.**

The example below creates the user account "laura", assigning the uid 103 and a gid of 10. Laura's home directory is on the server "blue" and will be using the **csh** login shell. Add the following line to the YP master's /etc/passwd file, and re-make the database.

laura::103:10:Laura's Davis:/home/blue/laura:/bin/csh

After the YP database is updated, create laura's home directory on the server blue, in the /home/blue directory as shown in Figure 4.21. This procedure must be done as root.

The first two lines in Figure 4.21 change the working directory to /home and make the directory laura. In the third line, the default initialization files are copied from the directory /home/blue/proto to the new account, as explained above. The remaining commands in Figure 4.21 change the ownership and group status for the new account, laura. A password should be created for this account as well. This is done using the **yppasswd** command, adding the new account as an argument.

A standard password convention should be employed when adding users for the first time. Their last name seems to work well in most situations. Instructions should be supplied to each new user, explaining how to login and change their password once they login to their account.

If you are using YP, then the **yppasswd** command should be

```
blue# cd /home/blue
blue# mkdir laura
blue# cp /home/blue/proto/.[clm]* laura
blue# chown -R laura laura
blue# chgrp -R staff laura
```

FIGURE 4.21. *Making a home directory.*

used to add a password to the new account. Remember, before any user can successfully execute the **yppasswd** command, the YP master server must be running **rpc.yppasswdd** which is not started by default. A procedure to start this daemon is supplied in Chapter 2.

Now, logging in to the machine "purple" as laura places you in the /home/blue/laura directory, completing the setup. You may wish to login as the new user to test the new account before informing the user.

4.1.7.3 Non-YP Accounts

Assume that you are not using the YP database. Each machine that uses a non-YP account must have its local */etc/passwd* file edited. The **vipw** utility was created for this purpose (see vipw(8)). Only root, the superuser, has the privilege of editing the passwd file. In this example, the passwd file on the machine "purple" will be edited. Purple is a newly created diskless client of the server "blue".

The client passwd file can be changed in two different places. You can edit the server's */export/root/purple/etc/passwd* file before purple is booted, or you may edit the passwd file on the diskless client using the **vipw** command. **Vipw** cannot be used on the server's /export/root/<client>/etc directory because it defaults to the */etc/passwd* file. You should also add the user account to the server's */etc/passwd* file so that proper file ownership is maintained.

Figure 4.22 illustrates the */etc/passwd* file from a fresh installation. The root login appears first. Next are a number of accounts needed by the system to function properly. The nobody account is used by NFS when the system cannot obtain a password entry for your current uid. The daemon, sys, bin, uucp, news, ingres, audit, and sync accounts are all used by the local system. Various files and daemons are owned by some of these accounts so they must be there. It is best to leave the standard accounts alone in the passwd file.

The last line in a generic */etc/passwd* file begins with the character "+". This entry is for the YP database. When a login is attempted on a machine with this line in the */etc/passwd* file, the local passwd file is scanned first. If a match is found, the login parameters from the local file are used. If no match is found, the

```
purple# vipw
root::0:1:Operator:/:/bin/csh
nobody:*:-2:-2::/:
daemon:*:1:1::/:
sys:*:2:2::/:/bin/csh
bin:*:3:3::/bin:
uucp:*:4:8::/var/spool/uucppublic:
news:*:6:6::/var/spool/news:/bin/csh
ingres:*:7:7::/usr/ingres:/bin/csh
audit:*:9:9::/etc/security/audit:/bin/csh
sync::1:1::/:/bin/sync
+:
```

FIGURE 4.22. *Generic* /etc/passwd *file.*

"+" sign instructs login to search the YP passwd map for such an entry.

4.1.8 Using a Home Directory Server

A home directory server is similar to the NFS resource server in that it supplies disk space over the network to its clients. The difference is that the directories are mounted with write permission. These directories need the most attention when performing backups.

Install a home directory server as you would any NFS resource server, leaving some partitions empty. It is best to balance the load between disks if at all possible. Make two or three partitions for home directories using a naming scheme such as /home/<server1>, /home/<server2>, and /home/<server3>.

When the installation is complete several options are available for exporting the home directories. You can export the whole parent directory, /home, thereby granting mount access to any machines. You can create or use an existing netgroup to limit mount access to a selected number of machines. This setup works well if the marketing people mount the same home directory server. Establish their home directories under a common file-system and export the parent to the marketing netgroup. Remember, filesystems attached on an exported directory are not usable unless specifically exported themselves.

Another option is to grant mount access on a per-machine basis. If the user "laura" always uses the workstation "green", you can export laura's home directory specifically to the machine green. This arrangement ensures that no other system can mount laura's home directory. If laura wanted to use a different workstation, other than green, you would have to add the machine to the */etc/exports* file and run **exportfs** again.

A sample */etc/exports* file using each of these options may be similar to Figure 4.23. Home directories living under /home/blue1 can be mounted by any machine. The home directories resident under /home/blue2 are only mountable by the marketing netgroup. The home directory /home/green/laura can only be mounted by the machine green.

4.2 Workstation Administration

Workstation administration can be defined as the administrative steps taken to configure a workstation into a network. As noted earlier, each workstation can be diskfull, diskless, or dataless. Configuring a diskless system to boot from a server can be considered workstation administration, but administrative actions are done on the server, not on the client. The ideas expressed over the next few pages will deal solely with procedures that apply to workstations, usually after it has booted SunOS. These steps may involve editing files, creating directories, and/or starting background processes or daemons.

One of the most common types of administration done to workstations is the setup of NFS mounts. In the previous pages, you have learned how to set up the NFS resource server. Now you

```
#
# Exports file for home directory server blue
#
/home/blue1
/home/blue2              -access=+@marketing
/home/blue/laura        -access=green
```

FIGURE 4.23. *Possible export options for home directories.*

will be shown how to use the resource server from the client's point of view. The procedure for setting up NFS mounts is exactly the same for both diskless and diskfull systems. The major rule governing NFS mounts states that you cannot mount a resource from a machine that is already mounting that resource from another system. Say, for example, the server blue was mounting the manual pages from the resource server dora. A client of blue also wishes to use the manual pages and tries to mount the resource from blue. The mount fails, giving the message: "too many levels of indirection". *Clients can only NFS mount resources from the machine where the resource actually lives.* In this case, resources can only be mounted from dora.

You can mount a resource from the command line to be used temporarily, or automatically mount resources by adding entries in the */etc/fstab* file. With the latter approach, NFS mounts occur during the execution of the rc scripts at boot time.

Before any NFS resources can be mounted, you must know several details; the hostname of the server, the complete path to the resource, any export restrictions the resource may have, and the mount point to which this resource will be attached on the local system. The hostname of the resource server may be hard to obtain without a naming convention which can be done by using nick-names in the YP hosts file. When this arrangement is used, a resource server may have the host nickname of "nfs_server". The complete path to the resource and export options can be obtained by using the **showmount** command. You can execute **showmount** from your local machine using the server hostname as an argu-ment. This also verifies that the network is working properly by using a remote procedure call on the NFS server.

The server of diskless clients is a good example of how NFS resources are used. The resources offered on this server are operat-ing system files which demonstrate the versatility of NFS. To see what is actually exported on a diskless client server, use the **show-mount** command, adding the diskless server's hostname as an argument.

Figure 4.24 shows the resources offered by the server blue. The /usr, /home, /export/exec/sun4, and /export/exec/kvm/sun4c directories are all accessible by everyone which means that any other hostname that this system knows about will be allowed to

```
purple# showmount -e blue
export list for blue:
/usr                      (everyone)
/home                     (everyone)
/export/exec/sun4         (everyone)
/export/exec/kvm/sun4c    (everyone)
/export/root/green        green
/export/swap/green        green
/export/root/purple       purple
/export/swap/purple       purple
```

FIGURE 4.24. *Demonstrating showmount.*

mount these directories. The root and swap directories exported for each client are only mountable by those clients. In a similar fashion, the exported resources of the NFS resource server "dora" can also be obtained by using **showmount.**

Figure 4.25 shows the five resources offered by dora: the on-line manual pages, two architecture-specific directories, sun3 and sun4, and two applications directories. To NFS mount the manual pages, enter the command below as root:

purple# **mount** -o ro dora:/usr/share/man /usr/share/man

The command line breaks down as follows: **mount** is the command that attaches the named directory to the local mount point, "-o ro" is the option to mount the directory read-only, and "dora:/usr/share/man" is the complete path to the resource in the format:

server:<pathname-to-resource>

```
purple# showmount -e dora
export list for dora:
/usr/share/man        (everyone)
/export/local/sun3    (everyone)
/export/local/sun4    (everyone)
/export/whizbang      market
/export/newcomp       source
```

FIGURE 4.25. *Listing NFS resources on the server dora.*

The last argument is called the mount point. This is a directory where the NFS resource is attached to your system. As with any mount, both the path to the resource and the mount point must already exist or the mount will fail. Files residing in a directory where a mount occurs are hidden until the mount is detached. In the example above, it was not necessary to make a mount point because the directory /usr/share/man is created during **suninstall.** The directory /usr/local is also created by default on all Sun machines to be used as the mount point for NFS resources. The directories exported by the resource server dora are meant to correspond with applications used by workstations. The machines in the marketing netgroup NFS mount the whizbang directory, while the programmers mount the newcomp directory.

4.2.1 Automatic NFS Mounting

Automatic NFS mounts are possible by adding an entry to the /etc/fstab file. NFS mount entries have much the same format as local mount entries. The major differences involve the NFS server and the full path to the resource. There are also many more options available to NFS type mounts mostly because of the network.

There are two types of NFS mounts, the hard mount and the soft mount. Hard mounts should be used if writing is done, or if the NFS resource is critical to the operation of the machine. Diskless clients hard mount their NFS resources because the directories connected are part of the operating system. When a machine hard mounts an NFS resource, the system pauses if the server goes down, and waits until the server is back up again before resuming. Hard mounts should be used sparingly, but cannot be avoided in some cases. Usually, any NFS mounted directory that is writable should be hard mounted. Home directories are another example of hard mounts.

Resources that are less critical should be soft mounted. NFS resources which are soft mounted complain if the server goes down, but do not stop the processing of jobs on the local machine, especially if they are mounted with the "intr" option.

Add the resources you want to mount automatically each time the system boots to the /etc/fstab file of the client machine. The resource(s) are mounted during the execution of commands in the */etc/rc.local* script, provided the resource has been exported, the mount point has been created, and the network is functional.

Setting up the diskless machine green to automatically mount resources from dora involves adding the following lines to green's */etc/fstab* file. This is accomplished by logging into the machine green as root to edit */etc/fstab*, or by logging into the server blue and editing the */export/root/green/etc/fstab* file. The same file is accessed using either method. Add the two lines below:

```
dora:/export/local/sun4     /usr/local nfs ro,soft,bg,intr 0 0
dora:/export/whizbang       /usr/whizbang nfs ro,soft,bg,intr 0 0
```

Be sure to select the correct executable path from the server. If green were a Sun-3 or Sun-3x machine, the /export/local/sun3 directory would be used. In this example, the system green is a Sun-4c machine, so the /export/local/sun4 resource is mounted.

The other automatic mount added to green's fstab file is the entry for the whizbang application, located in dora's /export/ whizbang directory. A mount point must be created on green to attach this resource. This is an excellent example to demonstrate exactly where to make mount points for diskless clients.

When diskless machines mount an NFS resource to a non-standard directory under /usr, as in /usr/whizbang, the mount point must be created on the server. Diskless machines do not have write access to their /usr directory. Mount points for clients of the same application architecture are made in the server's /usr directory. Mount points for diskless clients of unlike architecture must be created in the server's /export/exec/<arch> directory. After the directory is created, all clients have the mount point available. Each client must individually mount the resource, even if it is already mounted by the server. Diskless clients see resources mounted by their server as an empty directory.

4.2.2 Using Remote Printers

Adding a remote printer to network clients is simple. Each system that wishes to use any printer must have an entry in their own */etc/printcap* file, as well as the necessary spooling directories. Every machine must also have a hostname that is known by the print server, and have access to the print services through the server's */etc/hosts.lpd* or */etc/hosts.equiv* file. To add the services of a remote printer to any machine, study Figures 4.26 and 4.27. The lines that begin with a pound sign are comments.

The first un-commented line in Figure 4.26 indicates that the default line printer, lp, is also known on the local system as printer1. This printer is located on the remote machine minerva, "rm = minerva". The remote name printer on the remote machine is printer1, "rp = printer1". The spooling directory is the local /var/spool/printer1 directory. The log file for printer1 is */dev/null*, in other words, do not keep a log. After the printcap entry is complete, the spooling directory is made as in Figure 4.27.

After the printcap entry and spooling directories have been made, verify the new entry by using **lpq.** If you are calling the new printer lp, then **lpq** needs no arguments. If you have called it something other than lp, or it is a second or third printer on the system, use **lpq** -P<printer-name>. The response returned should be a list of queued jobs, or "no entries", meaning there are no jobs spooled. If the response to **lpq** is "your machine does not have lpd access", then make sure the */etc/hosts.lpd* file on the print server contains your machine name. You may need to recycle the line printer daemon on the print server when the contents of */etc/ hosts.lpd* or */etc/hosts.equiv* is changed. Chapter 8 has a section dedicated to recycling printer daemons.

Use the script in Figure 4.28 to add a remote printer to any networked client. This is a very basic script, but will install the necessary printcap entry and create the spooling directory to make the printer functional.

```
# /etc/printcap file for client "green"
# Entry for printer1
#
lp! printer1:\
    :lp=:\
    :rm=minerva:\
    :rp=printer1:\
    :sd=/var/spool/printer1:\
    :lf=/dev/null:
```

FIGURE 4.26. *Adding a remote printer to the* /etc/printcap *file.*

```
dora # mkdir /var/spool/printer1
dora # chown daemon /var/spool/printer1
dora # chgrp daemon /var/spool/printer1
```

FIGURE 4.27. *Creating the spooling directory.*

4.2.3 Electronic Mail

Electronic mail or email is a means of communicating to users in the local network, business community, or to other UNIX users around the world. In its most basic form, email operates on valid user accounts that are in the local password file, or in the YP password map. Email is only delivered to systems where a home directory is available unless an alias is established to forward the mail to another system or to redirect the mail to a file.

When email is addressed to a user that is not found in the passwd file or YP map, the local */etc/aliases* file is searched. If no matches were found, the YP aliases map is checked and the mail is either sent to that user or is returned to the sender by the mailer-daemon.

The **sendmail** daemon is responsible for sending and receiving email. It is started during the execution of the */etc/rc.local* file at boot time on Sun systems. This daemon monitors incoming and outgoing mail requests that are in the Simple Mail Transfer Protocol, SMTP format. This format, when used with no arguments, reads the standard input until an end of file (EOF) marker is found, such as <Control-D>, or until a line beginning with a single period is entered.

In small networks, mail can be passed around between machines without major problems providing all user accounts are known by each machine sending and receiving mail. Making sure all user accounts are known is best handled with YP in the YP password map. Once the YP aliases map is set up, mailing to a specific user at a specific machine is no longer necessary. When a master alias file is maintained, only a username is required when sending mail. The username can be aliased to always receive mail at one hostname.

```
#!/bin/sh
#
# This script adds a printer to your printcap
# and makes all the necessary spooling directories.
# Invoke as follows:
#
# # prt.script <printer-name> <printserver>
#
# This script must be run as root!
#
#
if [$# -ne 2]; then
echo "usage:"
echo "$0 printer printserver"
exit 0
fi
echo "$1:\
    :lp=:\
    :rm=$2:\
    :rp=$1:\
    :sd=/var/spool/$1:\
    :lf=/var/spool/$1/log:" >> /etc/printcap

mkdir /var/spool/$1;/usr/etc/chown daemon /var/spool/$1
/usr/bin/chgrp daemon /var/spool/$1
touch /var/spool/$1/log
```

FIGURE 4.28. *A shell script to add remote printers.*

4.2.4 Debugging Mail Problems

One way to resolve problems with electronic mail is by using the **mconnect** command. When invoked with no arguments, **mconnect** opens a connection on the local host that expects to speak the Simple Mail Transfer Protocol, (SMTP). You may connect to a remote host using the hostname of the machine as an argument to **mconnect** as in Figure 4.29.

Use **mconnect** to verify that **sendmail** is working on a local level. When you are sure that the local daemons are working correctly, start back-tracking to where the problem was found. Routing problems are the most prevalent in this case.

Another way of tracking down mail problems is by using the /usr/ucb/mail -v option. When **mail** is invoked this way, a verbose output is displayed as each connection is made.

If mail is not getting to a particular machine, you should first try to **ping** the machine. **Ping** simply sees if the system is up and running on the network. If no answer is received, find out if the remote system is booted. If the **ping** worked and the problem persists, **mconnect** to the machine to make sure that **sendmail** is running. Then you may wish to send some test mail using the -v option to **mail** to verify that mail is getting routed there.

4.2.5 Moving Machines Around

Most administrators are faced with moving groups of users and/or systems between sites or networks at some point in their careers. If you have ever done this you know it is no easy task. Moving one or two users to a different network is no problem, especially if their systems are standalone machines. Moving hundreds of systems around can be enough trouble to cause many hours of lost sleep or, even better, an early retirement.

There are a few precautionary steps that can be taken to plan for moves before they are even a twinkle in a VP's eye. Some

```
# mconnect green
connecting to host green (192.9.201.3), port 25
connection open
220 green.sunnet Sendmail 4.0/SMI-4.0 ready at Mon, 24 Jul 89 02:22:52 PDT
HELP
214-Commands:
214-  HELO   MAIL   RCPT   DATA   RSET
214-  NOOP   QUIT   HELP   VRFY   EXPN
214-For more info use "HELP <topic>".
214-smtp
214-To report bugs in the implementation contact Sun Microsystems
214-Technical Support.
214-For local information contact postmaster at this site.
214 End of HELP info
```

FIGURE 4.29. *Using mconnect.*

simple guidelines can save you from working late before the move occurs.

1. Keep systems and accounts that belong to the same workgroup within the same group of servers. When possible, designate one or two servers as a departmental server. Only add clients from that specific department.

2. Do not add the operating system support for a diskless machine to one server, and then use another server for a home directory. The most time consuming part in preparation of a move is copying home directories around. Some users can astound you with the amount of data stored in their home directories.

The major problems with moving concerns diskless machines. More often than not, the diskless machines currently configured on one server have separate destinations. This can cause quite a bit of juggling. It would be nice to have a few extra servers at your disposal to move selected clients onto so that the server and all of its clients can be moved together. However, this is usually not the case. You should only have to move a client once if planned correctly. This can soon turn into a big puzzle as the challenge becomes moving the least number of files as possible.

The first step should be to determine which server the client is on, how much disk space they are currently using, and where you should move them. Make sure that the home directory for the user fits before you start the move process.

Select the server with the highest number of clients moving to destination A as the server going to A. Also decide which servers are staying by determining what their clients are doing. If disk space for at least one client exists on every server, then you are home-free.

4.2.5.1 Moving Root Directory Files

Once you have decided who is moving where, a plan of action can be taken. For diskless machines, certain files must be modified to allow proper function on the new network. Therefore, you cannot copy the whole root directory to the new server. The contents of the */etc/fstab* file must change as the server changes since each server is included in the mount path. The contents of other files may need to change if the IP address and YP domain name are different.

The best procedure would employ a shell script to search each diskless machine's root directory for certain files and copy them to their home directory.

Then, the whole home directory can be copied across the network, or archived to tape. The same script could then be used to extract the root files from the home directory, and place them in the client's new root directory.

The steps taken when moving diskless machines from one network to another are listed below.

1. Halt the diskless machine.
2. Copy the needed root files to the user's home directory.
3. Copy the home directory over the network to its new destination.
4. Run **setup_client** on the new server.
5. Edit the new client's root files, using the saved files as reference.
6. Boot the diskless machine from the new server.

The root files that need to be saved may be all or some of the following:

/etc/fstab
/etc/passwd
/etc/licenses
/etc/aliases
/etc/printcap
/var/spool/mail/<login>

4.2.5.2 Moving Home Directories Moving home directories from one server to the next is quite painless given enough network bandwidth. Large data transfers over the net should not be done during periods of high activity.

The combination of **rsh** and **cpio** allows you to replicate a user's home directory on a different machine. **Cpio** in this case works much better that **rcp** and **tar** since user and group ownership can be maintained. **Cpio** also preserves any hard or symbolic links which may be present, as well as retaining modification times on all files.

To move the user account "tims" from the server baltic to the server blue you need to first verify the size of the user directory and then see if it can fit on the new server. Use the **du** utility to check directory and file sizes. Allow root access on baltic for the machine blue since this is where the remote command is instigated. This is done by adding the hostname blue to baltic's */.rhosts* file. When this is accomplished, root can login to baltic without entering a password. Run the two commands below to replicate the user account "tims".

```
blue# cd /home/blue
blue# rsh baltic "cd /home/baltic;find tims -print ¦ cpio -o' ¦ cpio
-ildumv
```

If you prefer to use **tar** instead of **cpio,** use this command line to copy a home directory over the net:

```
blue# rsh baltic "cd /home/baltic;tar -cf - tims" ¦ tar xfBp -
```

4.3 Wrap-Up

In conclusion, Sun administrators must be adaptive to almost any situation. There are certainly more problems encountered than can be discussed in this forum. Hopefully, a solid basis can be formed from the examples discussed earlier. Each piece of the administrative puzzle is connected to another. Always understand how to return any changes made to their original configuration before a change is attempted.

Basic Networking

5

A network is a collection of two or more systems connected together by a common wire. The systems connected to this wire can transfer data, share files, and run programs among each other. Programs executed on remote systems act as if they were running locally. There are many layers and protocols involved in networking. It is not the intent of this book to investigate what is occurring on the wire, but to show some of the basic commands necessary to maintain a network from the administrator's view.

Much of Sun administration deals with logins to a remote system, and changing or editing a file or group of files to allow communication between machines. Of course, no communication can exist if the systems are not connected properly to the common wire. The next section briefly explains the hardware necessary to allow connectivity among all machines in your network. The way explained here is not the only way, but has been found to be the easiest to debug when problems arise.

A network number is by no means architecture, vendor, or even network specific. The network could be Ethernet, token-ring, or FDDI. Each machine or node that is connected to a network must have a unique name and address regardless of its make or model.

5.1 Network Hardware

Every Sun system has included some form of network interface in its design. The main component of Sun networking is Ethernet, a 50 Ohm coaxial cable allowing a data transfer rate of 10 megabits per second. The cable is actually approximately 1/2 inch thick, but is quite large given the fact that it only contains one wire. This is why Ethernet is often called thick-net. Each Ethernet cable segment must have a 50 Ohm terminator installed on both ends. Everything connected between these two terminators is part of one network segment. The maximum length limitation on each network segment is 500 meters, unless you boost the signal using repeaters. Machines cannot be connected directly to the 50 Ohm cable without the help of a tranceiver tap.

The tranceiver tap is an intelligent device that connects directly into the Ethernet cable. It transfers the activity from the Ethernet wire into a number of different signals on the tranceiver cable. The transceiver cable can then be connected directly into a Sun system. There are different types of tranceiver taps. Some are called "vampire taps" since they tap into the wire through a small hole cut out of the Ethernet cable. Other taps are called "in-line" taps because there is actually a connector on both ends so that the Ethernet wire can be connected in-line. The latter type of tap has been found to be much more dependable because it is less prone to failure when moved or jarred. Spacing between taps on the Ethernet wire must be on multiples of 2.5 meters to prevent reflections and decoding problems. Most Ethernet cables are marked with black bands every 2.5 meters. Make sure to install the terminators and all taps on these bands so that the signal can be reflected properly. It is optimal for larger networks to connect the tranceiver taps into what is called a multiplexer or MUX box.

The MUX box is a way of connecting a number of machines, usually eight or sixteen, to the Ethernet cable through one single tranceiver tap. It is intelligent enough to control the flow of traffic from the network to the machines and from the machines to the network. Some multiplexor boxes can act as the network themselves, eliminating the need for the Ethernet wire. In this situation the MUX box would replace the taps and the Ethernet cable. While this does work, problems may result. Once a multiplexor is designated as the main Ethernet box, only single nodes should be connected to it. Do not connect another mux to it. Most MUX boxes are built to handle the traffic for a specific number of hosts; doubling that number can severely hamper network throughput.

Some Sun machines are equipped with a BNC connector for connecting to thin-net. This network configuration is sometimes called "cheaper-net" because it requires less hardware to set up. In the thin-net environment, machines connect directly to the cable, thus eliminating the MUX box and tranceiver cables. It may be cheaper, but it is also less responsive. As with thick-net, thin-net must also be terminated on each end with a 50 Ohm terminator. In order to use thin-net, some configuration settings must be changed on the system CPU board, mainly to instruct the system as to which connector to use when sending and receiving packets.

There are many contracting firms that will install your network for you. If you have little experience in this area, it is best left to the professionals.

5.2 Network Software

After your network hardware has been installed and tested, your systems can be installed and booted. Each system's network interface is started by the /etc/rc scripts at boot time. The **ifconfig** command (see ifconfig(8c)) is used to turn the interface on and off. There are a number of other options to the **ifconfig** command. One of these is the hostname or IP address. When initializing an interface a hostname is required. The other options are setting the subnet mask (discussed below), the broadcast address, and a flag called "arp" which enables the use of the Address Resolution Protocol for mapping between network level and link level addresses. The "arp" flag is the default; thus it does not need to be specified when starting the Ethernet interface.

Each time a system begins the boot process, the kernel is loaded and the devices polled. The */etc/rc.boot* file sets the hostname of the machine with the name specified in the line:

    hostname=harlie

Later in the file, the primary Ethernet interface is started using the hostname as an argument.

    ifconfig xx0 $hostname -trailers up

The xx should be any one of the following device names: ie, ec, or le. If you are not sure which Ethernet interface you have installed leave all three lines in the file. The extras will silently and harmlessly fail. The hostname must exist in the local */etc/hosts* file in order for the interface to be started properly. If the wrong address is associated with the hostname, communication on the network is affected. Be sure that the YP entry and the entry in the local file match. If they do not match, all other network requests will not work, including **ypbind** which binds to a YP server. Once the system has contact with YP another call is made to establish the netmask for the interface:

ifconfig xx0 $hostname netmask +

This command employs the netmask YP map to establish the netmask for your local net. It is important that this address is set right if you have used subnetting. It is a good idea to change this line to read as follows:

ifconfig xx0 $hostname netmask + broadcast #.#.#.0

Substitute the network number for the "#.#.#.0". This will explicitly set the broadcast address for this interface to the network number that is appropriate for the network it is attached to. You can check to make sure that the interface is configured properly by entering the **ifconfig** command with only the interface name as an argument:

```
harlie# ifconfig le0
le0: flags = 63<UP,BROADCAST,NOTRAILERS,RUNNING>
    inet 192.9.200.1 netmask ffffff00 broadcast 192.9.200.0
```

The values displayed here are appropriate values for this network. The values used for your network depend on the type of network number that you use and whether you install subnetting or not. In some cases the netmask option does not work properly. To fix this problem change the " netmask +" entry to be "netmask x.x.x.0", where x.x.x.0 is 255.255.255.0 or some other appropriate netmask entry.

5.3 Choosing a Network Class

Internet hoot numbers consist of four fields, or octets, separated by periods as in 192.9.200.1. There are three classes of network numbers available, class A, class B, and class C. The network class you choose depends on the size of your installation. Each IP address is made up of two parts. The first part is the network number. This number is made up of some portion of the first three octets. The second part is the host number, which occupies the octets that are not used to define the network number. You need to know which part of the address to use for each number during the install process.

Class A network numbers occupy the first octet beginning at 1, and ending at 126. This means that if you were given the network number of 1, all the host addresses from 1.0.0.1 to 1.255.255.254 are yours to assign as you please. A Class A number would be used if you were a very large company starting an international net. The network would be one network with several millions of hosts (most likely gateways to smaller nets). The larger networks, such as the Internet, use one class A number for all of its hosts. All of these systems are in one network and they all have complete hostfiles for the rest of the net. Setting up a network of this size is beyond the scope of this book.

Class B network numbers begin at 128.1 and end at 191.255. The Class B number 128.1 contains all the possible host addresses between 128.1.0.1 and 128.1.255.254, somewhat less than 65,000 nodes. This size network is also much larger than many companies need. Establishing a network with this many hosts is difficult. Adding too many machines on one piece of wire without additional network equipment could bring your network to a crawl. Performance problems will lessen when optical networks are more readily available. (See the discussion below on subnetting for a more efficient use of a Class B network number.)

Class C numbers are probably the most common. This is true because there are more of them. Class C network numbers start at 192.0.1 and end at 223.255.255. Each class C network has a possible 254 host or node addresses available. This is the maximum size of one network.

Under normal circumstances adding many more than 100 nodes to a network is often enough to saturate the network. How many hosts you can add to one network depends on the types of applications that you are using, the number of diskless or dataless clients on the net, and the amount of data that is NFS mounted from other systems. In some instances, a network saturates with 60 nodes, where in other cases, you can reasonably run over 150 nodes.

Each network segment should be assigned one network number. You will have problems if you try to use two network numbers on one piece of cable. The x.x.x.0 or x.x.x.255 addresses should not be used when assigning hosts. They are used for broadcasting and should never be assigned to a specific host. The first can be used to name a network, but a host should never use the x.x.x.0 address for its host address.

The network address shown as an example during the installation of a Sun workstation is the class C number 192.9.200. If you never plan to connect your network to the outside world, this number works just fine. But chances are, you may want to connect to another machine outside your local network at one time or another. Changing the IP addresses for all the systems on your net can be quite a chore depending on its size. Before you start building a network, contact:

DDN Network Information Center
SRI International
333 Ravenswood Ave.
Menlo Park, CA 94025

to request a registered network number. It costs nothing and will keep everyone else currently connected to the Internet quite pleased since you will not cause great confusion by using some bogus Internet number. These folks can also give you instructions on how to join the Internet.

5.4 Subnets

Subnetting is a way of using one assigned network number for many networks. For instance, a class B number should be used for one network with up to 64,770 nodes. By employing subnetting you can change this one network number to 255 networks with 254 nodes each. When you are given a class B number, for instance 129.9, you can assign 129.9.0.1 to 129.9.255.254 as nodes on your network. Through the use of subnets, you can tell your servers that their network number are 129.9.x instead of 129.9. This allows you to set up 255 separate networks using the 129.9 number.

One advantage of using subnets is the reduction of traffic. In this example, without subnetting, all 64,770 nodes would have routing information for all other nodes in the network. Through the use of subnets, each node would contain routing information for a maximum of 254 nodes on its local network and information on how to get to the other 254 networks. Thus, using subnets can reduce the amount of routing traffic that is broadcast on the network.

Another advantage to subnetting is that all of the hosts do not have to be on one physical network. This allows for the expansion of your network to another town, without having to request another number from SRI. Also, this allows you to separate network hogs from the rest of your networks. For instance, if you know that one group is using an application that is particularly network intensive, you would probably want to isolate these users from the rest of your normal users so the program does not degrade the performance of the entire network. If you were not using subnetting you would again need to request another number for the network hogs.

When considering subnets, it is best and easiest to subnet using the full octet. It is possible to mask out only part of the octet, but assigning host addresses and figuring out the broadcast address can become a nightmare if only part of the octet can be used. In general, subnetting with the full octet is simple.

Another point is that you should subnet all of the networks associated with one number. Do not try to have one half of 129.9 be subnetted and the other half non-subnetted. This causes serious routing problems. You can, however, leave some of your numbers as class C as you move towards a subnetted class B network.

5.5 Setting Up a Single Network

A single network site is an installation of machines connected to one network segment. This is usually a one office or one building business that needs to share programs and files between machines. Every machine on this network is connected in one way or another to the same piece of wire. The network is isolated from the rest of the world. As an example we will use a small network called "sunnet". There are seven machines on sunnet; harlie, minerva, dora, athene, hal, nomad and mike. The /etc/hosts file for "sunnet" would look like this:

```
192.9.200.0    sunnet             # sunnet network
192.9.200.1    harlie ypmaster    # YP master
192.9.200.2    minerva            # print server
```

```
192.9.200.3    dora        # resource server
192.9.200.4    athene      # modem server
192.9.200.5    hal         # source machine
192.9.200.6    nomad       # backup server
192.9.200.7    mike        # YP slave
```

All machines on sunnet will be able to talk to each other as long as each system's hostname and IP address is known. If YP is not being used, each system's host file must have every other system's hostname and address. The network name is irrelevant on a single network.

When using YP, only one system, the YP master, needs to contain the complete */etc/hosts* file. This file is used to create the YP hosts maps. If not using YP, every system connected to this network needs the same */etc/hosts* file and when any additions are made to this file, such as a new machine, each existing machine needs to be updated as well.

5.6 Adding Multiple Networks

Sites that have more than 100 machines should use more than one network segment. Each network segment uses a different network number. The class C network number 192.9.201 will be used to connect a new network segment, the marketing group, to the sunnet network. The new network will be called netb. Now the problem is getting these two networks to communicate. This is done with a system set up as a router or gateway.

A gateway machine has two Ethernet interfaces. One is used as its primary Ethernet interface, usually ie0 or le0. The other is the gateway connection, usually ie1 or le1. The primary interface connects to the local network segment, while the gateway interface connects to a different network segment that contains other machines. Do not install both Ethernet interfaces on the same network segment.

To install a gateway, obtain a second Ethernet interface for one of the machines. This usually entails purchasing a new Ethernet card. In this example, the machine "red", on the new network, has two Ethernet interfaces installed. The ie0 interface is attached to its local net, using the "netb" address "192.9.201.1", while the gateway connection, ie1, is attached to the "sunnet" using the address "192.9.200.8". Unique hostnames must exist for both connections. A common naming convention for the gateway connection is appending a "-gtw" to the base hostname. On the gateway system, lines would need to be added to */etc/rc.local* and */etc/rc.boot* to run **ifconfig** on the new interface as illustrated below:

```
#@(#)rc.boot
  .
  .
  .
ifconfig le0 $hostname -trailers up
* ifconfig ie1 $hostname-gtw -trailers up
  .
  .
#@(#)rc.local
  .
  .
  .
ifconfig le0 'hostname' netmask +
* ifconfig ie1 'hostname'-gtw netmask +
```

The lines with the "*" show the entries for the new ie1 interface. Once the changes are made to the hosts file on the YP master, the last step on the gateway would be to either boot the generic kernel or to create a kernel with the appropriate driver for the second interface. Please look at Chapter 2 for a discussion on the reconfiguration of kernels. The resulting */etc/hosts* file which combines the hosts for neta and netb is shown in Figure 5.1.

Once this host map is propagated, you should be able to boot the server named red. Now, machines on the sunnet network can communicate with machines on the netb network via the red-gtw gateway. If the machine blue "knows" how to get to the machine red, it can also get to dora as well. Since red is connected to both networks, it allows the communication between both network segments.

When establishing an additional network, it is best to install two gateway servers. This configuration makes your network more fault tolerant. Your networks will continue to communicate even if one of the connections is bad. Without the double gateways, there is a single point of failure for each additional network you add. If one gateway crashes, all of the users on that net would be isolated.

If this two network segment design is expanded once again to add a group of programmers, another network number must be

```
#
# Main net
#
192.9.200.0    sunnet neta        # sunnet network
192.9.200.1    harlie ypmaster    # YP master
192.9.200.2    minerva            # print server
192.9.200.3    dora               # resource server
192.9.200.4    athene             # modem server
192.9.200.5    hal                # source machine
192.9.200.6    nomad              # backup server
192.9.200.7    mike               # YP slave
192.9.200.8    red-gtw            # gateway to netb
#
# Marketing net
#
192.9.201.0    netb               # marketing network
192.9.201.1    red                # gateway & slave server
192.9.201.2    blue               # netb client server
192.9.201.3    green              # blue client
192.9.201.4    yellow             # gateway & slave server
192.9.201.5    orange             # blue client
192.9.201.6    purple             # blue client
```

FIGURE 5.1. *Example host file for two nets.*

used. The new network uses number 192.9.202 for the programmers' net, and will be called netc. The resulting */etc/hosts* file is displayed in Figure 5.2.

Now there are three different network segments in this domain: 192.9.200.0, 192.9.201.0, and 192.9.202.0. All segments can be served by a single YP master, so that all the machines know the host addresses of the others. The gateway connections are red-gtw, which connects neta to netb; north-gtw, which joins the programmers net, netc, to neta; and yellow-gtw, which connects netb and netc together.

5.7 Useful Commands

There are two types of commands that are of particular interest when studying networking. The first type of commands are the ones that allow for network troubleshooting and the second type

```
#
#
# YP hosts file for domain sunnet
#
127.0.0.1        localhost
#
# Main net
#
192.9.200.0      sunnet neta          # sunnet network
192.9.200.1      harlie ypmaster      # YP master
192.9.200.2      minerva              # print server
192.9.200.3      dora                 # resource server
192.9.200.4      athene               # modem server
192.9.200.5      hal                  # source machine
192.9.200.6      nomad                # backup server
192.9.200.7      mike                 # YP slave
192.9.200.8      red-gtw              # gateway to netb
192.9.200.9      north-gtw            # gateway to netc
#
# Marketing net
#
192.9.201.0      netb                 # marketing network
192.9.201.1      red                  # gateway & slave server
192.9.201.2      blue                 # netb client server
192.9.201.3      green                # blue client
192.9.201.4      yellow               # gateway & slave server
192.9.201.5      orange               # blue client
192.9.201.6      purple               # blue client
#
# Programmers net
#
192.9.202.0      netc                 # programmers network
192.9.202.1      north                # gateway & slave server
192.9.202.2      baltic               # netc client server
192.9.202.3      weddell              # baltic client
192.9.202.4      caspian              # baltic client
192.9.202.5      bering               # baltic client
192.9.202.6      yellow-gtw           # gateway to netb
```

FIGURE 5.2. *Example host file for three nets.*

are those commands that make it easy to do things with the network. Several commands of both types are presented in the next couple of paragraphs. This is not intended to be an exhaustive list, but should provide an indication of the available functions.

5.7.1 Network Troubleshooting Commands

The **netstat** command displays information on the network status (see netstat(8C)). There are options available to display the state of sockets or connections and the routes that have been established. You can look at the current routing tables with "**netstat -r**". This command displays the names of the destination networks and the name of the gateway that your system is currently using to get there. If numbers show up in the destination column, it means that the IP address for that host is not in the local host file or in the host YP map. Using the options -rn shows the actual address numbers instead of the names for all hosts. This option is useful when you are looking for the route to a particular network number. In the releases before SunOS 4.0, the options in this example had to be entered as "-r -n instead of "-rn". The later versions of SunOS allow either syntax.

Another helpful option included with **netstat** is "-i". This displays some statistics on the interfaces that are started during the boot process. For instance, the following command shows that le0 is configured with the hostname "yellow" and is attached to netc.

```
yellow# netstat -i
```

Name	Mtu	Net/Dest	Address	Ipkts	Ierrs	Opkts	Oerrs	Collis	Queue
le0	1500	netc	yellow	34051160	3093	39022839	1	1083939	0
le1	1500	netb	yellow-gtw	31852492	3378	25529653	23	1311446	0
lo0	1536	loopback	localhost	1567	0	1567	0	0	0

It also shows that there have been some errors and collisions on the network. Each network has a certain error level associated with it. It would be best if the level is kept as low as possible, but a noise-free and perfect network is very unlikely. As the System Administrator, you should be aware of the level that is normal for your environment. Any sudden increase would indicate a problem. Usually these problems are caused by the network taps, the MUXs or the Ethernet interfaces. For le0 the total number of packets processed since the system was last booted is equal to the packets in (Ipkts) plus the packets out (Opkts) or 73,074,999 packets. The number of errors is 3,094 (add Ierrs and Oerrs) and the number of collisions is 1,083,939. The error rate is almost insignificant for this interface and the collision rate is about 1.5%. If any of these rates increase suddenly or are over 10% (at the most!) the network is not functioning properly and should be fixed.

The **route** command can be used to help troubleshoot when you have routing problems (see route(8C)). On the client named baltic you would normally have a route that uses the server north (IP address 192.9.202.1) to reach the server dora on the 192.9.200.0 network. If the gateway north was to hang so that the routes are not dropped, you would need to delete this route from your routing tables so that the other route through yellow-gtw can be used. The syntax of the command is:

> **route** delete destination_network gateway_address

where destination_network number would be 192.9.200 and gateway_address would be 192.9.202.1. Next, either wait for the route through yellow-gtw to be established automatically or if you are in a hurry add it with the following command:

> baltic# **route** add 192.9.200.0 192.9.202.6 2

Notice that the number of hops is now two. The number of hops is normally equal to the number of gateways you must go through to reach a specific network.

This command can also be executed with the "-f" option to flush the routing table on the system. There are occasions when the routing is so confused that manually deleting all of the bad routes would take too much time. In this instance, it is better to flush the routing table and allow the system to establish new routes. Do not do this if **in.routed** is not running because the system will not create any new routes (see routed(8C)). The **in.routed** daemon is normally started when a system is booted. It keeps the table which stores all of the routing information up-to-date. If this daemon is not running, then all routes must be entered by hand. Under most circumstances this daemon should be functioning on all systems.

5.7.2 Commands to Use the Network

Many commands are available to allow access to other resources in the network. Among these commands are **rlogin, rcp, rsh, rdate, rup** and **ping.** The first three commands allow for remote execution of **login, cp,** and **sh.** The **rdate** command is executed with a remote hostname as an option. The date on the local system is set to that of the specified remote host. You must be logged in as root to use this command. This command can be used to keep the time synchronized between systems.

The last two commands are used to determine if a remote system is up. The **rup** command followed with a hostname as an option shows the hostname, the amount of time that the host has been booted and the average number of jobs that have been in the run queue for the last minute, the last five minutes and the last fifteen minutes (see uptime(1)). These last numbers are displayed with the heading "load average" which tends to create the illusion that these values are out of 100% of something, when the reality is that a "load average" of over 10 normally means that the system is overloaded. The normal values for each server should be checked on occasion. This command uses the Remote Procedure Call (RPC) service. The error message:

    weddell: RPC: Port mapper failure

is reported if the system weddell is not reachable via RPC.

The **ping** command also can be used to check to see if a system is connected to the network; however, it uses the Internet Control Message Protocol (ICMP) instead of RPC. It needs the hostname of the system you are trying to reach as an option. It will respond with the message:

    no answer from weddell

if the host is not available.

5.8 Establishing a Subnet

Once you have made the decision to subnet, your first decision is which layout or network topology you wish to use. For example, if you were to get a class B number, 129.240, for the sunnet network described above, the first item to look at is the hosts file. Determine if you have too many hosts in any of the current networks. If you have had comments about systems being too slow, you should look at how efficiently the network routing is working and find better ways to balance the load. If you are changing all of the IP addresses to use subnets, the addition of another gateway or two is not a large amount of work.

Since this example network is small, it is easy to subnet the whole thing at one time. This procedure involves assigning new host addresses to all of the systems. Then, during some quiet time, you must halt all of the systems, or at least bring them all down to single-user mode. It is difficult to make changes to a network when part of it is running.

After halting all the systems, you should boot your YP master to single-user mode and make changes to some of the YP maps. Edit */etc/netmasks* on your YP master to reflect the following:

```
# Network    Netmask
129.240.0.0   255.255.255.0
```

This defines the network portion of your host address to be the first three octets, even though you have a class B address which normally uses the first two octets. Then change */etc/hosts* on the YP master to define the new IP addresses. After these two files are updated, make the maps and reboot the YP master to update its address.

Once the YP master is up, any gateways or standalone systems that are on the same network as the YP master can be booted to single-user. The IP address for each host must be changed in the local */etc/hosts* file, and then the systems can be rebooted. After the gateways are up, you should work on the YP slaves. While in single user mode, change the IP address in the hosts file, add the YP master's new address to the hosts file, set the domain name, run ypbind and then reinitialize the YP maps by using the following command:

```
# /usr/etc/yp/ypinit -s
```

If the YP slave is connected to a different network segment than the YP master, you may need to add a route so that the above command will succeed. See the discussion below on routing to determine the necessary options to the **route** command.

The addresses on all of the remaining systems need to be changed and the systems rebooted. This is not a difficult process on diskfull systems, but on diskless client servers and for dataless clients the process is a bit more difficult. For the diskless clients, each /*export*/*root*/<*clientname*>/*etc*/*hosts* file needs to be edited. This can be done while the server is in single-user mode by entering the following commands:

```
# mount -at 4.2
# cd /export/root
# vi */etc/hosts
```

The first command mounts all of the local filesystems. The last command allows you to edit the host files one right after the other. Since the files should already have the old IP address in it, all you need to do is swap the old address for the new one. The link in /tftpboot for each client has to be manually recreated. Each link connects the boot file for the architecture of the client to a filename which is determined by the IP address of the client. For example, before subnetting, the address for the client named weddell was 192.9.202.3. This address changed to hexadecimal format is C009CA03. In /tftpboot there should be an entry similar to the following:

```
lrwxrwxrwx   1 root         19 Oct 27  16:49  C009CA03 -> boot.sun3
-rwxr-xr-x   1 root     126912 Nov  2  08:14  boot.sun3
```

To change the entry for the new IP address, 129.240.3.3 (which is 81F00303 in hexadecimal), the following procedure should be used:

```
# rm C009CA03
# ln -s boot.sun3 81F00303
```

Please note the use of the capital letter for the F0 (which is 240 in hex.). Also, note that the entry for the .3 is padded to be 03. The link will not work correctly if these rules are not followed. Once the links are re-created the server and each of its clients may be booted. The other option is to remove and then reinstall each client, but this process can take too much time, especially if any of the files in each root partition have been changed by the user.

When converting dataless clients it is much better to change the IP address before the system is halted and the network goes down. The only way to change the IP address on a dataless client, after the client has been halted, is to either reinstall the system using the new IP address or reboot the system using MINIROOT and change the file by hand. Once MINIROOT is loaded and you have a prompt, enter the following commands:

```
# fsck /dev/rsd0a
# mount /dev/sd0a /a
# cd /a/etc
# ed hosts
# cd /
# umount /dev/sd0a
```

You need to substitute the proper device name for /dev/rsd0a if the root partition is not on a SCSI disk. The second command makes the files on the root partition available. These files will be found under /a instead of /. There are a limited number of commands available when running MINIROOT. You will not be able to use **vi** to edit the hosts file. **Ed** is the only editor available and it is a very basic editor (see ed(1)). Once it has been executed you may use a command such as the one below:

```
4s/192.9.201/129.240.1/
```

This command substitutes 192.9.201 for 129.240.1 on line 4. Practice with this command on a test file before you attempt to run it while running MINIROOT. Once the editing is done you should be able to reboot the system, as long as the appropriate server is up. Do not run **suninstall** after loading the MINIROOT, unless you plan on reloading the whole system. This whole process is long and tedious and it would be best to avoid the whole situation by changing the host address before you halt the system.

5.9 Routing

In the three network domain described above, in order for someone on the machine baltic to copy some files from the resource server dora, you can see a few different routes which may be taken to get to dora. One way might be through the gateway that is attached to its own network segment, north to north-gtw. This is the fastest way since it requires the fewest hops. In this case, only one hop is used, through north-gtw and on to dora. The other route might be through yellow-gtw, and on to netb. Then, from netb the machine red would be used to reach dora. This route involves two gateways so it uses two hops.

After a normal installation, each diskfull system does dynamic routing. This means that the software will constantly be monitoring the routes that are broadcast from the machines in the network. The shortest or quickest route will be selected if multiple routes are available. In the case described above, if north was to crash or the interface was to go down for some other reason, then **routed,** the routing daemon, would find the route available through yellow-gtw and would use it.

In cases where you have only one gateway, you can reduce the amount of traffic, by using static routing. These instructions must be done as superuser. You can also do this for diskless clients by having them automatically route to their server. This process involves two steps. The first step is to disable the dynamic routing, which is done by either moving */usr/etc/in.routed* to */usr/etc/in.routed.gen* or by commenting out the following lines in */etc/rc.local:*

```
if [ -f /usr/etc/in.routed ]; then
    in.routed;   (echo -n ' routed')   >/dev/console
fi
```

Make sure that you add a "#" in front of all three lines, or the script will not work properly. Directly below these lines the following line should be entered:

```
route add default IP_address 1
```

The IP address for the gateway system should be substituted for IP_address on systems using static routing. You may also use the diskless client server address as the IP_address for the route instead of the gateway. Once this change has been made you can then reboot the system. The problem with using static routing is that if the server or gateway that is defined as the default router should crash, the client will be hung. This is a good argument for dynamic routing and for multiple gateways for each route.

5.10 Special Networking

There are many Sun and third-party packages available that allow for special networking needs. These are not part of the standard OS and so must be purchased separately. Some of the packages allow for point-to-point networking, which can connect two remote sites. This makes it possible for your net to be much bigger than the Ethernet cable alone will allow. Other packages let your Sun systems connect with different types of networks (such as X25 and DDN) or with other non-Sun systems.

Security

6

Establishing the right level of security on the network is one of the most complex tasks that a System Administrator works on. A balance needs to be reached between ease of access and the need to restrict access. Usually the more security involved, the harder it can become to move files around and to share resources. The other side to this issue is that if a resource is easy to share, then it is not secure. Most environments will have some files that should not be open for everyone to read. Keeping those files secure while not hampering the accessibility of the rest of the system is a large job.

This chapter presents information about some of the files and processes that are available to help control security.

6.1 /.rhosts, /etc/hosts.equiv and ~/.rhosts

These files can make it possible for a user to login from one system to another without using a password (see hosts.equiv(5)). This practice should be discouraged, especially on any resource or home directory servers.

/.rhosts is consulted when someone attempts to **rlogin** as root on your local system. Each hostname listed in this file will be able to **rlogin** as root without supplying a password. This file should normally be empty. Each entry in this file may have one hostname per line. In environments where there are systems that serve as gateways, you need to include the gateway hostname (harlie-cnet) instead of just its hostname (harlie), because the routing takes the shortest path. The shortest path in this case could mean using the route through the harlie-cnet interface because the route through this interface has the fewest number of hops. If you are doing remote tape installs, you will need to add the hostname of the

system being installed to the /.*rhosts* of the tapehost in order to do the install. Remove this entry as soon as the installation is done.

/*etc*/*hosts.equiv* is checked when any other user attempts to **rlogin.** This file normally contains a "+". This means that anyone who is in the YP passwd map (except for root accounts) and is working from a system in the YP hosts map will be able to **rlogin** to the local system without a password. This file should also be empty. If necessary, entries can be of the form: hostname, +@netgroup, or -@netgroup. The +@netgroupa entry allows access to anyone who is logged in to one of the hosts in netgroupa. The -@netgroupb entry will require passwords from anyone logging in from the hosts in netgroupb.

The data in each ˜/.*rhosts* is included with the data from the /*etc*/*hosts.equiv* file. If you want to ensure that your users are using their passwords during any **login** session, do not allow this file in the top level of their home directory. Unfortunately, the only way to make sure that the users do not have this file is to create a process to find the file and then either remove it or to notify the appropriate people.

6.2 /etc/ttytab

Each terminal device in /dev should have an entry in /*etc*/*ttytab*. This includes the console, any terminal devices and all of the pseudo ttys that are used for network logins or when running **sunview** or any of the other windowing systems. The ttytab file is used to create /*etc*/*ttys* which should not be edited. All changes need to be made to /*etc*/*ttytab*. When **init** is reinitialized it will make the changes to /*etc*/*ttys*. Figure 6.1 shows a short example of /*etc*/*ttytab*.

Each line uses the form:

    devname command term_type   status # comments

Devname is the actual name of the special file in /dev. Command is the program that init should run on this device, normally /**usr**/**etc**/ **getty.** The quoting ensures that the command and its options are run by **init.** Term_type is the type of terminal that is attached to the device. All entries can be found in /*usr*/*share*/*lib*/*termcap*. The status field indicates whether the command should be run by **init**

```
#
# name    getty                      type      status comments
#
console  "/usr/etc/getty std.9600"   vi        on local secure
ttya     "/usr/etc/getty std.9600"   unknown   off local secure
ttyb     "/usr/etc/getty std.9600"   unknown   off local secure
tty00    "/usr/etc/getty std.9600"   unknown   off local secure
tty01    "/usr/etc/getty std.9600"   unknown   off local secure
tty02    "/usr/etc/getty std.9600"   unknown   off local secure
tty03    "/usr/etc/getty std.9600"   unknown   off local secure
tty04    "/usr/etc/getty std.9600"   unknown   off local secure
tty05    "/usr/etc/getty std.9600"   unknown   off local secure
tty06    "/usr/etc/getty std.9600"   unknown   off local secure
tty07    "/usr/etc/getty std.9600"   unknown   off local secure
tty08    "/usr/etc/getty std.9600"   unknown   off local secure
tty09    "/usr/etc/getty std.9600"   unknown   off local secure
tty0a    "/usr/etc/getty std.9600"   unknown   off local secure
tty0b    "/usr/etc/getty std.9600"   unknown   off local secure
tty0c    "/usr/etc/getty std.9600"   unknown   off local secure
tty0d    "/usr/etc/getty std.9600"   unknown   off local secure
tty0e    "/usr/etc/getty std.9600"   unknown   off local secure
tty0f    "/usr/etc/getty std.9600"   unknown   off local secure
```

FIGURE 6.1. *Ttytab file sample.*

or ignored. Including the secure flag in this field allows root to login directly. Not including the secure flag means that root logins are disabled. On the console entry, not adding the flag also means that you will be prompted for the root password when the system is booted into single user mode. Comments can be included throughout the file as either full line comments, or following each individual entry. All comments start with a "#".

6.3 Tightening Security

There are several items that should be considered if you wish to make your network more secure. Check the *./rhosts* and */etc/ hosts.equiv* files as part of your normal routine. Often these files are changed and the unneeded entry is left in the file. Keeping these files as clean as possible will help improve security.

Make sure that all users have a password. If YP is installed it is easy to check the passwd datafile on the YP master to see if a password has not been set for a user. See the example below:

```
harlie# grep :: /etc/passwd.yp
nobody:*:-2:-2::/:
daemon:*:1:1::/:
sys:*:2:2::/:/bin/csh
bin:*:3:3::/:/bin:
uucp:*:4:4::/var/spool/uucppublic:
news:*:6:6::/var/spool/news:/bin/csh
ingres:*:7:7::/usr/ingres:/bin/csh
audit:*:9:9::/etc/security/audit:/bin/csh
sync::1:1::/:/bin/sync
```

In this example, the entry for sync does not have a password. Normally this is acceptable, but if this was a user account entry, either the user should set a password or you should set one for the user. This is especially true if you have modems attached to any of your systems. You may also wish to check for the presence of "root" accounts by searching for ":0:" in the password file.

Occasionally a situation arises in which a user or a group of users needs access to only one system in your network. This can be resolved by adding the needed entry to the */etc/passwd* file on the system to which they need access, rather than adding the entry to the YP database. If, however, it is desirable to have all logins included in the YP maps, the same result can be created by using the following steps. On your YP master, create an entry for the user that looks like:

```
username::1010:10:User Name:/home/server/username:/bin/false
```

As usual, update the YP maps once the addition has been made. On the system that the user needs access to add an entry to */etc/passwd* such as:

```
+username:::::/bin/csh
```

This entry must precede the "+" entry at the bottom of the local passwd file. The entry on the YP master prevents the user from completing a successful **login** on all of the systems in the network. The second entry replaces the "/bin/false" in the YP entry with "/bin/csh" on the local system only, so that the user has login access locally but nowhere else.

Rlogin activity can also be controlled at a local level by removing the "+::0:0:::" from the bottom of the local passwd file. You will then need to add complete entries for each user who requires access (which defeats the purpose of YP!) or you can add the following to */etc/passwd:*

```
+user1
+user2
+user3
+user4
```

These entries will use the data that is in the YP maps, so that the user will not need to have a separate YP password and local password. This method utilizes the flexibility of YP without opening up the local system to everyone who has a login.

Another step that you can take to increase security is to change the exports file on the home directory servers so that only certain systems can mount each home directory. A standard */etc/exportfs* file looks like:

```
/                -access=servers
/usr             -access=biggroup,ro
/home/baltic     -access=biggroup
/home/baltic2    -access=biggroup
/home/baltic3    -access=biggroup
```

The following file would restrict the ability to mount each home directory:

```
/                    -access=servers
/usr                 -access=biggroup,ro
/home/baltic/larry   -access=weddell
/home/baltic/moe     -access=caspian
/home/baltic2/curly  -access=bering
```

The second file restricts NFS access to the home directories to the client system for each user. This can cause problems if the users share systems, since each host which mounts any home directories would have to be manually added to this file. The cost of increased time spent keeping this file updated would need to be compared with the increase in security, before using hostnames instead of netgroups.

Another item to look for is setuid files (set chmod(1)). The permissions on these files allows the user the same access as the owner of the file. This can cause major problems if the owner of the file is root. The following command will find all of these files on the local disks:

baltic# **find** . -fstype 4.2 -type f -perm -4000 -exec ls -l {} \;

All of the files that are displayed are potential problems. If the file is part of the normal Sun OS it is reasonably safe. If the file is in a home directory it should be investigated.

6.4 Installing Secure NFS

Secure NFS allows for a more secure environment than the standard Sun OS provides. In order to implement it you will need to be running YP and you will need to install an encryption kit (available in the U.S.A. only). The software when installed will check all RPC calls (including **mount** or **rlogin**) to verify both the user and the system that is making the request. This will help provide a higher level of security than is normally present in a standard YP installation.

Start the **rpc.ypupdated** process on the YP master if it is not running already. The standard */etc/rc.local* file starts this automatically when the server is booted. While this process is running, the */var/yp/updaters* file is checked to find out how to update the publickey.byname map or any other map that is included. This file is a standard makefile, and can be changed if you are familiar with the command syntax. If you move the YP datafiles from their standard locations, changes must be made to this file. Under most circumstances you will not need to change this file.

Once the process on the YP master is running, execute the **newkey** command for each user (**newkey** -u username) in the domain, and for each root login on a host (**newkey** -u hostname). You are prompted for the password of the user and then the keys are made.

Each user may change his or her password by using the **chkey** command. Adding a key for the username "nobody" allows users to create their own entries. Normally you do not add this account.

On each system in the domain, check that the **keyserv** daemon is running, as well as the **ypbind** daemon. The **keyserv** stores all non-root keys that are decrypted in */etc/keystore* and stores the

root key in */etc/.rootkey*. This means that the key is kept for each
user that logs in to a system.

After the setup is accomplished, in */etc/exports* on the NFS
servers add the -secure option to the exported directories. The
/etc/fstab on the systems mounting the NFS resource must be
changed to include the secure option.

6.5 Installing C2 Security

The C2 Security package was developed to follow the standards
set by the National Computer Security Center. It provides for
auditing of special events and stores password information in an
area that is not accessible to the average user. The files necessary
to run this package are part of the normal release and can be
selected for installation during the **suninstall** process. The files are
extracted by selecting the security category when doing an install.

To make the system functional, you must run the script called
/usr/etc/c2conv in single-user mode. The output from this script is
shown in Figure 6.2.

The first question is to verify that you are in single-user mode.
The question about the "SunDisk server" is asking if the system is
a server for diskless clients. If it is, the script asks for the path to the
clients' root partitions, which normally is /export/root. It also asks
for "additional exec locations". At this prompt, enter all of the
paths to the different exec directories that you have installed for
your clients, for instance, /export/exec/sun3 and /export/exec/
sun4. Enter "done" when finished with the exec list.

Next you are queried about the audit filesystems. If this system has a separate filesystem used for audit files then you would
answer yes. The script then prompts for the device name of the
partition that you want the files placed on. It is wise to have at least
two of these audit filesystems in a busy network. They do not have
to be on the same server. One audit file system per server is enough
in many situations. After entering the name of the local device,
enter the word "done". The next question asks you to identify
other audit file servers. You need to know the server name and the
device name for the remote audit partition. Entering "done"
brings up the next question, which lets you select "other audit
directories". Under most circumstances there should be none. The

```
# /usr/etc/C2conv
Is system single-user? [y¦n]: y
Is this a SunDisk server? [y¦n]: n
Is this an audit file server? [y¦n]: y
Enter audit device (e.g. 'xy1d'), or 'done': xy2d
Enter audit device (e.g. 'xy1d'), or 'done': done
Enter remote audit server name, or 'done': dora
Enter remote audit file system on dora, or 'done': /etc/security/audit/dora
Enter remote audit server name, or 'done': done
Specify other audit directories or 'done': done
OK to use audit flags 'ad,lo,p0,p1'? [y¦n]: y
OK to use soft disk space limit of 20%? [y¦n]: n
Enter soft limit percentage (e.g. '10'): 10
OK to notify 'root@harlie' when admin required? [y¦n]: y
Last chance to abort gracefully. Do you want to continue? [y¦n]: y

Update /etc/fstab

Update /etc/exports
Update /etc/security/audit/audit_control
Update /usr/etc/audit_warn
Split /etc/passwd into
    /etc/passwd and
    /etc/security/passwd.adjunct
Split /etc/group into
    /etc/group and
    /etc/security/group.adjunct
Set modes and owners
Do you want to set a local password for 'audit'? [y¦n]: y
Setting password for 'audit' . . .
New password:
Retype new password:
#
```

FIGURE 6.2. *Running the C2conv script.*

problem with using other audit directories is that they are not protected like the ones in /etc/security, which defeats part of the reason for installing this package. Entering "done" prompts for the audit flags.

A familiarity with the events that you want to audit is necessary to answer this prompt (see audit_control(5)). The audit flags set the type of events or audit class that will be audited. The options are shown in Figure 6.3.

The automatically configured flags are: ad, lo, p0 and p1. To change these flags, enter "no" after the "OK to use audit flags" question. You are then given a chance to enter in all of the flags that you wish to use. The next question shows the format that the entry should take. The "+ indicates that all successful attempts in this audit class should be logged and the "-" indicates that all unsuccessful attempts of that audit class are to be logged. A flag without either of these indicates that both successful and unsuccessful events should be logged. You may need to use only one or two of the flags. Remember that the more flags used, the more disk space necessary to capture the data.

The next questions, which ask about "soft disk space lets you select the point at which the system will send mail to warn of an almost full filesystem. When the soft limit is reached the system searchs for another directory to put the files in. These directories are the "other audit directories" which should have been entered earlier. You may answer "no" to the next question and enter a different value at the question: "Enter soft limit percentage". You may wish to decrease this value if the audit partitions are very large (200MB or more). Likewise, this can be increased if the partitions are small.

You are next asked if it is "OK to notify" root at the local system name when administration is needed. If you do not want mail going to the local root account, answer "no" and enter the email address for whom you want notified after the next prompt.

---

dr   - data read
dw   - data write
dc   - data create - **link, mkdir**
da   - data access change - **chmod, chown**
lo   - login and logout
ad   - normal administrative - **dump, fsck, su**
p0   - privileged operation - **quota, chroot**
p1   - unusual privileged operation - **mount, reboot**

FIGURE 6.3. *Audit flag options.*

The last question before the conversion asks: "Do you want to continue?". If you answer "yes", the actual conversion program is run. It updates several files, and most importantly creates a copy of the passwd and group files in /etc/security. The final question asks if you "want to set a local password for audit". It is wise to set passwords on any login account. You are prompted for a password if you enter "yes".

All future changes to the passwd and group maps must occur to the passwd.adjunct and group.adjunct files. In order to make sure that the passwd map is updated properly, change the rpc.yp-passwd entry in */etc/rc.local* on the YP master to:

/usr/etc/rpc.yppasswdd /etc/security/passwd.adjunct -m passwd.adjunct

Backups

7

7.1 Backup Concepts

Completing regular backups is probably one of the most, if not THE most important part of a System Administrator's job. Your users will depend on you to keep an up-to-date backup of all their files. This is especially true when you have a network of many diskless clients and a couple of big servers. In sites that have many computers, completing backups can be a very time-consuming job. Larger sites often have a backup operator or night shift, whose primary job is to get the backups done, usually in the evening or early morning when few people are using the computers.

A way of completing backups, without a backup operator, is to designate a server with as much disk as possible (within reason!!) and/or an 8mm tape drive, to use as a backup server. This server employs scripts and remote commands to pull files off from the other systems in the local network. These files can then be archived to the local disks or to the 8mm tape drive. The advantage of using disks, for short-term backup media, is that you can store a week's worth of data. This makes restoring files very easy. You still need to put these files on tape, but that can be done at your convenience.

The advantage of not using the disk is that you do not need to have "extra" expensive disks. Regardless of whether you install a backup server with extra disks or without, an 8mm tape drive is essential if the daily backups take up more than 500 MB. Sun does not support 8mm tape drives for all architectures running 4.0 or 4.0.3, but third party alternatives are available.

As far as backup media go, you can use disk or tape or some combination of the two. When you are ordering tapes be careful with using non-standard brands. If you decide to use non-standard brands, test them extensively before you start using them for your backup media. The preferred media for the 8mm tape drives are Sony® SP120. As this media becomes more popular more reliable tapes will be produced, but currently the Sony tapes are the best for the 8mm.

As part of the backup process it is absolutely necessary that you clean the heads on whatever tape drive you are using. For the 1/2″ and 1/4″ tape drives, a cleaning solution and a cotton swab are the necessary items. For the 8mm tape drive, purchase a head cleaning tape (use the one from Exabyte). Regardless of the tape drive that you use, you will get errors if you do not clean the heads regularly. How often you do clean the heads depends on how often you use the drive; once a month is probably the most you can delay it if the tape drive is used daily.

Plan to run your backups late at night or at other non-production times. All backup procedures are resource hogs. Tape writing and writing to disk takes a higher priority than many of the "normal" processes, so the server would appear slow to anyone using it during the backup. In addition, it is best not to have the files changing when you are running the backups, so planning the backups for a time when the systems are not being used is the best idea.

There are several factors to consider when choosing a backup scheme. One of the first factors is timeliness. How often do you need to run the backups and which files do you need to capture? With infinite resources and infinite time, you could do full backups every night, but this is usually not economically feasible and it is not necessary. What you need is to balance the resources you have available (including time, available media, and people) with the ultimate goal of having every file on one tape.

A backup scheme often includes three types of backups: full, weekly, and daily backups. A complete or full backup of every system is normally done once a month. This process usually occurs during the weekend because the systems should be down in single-user mode to get a clean copy. Weekly backups are run on Friday nights, to get a copy of the data that has changed in the last week. Daily backups can be done in two ways. The first is to capture all of the files that have changed since the last backup. The second is to capture all data that has changed since the last weekly or full backup. The latter type will require fewer tapes to go through if you need to restore files, but may use more tapes to complete the backup. For instance, if a directory is accidentally removed on Friday morning, you would need to restore from the last full backup and all weekly backups that have occurred since the full backup. In addition, in the first scenario, where you are capturing only one days worth of changed files, you would need to restore from the tapes made on Monday, Tuesday, Wednesday, and Thursday. In the second scenario, you would only need to use the tape from Thursday, but it could be spread over two or more tapes instead of one. This same sort of reasoning can be applied to the weekly backups to cut down on the number of tapes that you need to go through.

Deciding on which scheme to implement depends on the size of the systems that you are supporting and the importance of the files that are on those systems. You could decide to do only the full and weekly backups on a personal diskfull workstation if you are willing to take the one week penalty if your disk goes bad or if you accidentally delete something. If you have many diskfull workstations a home directory server is beneficial. In this model you could make each user responsible for doing the backups on their own OS files, but the files in their home directory could be on a large server that has a complete backup program. You could also note that your local NFS resource server is changed once in a great while, so this system could be sufficiently protected by a combination of weekly and full backups, or just full monthly backups alone.

Another factor to consider when establishing your backup procedure is the ease of restoring files. This is particularly important if you have someone who is not familiar with the system running your backups and restores. If you have the ability to do backups to disk, then simple restores become trivial. All you have to do is **rcp** the file. The procedure to do a restore from tape depends on which command is invoked when the tape is written. Each command is discussed in the next sections.

The level of difficulty involved in running the backups is another factor. In situations where the backups are running on more than two or three partitions, or require many tapes, you should implement a backup script so that you do not have to enter every command by hand. The script should be easy to manage or change. Having even a simple script can substantially reduce the difficulty and potential confusion.

Finally, the reliability of your backup procedure needs to be considered. Any backup that depends on network activity is inherently more error prone than those done to tape on your local system. Problems with gateways are often the cause of failure with network backups. The advantage of using the network for backups is that you can set up a script or a series of scripts to do most of the work, thus removing the need for someone to be there while the backups are running. Someone still needs to check for error conditions and to verify that the files were transferred properly. This person may need to re-run any commands that failed, but if an occasional manual backup is acceptable to you then there is no reason not to use network backups.

7.2 Output Devices and File Manipulation

One item that is often forgotten when discussing backups is that you can backup to a file, just as easily as you can backup to a piece of tape. All of the backup commands use a file that the program can write to. It does not matter if the file is on disk or on tape. In the situations where a disk is used as backup media, backups can be quickly written to the spare disk and then saved to tape later at your convenience.

Almost all tape functions use /dev/rst# instead of /dev/st#. The r indicates the use of the "raw" tape device. This allows you to write or read the tape in larger blocks which will cut down on the amount of time needed to write to the device. The current releases do not create the "cooked" or non-"raw" versions of the tape devices, but you might encounter them in older releases and in third-party software. If speed is an issue use the raw device when doing tape operations.

Several commands commonly used in backups require the use of the no-rewind device for the tape drive. This device is selected by placing a "n" in front of the normal tape device name; for example, */dev/nrmt0* instead of */dev/rmt0*. This device will not rewind the tape after the operation is complete. This is especially important when you have written several files to one tape. To access these files use the **mt** command (see mt(1)). The syntax of the command is:

mt -f device command

where:

-f device	is the device to be used; default is /dev/rmt12
command	is one of the following:
fsf #	skip forward "#" files
rewind	rewind the tape
status	give status of the tape unit
erase	erase the tape

The command "**mt** -f /dev/nrmt0 fsf 2" results in the first two files being skipped over, and the tape sitting at the beginning of the third file. If you type /dev/rmt0 instead by mistake, the first two files will be skipped over and then the tape will rewind to the beginning of the tape (BOT).

When writing data to tapes the density in which the data is written is often important. The higher the density, the more data that can be placed on one tape. For instance, if you are using a standard 1/4" tape drive, you may write to devices /dev/rst0, /dev/rst8, and on the newer tape drives /dev/rst24. The first two will write 60MB on a 600 foot cartridge tape, and the last will write 150MB. The 150MB tapes are special tapes, so you cannot use the older tapes with /dev/rst24. Using the larger densities will mean that you will use less tape for the same amount of data.

The amount of time each tape read or write takes can be greatly reduced by using appropriate blocking factors. Many of the commands used include options which will allow you to set the blocking factor. This factor determines how much data is written to tape at one time. In general, the larger the blocking factor the better. You can increase this factor too much, which will result in the addition of empty space to fill up the last block. Plus there is a limit on the amount of data that the system can transfer to tape at one time; but within reason the larger the blocking factor the faster your tape operations will occur.

You may place several tape files on one tape by using the /dev/nrst# option when creating the tape. This will allow the backups of several filesystems to be stored on one tape. The tape must be long enough to hold all of the data. You cannot split one tape file over two tapes on Sun systems. Currently, because of the many possible tape drives that can be installed on workstations, the software does not deal with the end-of-tape marker properly. This means that data may be written after the end-of-tape marker is encountered. The processes to restore however does not read beyond the end-of-tape marker so you will lose data if you cannot fit all of your data into one file on one tape. The only way around this problem is to use the **dump** command for backups as opposed to **tar** or **cpio.** Part of the command syntax for **dump** contains arguments which indicate the tape density and the length of the tape that you are using. The writing process is stopped at some point before where the end-of-tape marker is calculated to be thus avoiding it altogether. This process does not handle the end-of-tape marker properly either, but does allow you to spread your data over several tapes if necessary.

7.3 Backups Using **Dump**

The **dump** command (see dump(8)) is the backup command that many sites use. When run on a system with a local tape drive, it is very reliable. The usual errors with this command are caused by bad tapes or dirty tape heads. The **restore** command (see restore(8)) is used to extract files and/or directories from the backups created by **dump.** A backup procedure based on these two commands should be easy to work with and quite reliable.

On the negative side, the **dump** command is not very flexible, and should only be run on a non-active filesystem. It is also a good idea to run **fsck** on all filesystems before you start **dump.** You do not want to archive corrupt filesystems. Normally the two above requirements mean that the system should be in single-user mode. Running **dump** in multi-user mode can cause problems. If you cannot shutdown your servers every night to do the backups, you should consider using a different command for your backups. At least make sure that the level 0 or full dumps are done when systems are in single-user mode.

The **dump** command has many options available. The command syntax is:

   dump options arguments filesystem

where options can be a combination of the following:

0-9   indicates the dump level. All files since the last
                  dump at a lower level are copied. A full dump
                  is done using level 0.

b #   indicates that the next argument is a blocking
                  factor for the tape.

d #   indicates that the next argument is the tape
                  density.

f /dev/name   indicates that the next argument is name of the
                  device to be used.

s #   indicates the length of the tape.

Please note that some of these options require further arguments.
These arguments must be entered after all of the options, in the
order that the options are listed in the command line. For example,
the command:

dump 0sdbf 2400 6250 20 /dev/rmt8 /

runs a complete dump of the root filesystem (which is indicated by
the "0") to /dev/rmt8. The numerical values are the length of the
tape (required by the "s" option), the density ("d" option), and the
blocking factor ("b" option). These values are appropriate for a 1/2"
tape device.

Files archived with **dump** can be retrieved from tape using
the **restore** command (see restore(8)). This command only works
with tapes created using **dump**. The syntax of the command is:

restore -options filename

where options can be a mixture of the following:

i   interactive restore
r   restore the whole tape - do only on empty filesystems
R   resume restoring
t   table of contents
x   extract named files from tape
v   verbose mode
b   blocking factor
f   dump device
s   the next argument is the number of files on the tape to
        skip over

This command is most often run in interactive mode. This mode allows you to choose specific files and/or directories you wish to extract from tape. Extracting just a few files is much easier using this mode. The command:

restore -is 2

starts an interactive restore using the second tape file. Once in the interactive mode you may use these commands:

ls	list files in current tape directory
cd	change to a sub-directory on the tape
pwd	print the current directory pathname
add [filename]	add filename to the list of files to extract
delete [filename]	delete filename from the list of files to extract
extract	extract all files in the extraction list
quit	exit restore

Always make sure that you are in the appropriate disk directory before starting **restore.** For instance a restore tape file containing backups of either / or /usr would contain a /bin, but restoring the /usr/bin on top of /bin is not a good idea.

7.4 Backups Using Cpio

When you use the **cpio** command for backups you must do two separate steps. The first is to create a list of files to be copied. This is usually done with the ls command or with the **find** command. This list is then utilized by **cpio** to copy the files. **Cpio** is invoked to create the backups and to extract files from the backups. Any backup procedure based on these commands will be more difficult to do, but allows a greater flexibility than is available using **dump.**

One of the chief advantages to using **cpio** is that you can do active backups. The system does not need to be down in single user mode. It also lets you backup special files such as the files in /dev.

The major disadvantage to using **cpio** is that there is no interactive restore function. Also, you may not create a **cpio** file that is bigger than the tape you are using. The 8mm tape drives will help with this problem, since each tape can hold 2.3 gigabytes of data.

The following options are allowed with the command:

o   copy out to tape or file
i   copy in from tape or file
p   copy from one filesystem to another
B   set blocking factor to 5120
m   retain modify times
t   print table of contents
v   verbose mode
u   copy unconditionally; this replaces a new file with an
        older one

The command:

cpio -itvB</dev/rst0

displays a table of contents (**ls** -l format) for the tape file on /dev/
rst0.

There are several ways to create a list of files for **cpio** to use.
The most common method is to use the **find** command. The syntax
to the command is:

find dir option

where dir can be a directory in which to start the search, or a list of
file names and directories, and option can be a combination of any
of the options shown in Figure 7.1.

The command:

find . -xdev -ctime -3 -print

will make a list of files located in the current working directory or a
sub-directory on the current partition that have been changed in
the last 3 days. If the current working directory is /usr when you
start this command, you would get a list of files that have changed
in the /usr partition. None of the files located in filesystems
mounted on /usr would be included.

It is advisable to use relative directory names (like ".") as the
starting point for the find command. Not using "/" when creating
the backup files means that you can extract the files to any directory
you like. For instance, you can extract the files in /tmp and then
copy them over to a directory called ˜tom/RESTORE and then let
the user deal with them. In many instances this is better than
replacing the files when the user might be working with them.

-fstype type	the files will be added to the list if they are of a specified type; type can be nfs (for remote files) or 4.2 (for local files)
-name file	the files will be added to the list if the filename is "file"
-size n	the files will be added to the list if it is over "n" blocks long (512 byte blocks)
-ctime n	the files will be added to the list if it has been changed in "n" days; n can be
-xdev	restricts list to the partition that the command is started on
-print	print current pathname
-cpio device	write file in cpio format on named device

FIGURE 7.1. *Options to the find command.*

The list then needs to be fed to the **cpio** command. Allow the ctime intervals to overlap to get each file at least once; for instance, daily backups should use a two day interval, weeklys should use an eight day interval, etc. The next two command lines create the same result:

```
harlie# find . -ctime -3 -print | cpio -oB>/dev/rst0
harlie# find . -ctime -3 -cpio /dev/rst0
```

If you have generated a list of filenames by hand you may use the following command:

```
harlie# cat list | cpio -oB>/dev/rst0
```

Extracting files from a **cpio** backup can be difficult because you need to identify each file or directory that you want extracted from the backup with a complete path. This path must match the path as it appears on the tape.

```
harlie# cpio -iB etc/passwd </dev/rst0
harlie# cpio -idumB "tom/*" </dev/rst0
```

The first command will extract the file etc/passwd from the backup tape. The second command will extract all of the files and directories found under the directory tom. Notice that neither of the pathnames include a slash at the beginning of the pathname. The " " in the second command prevents the "*" from being interpreted by **csh,** if you are using **sh** you do not need them.

The **cpio** command includes a -p option which makes a copy of one directory hierarchy on another. The filesystems and directories must be mounted on the local system. You cannot use this option with **rsh.**

```
baltic# cd /home/baltic
baltic# find tom -print ! cpio -pdlumv /mnt
```

The second command makes a copy of the directory /home/baltic/ tom in /mnt. If you have NFS mounted another home directory on /mnt this command allows you to transfer a home directory without having to use tapes.

7.5 Other Archiving Commands

There are two other commands that are commonly used to create tape files. One is **dd** (see dd(1)). This command is most often used when creating images of root filesystems for boot tapes. It can also be used with **cpio** to read a tape if a header has gotten lost or if a tape is bad. It is not useful for your normal backup procedures, but this command is very versatile and should be studied.

A very common command is **tar** (see tar(1)). In many cases this command has been replaced by **dump** or **cpio. Tar** is good for creating archives of complete directories, but is less flexible for time dependent backups.

The following options are allowed with the command:

c	create a new tarfile
x	extract the data from the tarfile
t	produce table of contents for the tarfile
f /dev/name	the device to be used
v	verbose mode
b	blocking factor

This command can be used if you wish to make a tape with just a few files on it.

7.6 Selection of a Backup Scheme

When selecting a backup scheme, you do not need to consider include some filesystems. You will not need to backup /export/ swap on your client servers. It is much easier to re-create any missing file using **mkfile.** In addition you will not need to backup

/tmp or /var/tmp, if you have placed these directories on their own partitions. Also, if you have a filesystem that does not change very often, run the backups on a weekly basis instead of daily.

Many factors need to be considered when developing a backup scheme for a network. The most important of these are the resources that are available. You should develop a plan that makes the best of what you have. The scenarios discussed below are based on the assumption that your network contains many large servers (two gigabytes of data per server or more).

> Scenario 1: no night staff
> one 8mm tape drive mounted locally for each two gigabytes of data

This is the best situation. You can effectively do a full backup of each system every night. You can run the backups without using the network or without requiring a night crew. You may develop commands or scripts using **cpio** to backup the whole system every work night. The only physical task to be done is to place a different tape in the drive each day. Check the tapes every so often (at least once a week) to make sure that everything is functioning. Have the server start the scripts (use **cron**) or start the scripts each night when you go home. On a two gigabyte system the commands:

```
baltic# cd /
baltic# find * .[a-z]* -fstype 4.2 -print ¦ cpio -oB>/dev/rst0
```

will find all files on the server and write a backup copy to tape.

On larger servers, you will need to divide the data onto several tapes. Below is a sample disk configuration:

```
dora# df
Filesystem       kbytes      used      avail    capacity   Mounted on
/dev/xd0a         20209      3647      14541      20%      /
/dev/xd0g         60661     39977      14617      73%      /usr
/dev/xd0h        237607    194384      19462      91%      /build
/dev/xd1h        547697    544585          0     110%      /src
/dev/xd4h        547697    500539          0     102%      /src/os
/dev/xd5h        547697    416872      76055      85%      /src/os.old
/dev/xd6h        547697    372126     120801      75%      /src/os.beta
/dev/xd7h        547697    416872      76055      85%      /src.beta
```

Since this server has over two gigabytes of data it will have two 8mm tape drives (st0 and st1). The script in Figure 7.2 could be used to backup this server. Figure 7.3 shows the results from using this script.

```
#!/bin/csh
set tapelist0=(/src /src/os /src/os.old)
set tapelist1=(/ /usr /build /src/os.beta /src/beta)
echo "Backups for 'hostname'"
echo 'date'
echo " "
foreach filesys ($tapelist0)
    cd $filesys
    echo "$filesys"
    find * .[a-z]* -xdev -print !cpio -oB>/dev/nrst0
    sleep 10
    echo "$filesys done"
    echo " "
end
foreach filesys ($tapelist1)
    cd $filesys
    echo "$filesys"
    find * .[a-z]* -xdev -print !cpio -oB>/dev/nrst1
    sleep 10
    echo "$filesys done"
    echo " "
end
echo 'date'
```

FIGURE 7.2. *Sample backup script.*

This record can be appended to a file so that you will know which tape file holds the data that you want.

Scenario 2: no night staff
one 8mm tape drive per server

The best way to handle this situation is to make sure that only one tape worth of data changes can be made on the server per backup interval. For instance, in the example above you have a server, dora, with about 3 gigabytes of disk space. If there is only one 8mm tape drive attached to the server, then you would want to backup only those filesystems that are changing routinely. Say that the only filesystems that undergo continual change are the beta source directories, the build directory and root. In this case you would be able to backup /src/beta, /src/os.beta, and / on a nightly basis and only do the other filesystems on a weekly basis.

```
Backups for hal
Fri Jul 12 18:46:12 PDT 1990

/src
#### blocks
/src done


   . . .


/
#### blocks
/ done


   . . .


/src/beta #### blocks /src/beta done

Fri Jul 12 23:46:20 PDT 1990
```

FIGURE 7.3. *Sample backup script output.*

Scenario 3: night staff
    one 8mm tape drive per server

With a night staff, you should be able to use the script above to write to one tape at a time and require operator intervention before going on to the next tape.

Scenario 4: no night staff
    lots of unused local disk space
    no or very few 8mm tape drives

In this situation, use the disks as your daily backup media. Use the 8mm tape drives once a week to ensure that you have a copy of the backups that you can send off-site.

Scenario 5: night staff
    no or very few 8mm tape drives
    1/2″ drives on all servers

Shut all servers down each night. Use dump on the 1/2″ tape drives. In a site with many servers, the night operator will be very busy swapping tapes.

Scenario 6: no night staff
> no or very few 8mm tape drives
> no unused disk space

Get resources immediately! You will need one of these resources in order to backup the systems.

One of these scenarios should approximate your environment (hopefully not number 5 or 6). Often it is easy to justify the purchase of a dedicated backup server or some additional 8mm tape drives when the cost associated with training and sustaining a night staff is considered.

Troubleshooting

8

Two important factors aid while troubleshooting any problem are a knowledge of how things are supposed to work and a plan of action to fix the problem. Many System Administrators have mental or written lists that are used when a problem occurs. Developing this list takes a long time and the revision process for this list should be continuous. For some problems, like hung printers, the process to fix the problem is basically the same one that could have been developed and used with SunOS 3.2. New operating systems bring new problems and new error messages, so there is always something new to learn.

8.1 Error Messages

The following section presents some of the common error messages that are generated while running a Sun workstation. Each message is followed by a description of the probable cause and a way to fix it if it is a problem.

    1: panic: <bus error>

The panic message is displayed when the system receives a command or a set of commands that it can not handle gracefully. Often this occurs when a program tries to use resources that are already allocated to another process. This message is usually generated as the system is crashing. The second part of the message, "bus error" in this case, indicates which program or piece of hardware is causing the problem. You cannot do anything except possibly save the core image and get help.

    2: out of swap space

This message is displayed when too many processes are running on the system. Killing some of the extraneous windows will normally fix this problem. Check for processes that are hogging memory with "**ps -uC**". The third column of the output shows the CPU utilization for the process and the fourth shows the percentage of real memory that is being used (see ps(1)). These two columns will help you find rogue processes that can take up valuable memory. You may also want to check the data in the fifth column which displays the size of the data and stack segments for the program.

Many users believe that when a window is closed or is in the icon form, that it is not using resources. They will claim that they "only have two or three windows running". Make sure to find out how many processes they really are running. If the users do not have any extraneous processes and the systems have access to the configured amount of swap, then you must reconfigure each system to use more swap space. You can check the amount of swap that is available with this command:

green# **pstat** -s

The amount of swap space allocated and reserved will be displayed first (see pstat(8)). These two numbers are combined into a figure for the amount of swap space used, which is the next number. This figure is then subtracted from the total amount of swap space configured and a value for the swap space available is displayed.

Several procedures for increasing the swap space can be used. On diskless clients, if you have additional space in the /export/ swap partition, the size of the swap file may be increased with the **mkfile** command (see mkfile(8)).

blue# **mkfile** 30m /export/swap/green

In this example the swap file for the client named green is being recreated as a 30MB file. This is the simplest method for increasing swap space, but it only works for diskless clients. Only follow this procedure after the client has been halted.

The second way to increase swap space is to execute the swapon command (see swapon(8)). With this command, the free disk space on either a local disk or a remote disk can be allocated for use as swap space. This method can be employed on both diskless and diskfull systems. First a swap file needs to be created on the system with the free disk space by using the **mkfile** command described above.

```
blue# mkfile 16M /export/swap/green-2
blue# mkdir /export/root/green/swap
```

The second command creates a mount point for this new swap file for the client. Next, an entry like the one below should be added to the */etc/exports* file on blue and "**exportfs** -a" should be executed.

```
/export/swap/green-2 -access = green,root = green
```

On the client these lines must be added to */etc/fstab:*

```
blue:/export/swap/green-2 /swap nfs rw,hard 0 0
/swap swap swap rw 0 0
```

The first line allows for NFS mounting of the new swap file. The second line will be read by the **swapon** command. On the client the following commands should be executed by root:

```
green# mount -a
green# swapon -a
```

First the new swap file is mounted and then made available for swapping. The **swapon** command is included in */etc/rc* so if the entries are correct, the new swap file will be used automatically when the system is rebooted. This whole process can be done without halting any systems so the problem can be fixed without any down time.

The last two ways of increasing the amount of swap available include reconfiguring the local disk (for a larger swap) or reconfiguring the kernel to use an additional swap area. Both of these processes involve down time for the system so one of the first two options is best in most cases.

3: vfork failed

Vfork is called when some new processes are started (see vfork(2)). This system call fails if the user has too many processes running. Occasionally this is seen when a process continually spawns other processes, which then start other processes. Sometimes the only recourse is to reboot the system. If the system will not allow any new process to be executed, then the only choice is to **halt** the system.

4: xx0: no carrier,
5: xx0: ethernet jammed

In both of these messages the "xx" can be replaced with one of the following: le, ie, and ec. This is the Ethernet interface that is attached to the local system. The message could also be for "ie1" if a second Ethernet board is installed. The first of these messages (#4) indicates that the board is not receiving any response from the network. Usually this occurs because a cable is loose or a tap has gone bad. The second message is displayed when there is too much traffic on the network. It is more of a status message and should only be a cause for concern if many of them are generated. In a situation where you have many diskless clients booting at one time, many of these messages are liable to show up on the consoles. If this message is continually displayed then either something is wrong with the network or with the Ethernet hardware itself.

6: NFS server <systemname> not responding still trying,
7: NFS server <systemname> ok

Often these two messages are reported together. The first is displayed when the local system cannot reach another server system, normally when running **mount** during the boot process. The second message shows that the connection was successfully established. If many of the first messages are generated, then there is a problem with the remote system or with the network. Check to make sure that the remote system is booted and that any necessary gateways are functioning.

8: ypserver not responding

This message is generated when the local system is unable to reach a YP slave server. Generally there are two situations that cause this. One situation is when a slave server crashes. The fix for this is to bind manually to another slave server or to reboot the system that is down. The other situation is caused by incorrect host or domainname information on a rebooted system. The information must be checked if the system will not reboot by either editing the appropriate files after booting the system to single user mode or by editing the appropriate files in /export/root/<clientname> if the system is a diskless client. See the "client will not boot" section below for a more in depth discussion.

9: <partition>: file system full

The partition name displayed in the error message above can be any of those that are mounted on the local system. If it is the root or "/" partition you will need to search for files that can be deleted. Check in /tmp and /var/tmp (if they are not on a separate partition). Often files get left behind in these directories and are forgotten. Also check /var/spool/* for extraneous files. Occasional perusal of this directory will make you familiar with what is normal and what is not. Make sure to research the files if at all possible before removing them. Another directory that can have files that can be removed is /dev. Most of the files in this directory should be devices and so should not have a size associated with them. Often when running backups the device name will be entered in different ways due to problems with typing (for example, as /dev/rtm8 instead of /dev/rmt8), so your system will attempt to create a very large file. This file should be removed before you restart the backups.

Other things to check for are core files or large files.

find <partition> \(-name core -o -size +3000 \) -exec ls -l {} \;

This command will print out a list of all files named core in the current partition and any files that are over 1.5MB in size. You can substitute the "ls -l" with "rm -f" if you are sure that you want to remove any files that match these criteria.

10: 'su root' failed for <username> on /etc/tty#
11: 'su root' succeeded for <username> on /etc/tty#
12: ROOT LOGIN console

These three messages are generated to show when a user uses the **su** command or when someone logs in as root. These messages can be useful to track down system break-ins and to find out who has the root password.

13: /var/spool/<printer>: No such file or directory
14: /var/spool/<printer>/log: No such file or directory

/usr/lib/lpd, the line printer daemon, generates these messages when a directory or a log file described in */etc/printcap* is not present. To get rid of these messages, either the file or directory should be created or the entry should be removed from the printcap file.

15: duplicate IP address!! Sent from ethernet address: 8:#:#:#:#:#

The only time this message is generated is when you have two
systems trying to run using the same IP number. If the ethers YP
map is kept up-to-date then it can be quite easy to find the second
system. Otherwise a search must be made. If the second machine
succeeds in booting to multi-user mode, then the communications
to the first system will be redirected to the second. Once this has
occurred, both systems must be rebooted. The first should be
rebooted to re-establish communications and the second should be
booted to single-user mode so that the IP number can be corrected.
Only one system at a time can use an IP address.

8.2 Problems with Booting

Occasionally a system will not boot or reboot. Debugging this
problem can be very involved, but the following checklist should
provide some help.

8.2.1 Check the hardware

In all cases make sure that the network and/or the disk hardware is functioning properly. Loose cables and power that is not
turned on cause many of these failures. Also run a check on the
memory installed on the system. There are occasions when bad
memory prevents a system from booting, but no memory error is
generated.

8.2.2 Boot to Single-User Mode

Check the IP address in */etc/hosts* and the domain name in
/etc/rc.local. The IP address must match the entry in the YP host
map. The domain name must be entered exactly (capital letters are
significant). Problems with these two entries cause many of the
booting problems. For diskless clients you may check this data
from the the client's server by looking at */export/root/<client>/
etc/hosts* and */export/root/<client>/etc/rc.local*.

If these entries are correct, but a diskless client still will not
boot, assure that the tftpboot link on the server is using the correct
address. The link in /tftpboot on the server should use the hexadecimal equivalent of the IP address (for example, 192.9.202.3

should be C009CA03). Note that each octet in the host address should be represented by two characters (in this example, 3 is 03). These links are usually only bad if the host address was incorrect during the client install or the network number has been changed, but the links were not updated.

If the hardware looks fine, but the diskfull system still cannot make it to single-user mode, reboot the system using the MINI-ROOT on the installation tapes. Once you are booted you can run **fsck** on the root and usr partitions and you can mount these partitions to look for missing files. If the root partition does not have a /dev/null the system will not boot properly. The command

> **mknod** /a/dev/null c 3 2

will re-create the file if the root partition has been mounted on /a.

8.2.3 Boot to Multi-User Mode

Watch the output from the booting process and see where the process hangs. If the booting process does not go through all of the rc files then there could be a problem with the binaries that are executed from the scripts. If the system reaches single-user without any problems but cannot go further, then you probably have a problem with the network or with the software. At this stage, you should run the commands in */etc/rc.local* manually to see where the system is hanging. Sometimes a binary has been removed or re-named but the */etc/rc.local* file has not been changed to reflect this.

8.3 Problems with Printing

Often a printer will hang because a weird file is in the spool directory. Core files can confuse the line printer daemon and prevent it from functioning correctly. The commands listed below should fix this problem:

> minerva# **/usr/lib/lpc** abort all
> minerva# **rm** /var/spool/<printer>/core
> minerva# **/usr/lib/lpc** start all

When there are not any core or other strange files in the spool directory, sometimes the daemon needs to be restarted with the commands below:

```
minerva# /usr/lib/lpc abort all
minerva# kill -9 <pid for /usr/lib/lpd >
minerva# /usr/lib/lpd &
minerva# /usr/lib/lpc start all
```

The first command turns off the line printer daemons for each printer (if they are running). The second command needs the process ID for the main daemon that is running. This number can be found using "**ps** -aux ¦ **grep lpd**". The next command re-starts the main line printer daemon and the last command spawns off additional daemons for each printer.

If this does not clear the printer, repeat the first two commands from the example above. When the line printer daemon has been killed, power cycle the actual line printer, and then reinitialize the software using the last two commands in the example. While you are working with the hardware you may want to check the printer to make sure that it has not been broken. Often with the Laserwriter(TM) I, too much paper placed in the paper tray will cause the printer to jam. In this case, just removing the extra paper is enough to get things going again, but on occasion you will need to stop and restart the software too.

Set up a maintenance schedule so that the printer is checked and cleaned every time a new toner cartridge, a new ribbon or a new box of paper is added. All printers are prone to failure because of paper dust and other forms of dirt. Routine cleaning will prolong the life of the printer.

After installing a printer make sure that all spool directories and files are owned by daemon.

8.4 Forgotten Passwords

To change a forgotten YP password, as root on the YP master, you will need to edit the password YP datafile, remove the encrypted password entry for that user and make the new YP password map. Be careful to remove all of the password and not to remove anything else when editing the file. After the **make** has completed, ask the user to set their password with the **yppasswd** command or do it for them. If you are not using YP, edit the local */etc/passwd* file, remove the password from the entry and have the password reset using **passwd.** The password cannot contain any spaces or tabs.

Since root passwords are not normally included in YP, there are different mechanisms for correcting this password. On diskless clients, the following command may be used:

blue# **passwd** -F */export/root/<client>/etc/passwd* root

On diskfull systems, you will either need to reboot to single-user mode or load MINIROOT so that you can edit the */etc/passwd* file. The only other option is to reload the whole system, but this is a little drastic.

8.5 Problems with Mail

There are many situations that can disturb the delivery of mail. One common problem occurs when a user receives too much mail to load on their local system. To remedy this problem, you should use the steps listed below:

1. As root on the diskless client, kill the **/usr/lib/sendmail** process. This will prevent any new mail from arriving.

2. As the user, copy */var/spool/mail/<username>* to ˜home/ <username>.mail

3. As the user, remotely login to a system that has the users' home directory mounted and has enough space in /tmp to load the mail file. Use "**Mail** -f <username>.mail" to read the mail file. The **Mail** command is linked to **/usr/ucb/mail** which is a more user-friendly version than **/usr/bin/mail.** Once the user has deleted or otherwise dealt with the mail and has reduced the mail file follow the next step.

4. As the user, on the users' system copy˜home/ <username>.mail to */var/spool/mail/<username>*

5. As root, start mail again by typing:

/usr/lib/sendmail -bd -q1h &

In the instance where mail is loaded on a mailhost or on the client server, the user should be able to login to the server remotely and process the mail there.

There are several things that will prevent mail delivery. Make sure that the users' home directory is mounted on the system that they need to receive mail on. The program checks for this and will not deliver the mail unless you force it to by changing the local *letc/aliases* file. Also make sure that the mail file is owned by the user. One last thing to check: make sure that the file is not a link to another file. Mail will not be delivered to the user if the file is owned by root or if the file is a link.

8.6 Problems with Lockscreen

The **lockscreen** program is used by many users to lock up their system when they are not in their office. Sometimes the system fails to let the user back in when they return. Occasionally the process will have hung, which means that the process will have to be killed from another system. Normally the cause of this problem is that the keyboard is set to type in capitals only. On the Sun3 keyboard both the "F1" and the "Caps" key can be used to toggle this, so some experimentation is necessary to fix the problem. Another reason that **lockscreen** will not unlock is that the cursor is not present in the screen. This occurs when someone has accidentally bumped the mouse. If this happens all you need to do is find a way to get the cursor back on the screen. Either one of these situations can be fixed by killing the process after a **rlogin** from a remote system, but often the increase in user awareness when they are shown how to fix the problem is worth the extra effort.

Other Important Files and Issues

9

The topics discussed in the next chapter do not fit in well with other subjects in this book but include important of information. The first section is a discussion of some of the important files that you should be aware of. Next, serial communications will be explored, followed by a section on disk recovery.

9.1 /etc/rc Scripts

The rc scripts in /etc are run by **init** when a system is booted. These scripts initiate many of the network services that are needed in order to make your system function. A basic understanding of these scripts is necessary to comprehend what is happening during the boot process.

The first script that is run is */etc/rc.boot*, which starts by establishing a path. Then the hostname of the system is set. Next the appropriate ethernet device is turned on using the hostname as an argument. Finally the script checks to see if a filesystem check needs to be run. Normally, unless the system has been shutdown using **fasthalt** or **fastboot,** a filesystem check will be run. This will give you a chance to fix any errors on the filesystems before you bring the system up to multi-user. If an error is found on the root filesystem, it is corrected and the system is automatically rebooted for you. If there is an error on any file system that **fsck** can not resolve, both the root and user filesystems will be mounted read only and a warning message will be displayed.

Normally the filesystems are fairly clean and do not take human intervention to get things running again. When this is true, the */etc/rc.single* script is run. This scripts' purpose is to *mount* the root and user partitions in a writable mode and to clean up some possible error conditions.

The only reason that either of these two scripts should be edited is if you are changing the hostname of your system. Otherwise it would be best never to touch these files.

If everything is successful up to this point, the */etc/rc* script is run. This script attempts to do some correcting of the passwd file, mounts all of the local filesystems and starts the next script, which is */etc/rc.local.* The rc.local script is started before the */etc/rc* script has finished. The rc.local script must run successfully before the rc script can continue. While the rc.local script is running, the domainname is set, YP is turned on and many of the network activities are initiated. When the "local" script is done, the last part of the rc script is run. This last part finishes the clean-up process and starts the last services, such as **cron, inetd,** and the line printer daemon. NFS mounts can then be made since most of the network services have been started.

9.1.1 Editing the rc Scripts

Special care should be taken whenever these scripts are edited. Many boot failures are created when someone edits these files without knowing what they are doing. A good knowledge of shell programming will help with this process (but then that's another book. . .). In general, don't touch unless you must. If you have to, make a copy of the file before you edit it so that you can easily go back to the old version. Pay special attention to the spacing and the grouping of the commands. For instance, if you delete the spaces in the if statements, the test will not work and the script will fail. The correct syntax for a test is:

    if [-s /etc/ptmp]; then

An incorrect syntax is:

    if [-s /etc/ptmp]; then

This typographical error is the most frequent cause of problems with the rc scripts. The second most common error is the placement of new text or comments in the wrong spot in the file. You want to make sure that the command that you are trying to start will run at this point in the boot sequence. Also make sure not to disturb any of the text that is already there. Most of the file is in this format:

```
if [ -f somefile ]; then
    run a command
else
    echo an error message
fi
```

which would test to see if somefile exists; if it does, then the script would "run a command". If the file does not exist the script would "echo an error message". The "fi" is the end of the if statement. While adding text to this file, do not add text into the middle of one of these sets of commands. A good rule to go by is that you can add text to the rc scripts on the line before an if statement. Make sure that necessary network processes have already been started. For example, **ypbind** will not function if the network interfaces are not turned on. If all else fails, add the new commands before the "exit 0" in the */etc/rc* script.

9.2 /dev/MAKEDEV

This is the script used to make the special files located in /dev. Options include:

std	for standard devices
local	uses */dev/MAKEDEV.local*
st*	for SCSI tape
xt*	for Xylogics 472 1/2" tape
ip*	for IPI disk
sd*	for SCSI disk
pty*	for pseudo terminals

Normally, this command is invoked for you when you run **sun-install.** However, if you add a new board or device you will need to create the device files. A file named */dev/MAKEDEV.local* can be created to allow for the creation of any third party devices. The script invokes **mknod** which actually makes the device special file or files.

9.3 /etc/inetd.conf

This is the default file used by **inetd** to initiate any new services that are being requested. This file ties together the */etc/protocols* and */etc/services* files. Each entry contains:

service_name socket_type protocol wait_status uid program arguments

where service_name is the name of a service that can be run on this server (it must be in */etc/services* or the YP map); socket_type is self-explanatory; protocol is the name of a protocol (this should be in */etc/protocols* or the YP map); wait_status is usually set to nowait; uid is the user ID that the server program should run as; program is the name of a server program to be run to provide the necessary service; and arguments are any command line arguments to the server program.

9.4 Crontab

In the old UNIX releases crontab was a file that was checked when **cron** was run. **Crontab** is now a command which allows you to view or make changes to each individual crontab file. Many critical housecleaning processes are listed in the crontab file for root.

The **crontab** command (see crontab(1)) is often invoked with one of the following options: -e to edit and reinitialize, -l to list or -r to remove. These options will give you access to one crontab file at a time. You can select a specific crontab file by including the username after the required option. Normally this can only be done by root. Calling **crontab** without any options and with a filename will cause that file to be copied as the current user's crontab file. These files are all placed in the directory /var/spool/cron/crontabs.

Other files that are of interest are *at.allow* and *at.deny*. These two files can be found in /var/spool/cron. The *at.allow* file, if present, lists all of the users that can use **crontab**. The *at.deny* file lists all of the users who cannot run **crontab.** If both of these files are zero length then everyone can run **crontab.** If neither of these files are present then only root can run the command. The default installed setup is for all users to have access, because both files are zero length.

The formatting of each line in the crontab file is very important. The correct amount of information must be present to make sure that the command is executed at the proper time (see crontab(5)). Each line should be formatted as follows:

minute hour d-o-month month d-o-week command

in which minute and hour indicate the time that you want the command to run. The hour field can have values from 0 through 23. There is not an AM or PM option available. The next field, called d-o-month, is the day of the month. Month is the month of the year. The last numerical field is the d-o-week, or the day of the week field. This field should be used to run processes that only run once a week (Sunday is day 0). The last field is the command to be run.

An asterisk "*" can be placed in any of the numerical fields. This will indicate that all possible values for this field are valid. It is doubtful that you would ever want to use a crontab line with:

* * * * * command

because the system would attempt to run the command every minute. Each numerical field can alternatively contain a list of values separated by commas, which indicates a list of valid values, and/or two numbers separated by a hyphen, which indicates a range of values.

```
0 0 1,16 * * * semi.monthly
0 0 * 6 * * june.only
0 0 * * * 5 weekly.backups
0 0 * * * 1-4 daily.backups
1 4 * * * * rdate datehost 2>&1&
```

The last entry in this example will update the time on the local system to be synchronized with the time set on the system called datehost. This provides an "auto-magic" way to keep the systems synchronized in your network.

9.5 Serial Communications

UNIX-based systems are known for their ability to allow multiple users to simultaneously use the same system, usually accomplished through serial communication. Sun systems are based on a multi-processing environment where each workstation is a multi-user system. Instead of attaching many serial lines to each system, a windowing and/or networking environment is used.

Some installations prefer to use the serial model, connecting vast numbers of ASCII terminals to one common system. This is certainly less expensive than a workstation on each desk, but is more efficiently handled by a device called a bridge-box.

A bridge-box is a device connected to the network that has several serial connections. Each bridge-box occupies an IP address, and is intelligent enough to understand how to connect to other hosts on the network. This arrangement is good for networked sites. For non-networked installations, the only way to connect ASCII terminals is through hard-wired serial lines.

The basic steps to install a terminal to a serial port are simple. The hardware needed is the terminal, the open serial port, and a data cable, usually a 25 pin connector with pins two and three crossed, and pin seven straight through. The software needed is already native to UNIX. Enabling a tty port involves editing a few files, and sending a signal to **init.**

When installing an ASCII terminal as the system console, you are presented with two problems. The first is telling the system which port to use, the second is how. Every Sun computer has some form of serial port included in its design, usually no less than two. Most systems also have a toggle switch on or near the back panel of the CPU board that enables or disables the extended power-on diagnostics. When the "diag" switch is on, serial port A is the default console device set at 9600 baud, 7 data bits, 1 stop bit, no parity. If you connect an ASCII terminal to port A, flip the diag switch to enable diagnostics, and power on the system, then you should see the diagnostic messages scroll on the terminal. When the tests are complete, you are given ten seconds to interrupt the "diag-boot" sequence by typing any key. When this is interrupted, the monitor prompt is displayed, ">".

9.5.1 Setting the Console Port

To set the console location on every Sun machine except the SPARCstation 1, do the following at the monitor prompt, ">".

```
> q1f<CR>
EEPROM 01F: 00? 10<CR>
EEPROM 020: 00? q
```

The above commands set the primary console to serial port A. To set the console port to serial port B, enter 11 instead of 10. Other values in location 1F set the console device to a Sun bitmapped display (00 is for monochrome and 12 is for color monitors).

Once the PROM is set, you can power the system off and return the "diag" switch to its normal position. When the system is turned on, the ASCII terminal is now the console.

To enable the other on-board serial line for use as a login terminal, follow the steps for adding additional serial lines below, editing only the appropriate lines in the */etc/ttytab* file.

9.5.2 Adding Additional Serial Lines

Additional serial ports are available on Sun systems through various hardware products. The Sun-produced Multiple Channel Processor , or MCP, allows an additional 16 serial connections to the system. Installing the hardware involves connecting a board to the backplane and attaching a cable from the board to the unit that contains the 25-pin ports.

To enable the software, you must first verify that the driver is configured into the kernel. The generic kernel is configured with all known devices so begin by booting the generic kernel. Next, observe the boot output to determine the new board's ID number because this number is used in the following step to create the device nodes in the /dev directory.

The **MAKEDEV** script can create eight possible MCP devices. The first board installed is usually called mcp0. Viewing the boot output is one way to confirm the device name. Make the appropriate device by becoming root, changing directories to /dev, and executing "**MAKEDEV** mcpX", where X is the mcp device shown at boot time.

Next, enable logins on the ports by adding the new device names to the /etc/ttytab file, as shown in Figure 9.1 below. The getty field contains the full path to a command, in this case **getty,** and any parameters describing characteristics of that port. For **getty,** the baud rate parameter should be described in the */etc/ gettytab* file. The type field is the terminal type, found in the */usr/lib/termcap* file. Entries in the status field toggle the tty line on or off, specify the port to be local or remote, and enable or disable root logins from the port. Secure indicates the environment

# name	getty	type	status comments
#			
console	"/usr/etc/getty std.9600"	sun	on local secure
ttyh0	"/usr/etc/getty std.9600"	925	on local secure
ttyh1	"/usr/etc/getty std.9600"	vt100	on local secure
ttyh2	"/usr/etc/getty std.9600"	925	on local secure
ttyh3	"/usr/etc/getty std.9600"	925	on local secure
ttyh4	"/usr/etc/getty std.9600"	w30	on local secure
ttyh5	"/usr/etc/getty std.9600"	925	on local secure
ttyh6	"/usr/etc/getty std.9600"	925	on local secure
ttyh7	"/usr/etc/getty std.9600"	925	on local secure
ttyh8	"/usr/etc/getty std.9600"	925	on local secure
ttyh9	"/usr/etc/getty std.9600"	925	on local secure
ttyha	"/usr/etc/getty std.9600"	925	on local secure
ttyhb	"/usr/etc/getty std.9600"	925	on local secure
ttyhc	"/usr/etc/getty std.9600"	925	on local secure

FIGURE 9.1. *Enabling ports in the /etc/ttytab file.*

to be secure, allowing root logins. An "unsecure" entry disables root logins on that port.

The gettytab file is checked by **/usr/etc/getty** to determine at which baud rate to run the port. Other generic terminal characteristics can be set in this file. Generally the only time this file needs to be changed is if you have a modem that requires a different baud rate or if you want the rotary entries to cycle through different baud rates than those listed in the generic file. It is best to add new entries instead of changing old ones.

Each entry should be of the form:

```
# | alias | description:\
    :option:option:
```

where # is a unique one character identifier for this entry. Always check to make sure that you are not reusing a number or letter. Alias should be a short four-to-six letter name for this entry. The description can be several words and should explain what this entry should be used for. Please note that a " | " separates each of these naming fields. A ":" is used to separate any required options. The "\" includes the information on the next line in the current entry. Each entry can be several lines if necessary, but normally all that is needed is one or two options. You may use any of the options in the manual page (see gettytab(5)).

After the tty entries have been made, start **getty** by sending a hangup signal to the **init** process, as shown below.

```
# kill -1 1
```

9.5.3 Attaching a Modem

In the early days of networking, systems could only connect through serial lines. To communicate with systems beyond the local site, a modem attached to a phone line was, and still is used today (see tip(1C), remote(5), and phones(5)).

Attaching a Hayes® compatible modem to Sun equipment is accomplished by first selecting a serial port, and locating a phone line. You need a cable to connect between the modem and the serial port, and the cable from the phone line to the modem.

Determine if the modem is to have dial-in or dial-out capabilities, or both. To enable dial-in capabilities, you must perform the steps outlined above, being sure to set the correct baud rate in the */etc/ttytype* file.

```
#
# name    getty                       type      status comments
#
console  "/usr/etc/getty std.9600"    sun       on local secure
ttyd0    "/usr/etc/getty D2400"       dialup    on remote
```

To enable both dial-in and dial-out capabilities, perform the steps above, and some additional steps. Create a new device node in the /dev directory, using the same major device number as the dial-in port, adding 128 to the minor device number. Observe the following:

```
crw-------  1 uucp 12, 128 Feb 19 14:01 /dev/cua0
crw--w--w- 1 root  12,   0 Feb 16 08:54 /dev/ttyd0
```

Both nodes are connected to the same physical port whose major number is 12. The dial-in port, ttyd0, has a minor number of zero. The dial-out port has a minor number of 128. If the dial-in port had a different minor device number, such as four, the dial-out minor number would be 132.

Use **mknod** in this manner to create a dial-out port:

```
# cd /dev
# mknod cua1 c 12 132
#
```

After setting up the dial-out node, create entries in the */etc/remote* file for automatic dialing. For example, you often call company X over the modem using the number 555-1234. When you create an entry for X in */etc/remote*, one command connects to the port, and dials the number.

```
# tip X
```

The entry for X in the */etc/remote* file is similar to Figure 9.2 below.

9.6 Disk Recovery

Preparing for a disk crash is like insurance: making arrangements for something you never want to do. But when a disk fails, you are happy that the necessary information was saved. Redundancy is the key. It is acceptable to keep needed information on-line, but do not put it all on the same machine. What if that machine loses its disk?

Some things you can do to prepare for disk troubles are:

1. Store the label information for each and every disk on one other machine, and off-line on paper.

2. Store defect list information for all your disks on another machine.

```
#
# /etc/remote
#
X:Company-X Xcom:\
    pn=5551234:tc=UNIX-2400
Y:Company-Y:Ycom:\
    pn=5552234:tc=UNIX-2400
```

FIGURE 9.2. *Sample entries in the /etc/remote file.*

3. Make copies of your */etc/fstab* files, from all your machines, and print them out.

4. Perform preventive maintenance on your disks, especially the rack-mounted disks.

5. Maintain a rigorous backup schedule.

If you start having problems with a disk, keep a listing or a log of the errors. This list can be invaluable in diagnosing the problem. For instance, if the errors are random and do not repeat regularly, then the problem is most likely to be something wrong with the controller or the cable. Trying to run **format** on any disk under these conditions would cause more problems. If the errors are continually repeated or the disk will not work, then you will either need to reformat or replace the disk.

9.6.1 Storing Label Information

Use the **dkinfo** command to display the label information. Redirect the output into a local file, and append the label information for each disk on the system to that file. Print it out and put the paper in a file cabinet. Copy the file to at least two other machines. Maintaining a copy of the label information is the best way to protect yourself from disaster.

9.6.2 Storing Defect Information

Store each disk's defect information by starting the **format** program, and entering the defect menu. Since there is an option to save the defect list to a file, select that option and again, store the file on a different machine.

The defect information, while important, does not help you as much as the label data. The label information can be transferred to a different disk of the same type while the defect information is specific to one disk. Still it is good to have the defect list on-line.

9.6.3 Copying Your */etc/fstab* Files

The label information is the most important because it defines the start and end of partitions. The */etc/fstab* file shows how the partitions were used, their mount points and names. The same information can be obtained in other ways, but maintaining a copy of the */etc/fstab* file for each system is the easiest.

One other way is to run **fsck** on each partition, noting the "last mounted on" line. This procedure is very time consuming and possibly misleading.

9.6.4 Preventive Maintenance

For most winchester type disk drives, little maintenance can be done other than providing a proper air-flow in and around the disk enclosure. Some of the rack-mounted drives have their own blowers, along with a filtering system, just for cooling. Many times, the filters become clogged, constricting the proper air-flow to the electronics of the disk. It is at this point when error messages start appearing in the console, usually recoverable errors. Clean the filter on the Fujitsu-M2351, and the Fujitsu-M2361 regularly to avoid this type of problem. In most cases, soft errors are destined to become hard errors.

9.6.5 A Rigorous Backup Schedule

How well you recover from a disk crash is only as good as your last backup. None of the above procedures help if you do not keep your systems backed up well. The backup program you choose dictates how to reconstruct when a disk is replaced.

If you use **dump** to capture your data, you must use **restore** to put it back. These two programs, while probably the most common, are more limiting when restoring everything. **Dump** takes a snapshot of the filesystem, inode numbers included, and puts them onto tape. If you need to restore the files to a completely different disk, the size of the filesystem you are restoring to must be exactly the same size, or larger.

If you use **cpio** or **tar,** you have more options available, but only if explicit paths are not used when archiving the data (such as home/sys instead of /home/sys). Either utility enables you to re-store data to any filesystem when explicit paths are not used.

Keep custom files, and those that are not part of the original filesystem on separate media when at all possible. If you need to restore the root and /usr files, you can use **suninstall.** Then, restore your custom files on top of the OS files. This is especially helpful when the primary system disk fails.

9.6.6 Replacing a Disk

When a disk fails and is replaced, the administrator is left with the task of turning the new disk to a mirror image of the original. This is only possible if the replaced disk is the exact make and model of the original. To accomplish this task you must have the original label information available, the filesystem names, and, of course, the archived data from the filesystems that were on the original disk.

If the replaced disk contained the root filesystem, you will need to run **suninstall,** only configuring the partitions used by the OS (such as /, /usr, /var). Be sure to use the same partition arrangement if **dump** was used to archive data. After the installation is complete, restore the other filesystems on the replacement disk from backups by first running **newfs** on the partition, and then mounting it. This is where the */etc/fstab* information is needed. Restore each filesystem, update the */etc/fstab* and create the mount points.

Be aware that filesystems on other disks should not be affected. You should only have to re-create the mount point and mount those partitions to make the data available.

If the replaced disk does not contain the root filesystem, determine if you can boot the OS. If so, boot into single-user mode and comment out any lines from the */etc/fstab* file that attempt to mount the new disk. Once the comments are blocked, you can complete booting into multi-user.

Start the **format** utility, selecting the replaced disk. Re-label the disk, using the **dkinfo** output explained above. Run **newfs** on each filesystem, mount the filesystem, and restore from backup media.

If you cannot boot the OS, your options are: to boot the MINI-ROOT and attempting to restore from there or to temporarily make the system a diskless client. The later may be of most benefit as all of the networking and OS utilities are available. Another benefit to restoring disks while running as a diskless client is that you can copy the /usr files to disk.

Reference Library

As a System Administrator, you will not be able to remember everything, so it is wise to have a good library available. This is not meant to be an exhaustive list but should provide some direction.

The first thing that you should get is the SunOS documentation set and full documentation for any unbundled or third-party products you must support. A personal copy of the manual pages and the installation manual in which you can write notes is invaluable. One skill that you will need to develop is the ability to read the manual pages. All sorts of information can be found in them, but you will probably need to spend some time with them, before they can be useful for you. Spend time reviewing the commands that you are familiar with and check out any options that are new. Also follow the references to additional manual pages. These additional pages can sometime make necessary information available, even if it is missing from the first manual page. For the quick review nothing is better than the manual pages.

A series of books that has a lot of useful information is the *Nutshell Handbooks* which are published by O'Reilly and Associates, Inc. There are many books in this series. Select those that are interesting to you or that you think you will use (hopefully they will be the same).

A general UNIX System Administration book that is quite good is *UNIX System Administration Handbook* by E. Nemeth, G. Synder and S. Seebass, published by Prentice Hall. It does not go into great detail about the SunOS, but it is good for generic UNIX.

If you want to learn more about kernels and other "internal" subjects get *The Design and Implementation of the 4.3BSD UNIX(R) Operating System* written by S. Leffler, M. McKusick, M. Karels and J. Quarterman, published by Addison Wesley. It is not specifically about SunOS but is still very useful.

For information about the **csh,** read *The UNIX C Shell Guide* by G. Anderson and P. Anderson, published by Prentice Hall. This book is indispensable.

If you want to do some *awk* programming, you should look into *The Awk Programming Language,* written by A. Aho, B. Kernighan and P. Weinberger and published by Addison Wesley. It goes into great detail about the things you can do with this command.

Last but definitely not least, for information on **nroff** or **troff** look at *UNIX(TM) Nroff/Troff: A User's Guide* written by K. Roddy and published by Holt, Rinehart and Winston.

Index

A

Alias files, 115–118
  sample, 116
Application software, 161
Archiving commands, 251
ASCII datafiles, 109
  formatting, 112
ASCII terminals, 164, 272
Audit filesystems, 237
Audit flags, 238–240
The Awk Programming Language,
  282

B

Backup, system, 13–14, 241–255
Backup commands, 244–251
Backup concepts, 241–244
Backup media, 241–242
Backup schedule, 278–279
Backup schemes, 242–243
  selecting, 251–255
Backup script, 243–244
  sample, 253
  sample output, 254
Berkeley Software Distribution
  version 4.3, 2
Binary files, 9
Blocking factor, 245
Blocks, 18–19
BNC connector, 212
Booting, problems with, 262–263
Booting MUNIX, 35
  on SPARCstation 1, 51
  from tape, 38, 39

Bootparams files, 126–129, 182–183
  sample, 128
Bridge-box, 272
Broadcast address, 167, 214
"Bundled" software, 169

C

C2 security makefile changes, 140
C2 Security package, 237–240
C2conv script, 238
C2secure maps, 38–139
Class A addresses, 215
Class B addresses, 215
Class C addresses, 163, 167, 215–216
Client form, 75–78
Client machines, 2–4
Client servers, 177–191
Communications, serial, 271–276
Configuration file, 91–96
Console ports, setting, 272–273
Cpio command, 248–251
Crontab command, 270–271
Cylinders, 17

D

Dataless clients, 3, 4
Defect list, 15
  storing, 277
  viewing, 41–42
Defect menu, 43
Density, tape, 245
Deskside machines, 1–2
Desktop workstations, *see*
  Workstation *entries*

/dev/MAKEDEV, 269
Device information, 88–90
Device removal, 94–95
Dial-in and dial-out capabilities,
    275–276
Disk labels, 20, 50–51
    modifying, 47–50
Disk layouts, 21–35
    diskless client server, 26–33
    print server, 34–35
    resource server, 33–34
    standalone, 21–26
Disk recovery, 276–277
Diskfull machines, 2, 4–9
Diskless client kernels, 96–103
Diskless client server layout, 26–33
Diskless client servers, 6–7
    with two disks, 32–33
Diskless clients, 3
    adding, 178
    booting, 186–191
    hung in boot process, 155
    removing, 184–186
    running format as, 51–52
Disks
    formatting, 42, 44
    labeling, *see* Disk labels
    partitioning, 14, 18–19, 44–47
    replacing, 279
    selecting, 40–41
Dump command, 246–248
Dynamic routing, 228

E

Electronic mail (email), 204–206
End-of-tape marker, 246
Entering format, 38–40
Error messages, 257–262
/etc/fstab files, 277–278
/etc/inetd.conf, 269–270
Ethernet, 211
Ethernet address, 129
Ethernet interface, 6
Ethers files, 29–131
    sample, 130

Export directory, 29
/export partition, 26–30
Exporting, 5

F

Fiber Distributed Data Interface
    (FDDI), 6
Files
    restoring, 243
    saving, 13–14
Fileservers, 1, 5–9
Filesystems, 19–20
Format
    entering, 38–40
    running, as diskless client, 51–52
Format concepts, 14–20
Format main menu, 42
Free-hog disk partition, 37, 67–68

G

Gateway machines, 218
Gateway servers, 219
GENERIC kernel, 87–103
gid (group identification number),
    118, 119, 194
Group files, 118–120
Group identification number (gid),
    118, 119, 194
Group map, 131

H

Heads, 17
Heterogeneous servers, 7
Home directories, 191–197
    moving, 208–209
Home directory server, 197–198
/home partition, 31–32
Homogeneous servers, 7
Host number, 120, 214
Hostfiles, 120–124
    example for three sets, 221

example for two nets, 220
sample, 22, 166
Hostnames, 120–121

I

In-line taps, 212
Internet protocol (IP) number, 13
    duplicate, 262

K

Keys, 112

L

Label information, storing, 277
Labels, disk, *see* Disk labels
Laserwriters, 173–174
Library, reference, 281–282
Local network, 111
Lockscreen, problems with, 266
Login accounts, 6
Lost+found directory, 19
Lpc utility, 176, 177

M

Mail problems, 265–266
    debugging, 205–206
Maintenance, preventive, 278
Maintenance schedule, 264
Makedbm command, 144
Manufacturer defect list, *see* Defect
    list
MINIROOT filesystem, 35, 37,
    54–55, 226–227
    booting, 57, 58
    booting, from tapeless machine,
        82–83
    copying, 56
    installing, 55–57
    loading, from MUNIX, 52–53
    remote copy of, 82
Modems, attaching, 275–276

Motorola MC680X0 family, 10
MUNIX, 37
    booting, *see* Booting MUNIX
    loading MINIROOT from, 52–53
MUX box, 212

N

Netgroup files, 131–134
    sample, 133, 168
    short sample, 134
Netid files, 137–138
Netmasks files, 134–135
Network, 1
    adding more than one, 218–220
    defined, 211
    local, 111
    single, setting up, 217–218
Network classes, 14–216
Network commands, 220, 222–224
Network File System, *see* NFS
    entries
Network hardware, 211–213
Network Information Service (NIS),
    109
Network number, 211, 214
Network routing, 227–228
Network security, *see* Security
Network software, 213–214
Network troubleshooting commands,
    222–223
Network usage commands, 223–224
Networking, 211–229
    point-to-point, 229
    special, 228–229
Networks files, 135
NFS (Network File System), 2, 4
    secure, 236–237
NFS information, 172–173
NFS mounting, automatic, 201–202
NFS resource server, 168–172
NIS (Network Information Service),
    109
Non-YP accounts, 196–197
Nutshell Handbooks, 281

P

Panic message, 257
Partition "c," 24, 46
Partition "g," 46–47
    changing, 49–50
Partition menu, 45
Partitioning disks, 14, 18–19
Password, YP, *see* YP password
Password files, 124–126
    editing, 194–196
Point-to-point networking, 229
Pre-installed systems, 101–104
Preventive maintenance, 278
Print server layout, 34–35
Print servers, 4, 8–9, 173–177
Printer access, controlling, 176–177
Printers, remote, using, 202–205
Printing, problems with, 263–264
Protocols files, 135–136
Prototype files, 193
Publickey files, 137

R

Race conditions, 160
Rack-mounted fileservers, 2
RARP (Reverse Address Resolution
    Protocol), 187–188
Rc scripts, 267–268
    editing, 268–269
Reference library, 281–282
Remote printers, using, 202–205
Resource server layout, 33–34
Resource servers, 8
Restoring files, 243
Reverse Address Resolution Protocol
    (RARP), 187–188
/.rhosts, 231–232
Root directory, 23
Root directory files, moving, 207–208
Root partition, 21–23
Root passwords, 124–125
Routing, network, 227–228
Rpc files, 136

S

Saving files, 13–14
Sectors, 18–19
Secure NFS, 236–237
Security, 231–240
    tightening, 233–236
Serial communications, 271–276
Serial ports, additional, 273–275
Server administration, 162–198
    client servers, 177–191
    home directories, 191–197
    NFS information, 172–173
    NFS resource server, 168–172
    print servers, 173–177
    server room set up, 163–164
    YP master server, 164–168
Server room set up, 163–164
Servers, 4–9
    client, 177–191
    diskless client, *see* Diskless client
        servers
    fileservers, 1, 5–9
    gateway, 219
    heterogeneous, 7
    homogeneous, 7
    print, 4, 8–9, 173–177
    resource, 8
Services files, 136–137
Setup_client script, 178–182,
    183–184
Slash (/), 21
Slip sectoring, 16
SMD (storage module disk)
    devices, 16
SPARC microprocessor, 9
Spooling directories, 175
Standalone layout, 21–26
Standalone machines, 4, 5
Static routing, 228
Storage module disk (SMD)
    devices, 16
Subnetting, 216–217
    establishing, 224–227
Sun administration, ix, 161–209

server administration, 162–198; *see also* Server administration
workstation administration, 198–209; *see also* Workstation administration
Sun architectures, 9–11
Sun computer systems types, 1–11
Sun workstations, *see* Workstation *entries*
Sun-3x, 10
Sun-4c, 11
Suninstall, 47, 54–83
  aborting, 83–84
  adding more software, 104–108
  booting from local tape, 55
  disk form, 64–67
  display unit, 68–71
  entering, 57–79
  free-hog disk partition, 37, 67–68
  host form, 61–63
  main menu, 60
  post-installation issues, 84–87
  pre-installed systems, 101–104
  remote instalation, 79–83
  setting YP type, 63–64
  software form, 71–75
Sunnet domain, 167, 168
SunOS, ix
SunOS relcase tapes, 35–38
Swap-local clients, 4
Swap partition, 23–24
Swap space, increasing, 258–259
System administration, ix
System backup, *see* Backup *entries*
Systems
  moving, 206–207
  pre-installed, 101–104

T

Table of contents (TOC), 36, 37
Tape files, 35
Tapes, density of, 245
Tightening security, 233–236
TOC (table of contents), 36, 37

Tracks, 17
Transceiver tap, 212
Transcript software, 174
Troubleshooting, 257–266
  network commands for, 222–223
/ttytab, 232–233

U

uid (user identification number), 193–194
"Unbundled" software, 169
The Unix C Shell Guide, 282
UNIX kernel, 9
UNIX System Administration Handbook, 281
UNIX Systems Administration, ix
UNIX (TM) Nroff/Troff:A User's Guide, 282
User accounts, 191–192
  adding, 192–194
User identification number (uid), 193–194
/usr partition, 24–26, 30–31

V

Vampire taps, 212
/var directory, 31
/var partition, 30
/vmunix, 96

W

Workstation administration, 198–209
  automatic NFS mounting, 201–202
  electronic mail, 204–206
  moving machines around, 206–207
  using remote printers, 202–205
Workstation installing, 13–108
  format concepts, 14–20
  preparation, 13–20

Y

YP, 109–160
  description, 109–111
  problems when using, 153–155
YP clients, 153
YP commands, 141–149
YP concepts, advanced, 155–160
YP domain(s), 109–110
  many, on one net, 156
  one, on many nets, 155
  several, on one ypserver, 156
YP makefile, 112–114
  sample, 114
YP maps, 110, 112–113
  adding, 157, 159–160
  automatic updating of, 155
YP master, 4, 110
  booting, after installation, 85–87
  changing YP slave into, 156–157
YP master script, 158–159
YP master server, 164–168
YP master server initialization,
      149–151

YP password
  forgotten, 154–155, 264–265
  not working, 154
YP slave, 110
  as master, 154
  changing, into YP master, 156–157
YP slave server initialization,
      151–153
YP type, setting, 63–64
Ypbind command, 141–142
Ypcat command, 147
Ypinit command, 142–143
Ypmake command, 143–144
Ypmatch command, 147–148
Yppasswd, *see* YP password
Yppasswd command, 149
Yppasswdd command, 148
Yppoll command, 145–146
Yppush command, 145
Ypserv command, 141
Ypservers map, 139, 141
Ypset command, 142
Ypwhich command, 146
Ypxfr command, 145